BOOK 4 – ALTERNATIVE INVESTMENTS AND FIXED INCOM

SCHWESERNOTES™ 2013 CFA LEVEL II BOOK 4: ALTERNATIVE INVESTMENTS AND FIXED INCOME

Published in 2012 by Kaplan Schweser.

Printed in the United States of America.

ISBN: 978-1-4277-4249-0 / 1-4277-4249-9

PPN: 3200-2852

READINGS AND LEARNING OUTCOME STATEMENTS

READINGS

The following material is a review of the Alternative Investments and Fixed Income principles designed to address the learning outcome statements set forth by CFA Institute.

STUDY SESSION 13

Reading Assignments

Alternative Investments and Fixed Income, CFA Program Curriculum, Volume 5, Level II (CFA Institute, 2012)

STUDY SESSION 14

Reading Assignments

Alternative Investments and Fixed Income, CFA Program Curriculum, Volume 5, Level II (CFA Institute, 2012)

STUDY SESSION 15

Reading Assignments

Alternative Investments and Fixed Income, CFA Program Curriculum, Volume 5, Level II (CFA Institute, 2012)

LEARNING OUTCOME STATEMENTS (LOS)

The CFA Institute Learning Outcome Statements are listed below. These are repeated in each topic review; however, the order may have been changed in order to get a better fit with the flow of the review.

STUDY SESSION 13

The topical coverage corresponds with the following CFA Institute assigned reading:

38. Private Real Estate Investments

The candidate should be able to:

a. classify and describe basic forms of real estate investments. (page 9)
b. describe the characteristics, the classification, and basic segments of real estate. (page 10)
c. explain the role in a portfolio, the major economic value determinants, investment characteristics, and principal risks of private real estate. (page 12)
d. describe commercial property types, including their distinctive investment characteristics. (page 14)
e. compare the income, cost, and sales comparison approaches to valuing real estate properties. (page 15)
f. estimate and interpret the inputs (for example, net operating income, capitalization rate, and discount rate) to the direct capitalization and discounted cash flow valuation methods. (page 17)
g. calculate the value of a property using the direct capitalization and discounted cash flow methods. (page 17)
h. compare the direct capitalization and discounted cash flow methods. (page 25)
i. calculate the value of a property using the cost and sales comparison approaches. (page 26)
j. describe due diligence in private equity real estate investment. (page 31)
k. discuss private equity real estate investment indices, including their construction and potential biases. (page 31)
l. explain the role in a portfolio, the major economic value determinants, investment characteristics, principal risks, and due diligence of private real estate debt investment. (page 12)
m. calculate and interpret financial ratios used to analyze and evaluate private real estate investments. (page 32)

The topical coverage corresponds with the following CFA Institute assigned reading:

39. Publicly Traded Real Estate Securities

The candidate should be able to:

a. describe types of publicly traded real estate securities. (page 42)
b. explain advantages and disadvantages of investing in real estate through publicly traded securities. (page 43)
c. explain economic value determinants, investment characteristics, principal risks, and due diligence considerations for real estate investment trust (REIT) shares. (page 45)
d. describe types of REITs. (page 47)
e. justify the use of net asset value per share (NAVPS) in REIT valuation and estimate NAVPS based on forecasted cash net operating income. (page 51)

f. describe the use of funds from operations (FFO) and adjusted funds from operations (AFFO) in REIT valuation. (page 53)
g. compare the net asset value, relative value (price-to-FFO and price-to-AFFO), and discounted cash flow approaches to REIT valuation. (page 55)
h. calculate the value of a REIT share using net asset value, price-to-FFO and price-to-AFFO, and discounted cash flow approaches. (page 55)

The topical coverage corresponds with the following CFA Institute assigned reading:

40. Private Equity Valuation

The candidate should be able to:

a. explain sources of value creation in private equity. (page 70)
b. explain how private equity firms align their interests with those of the managers of portfolio companies. (page 71)
c. distinguish between the characteristics of buyout and venture capital investments. (page 72)
d. describe valuation issues in buyout and venture capital transactions. (page 76)
e. explain alternative exit routes in private equity and their impact on value. (page 80)
f. explain private equity fund structures, terms, valuation, and due diligence in the context of an analysis of private equity fund returns. (page 81)
g. explain risks and costs of investing in private equity. (page 86)
h. interpret and compare financial performance of private equity funds from the perspective of an investor. (page 88)
i. calculate management fees, carried interest, net asset value, distributed to paid in (DPI), residual value to paid in (RVPI), and total value to paid in (TVPI) of a private equity fund. (page 91)
j. calculate pre-money valuation, post-money valuation, ownership fraction, and price per share applying the venture capital method 1) with single and multiple financing rounds and 2) in terms of IRR. (page 93)
k. demonstrate alternative methods to account for risk in venture capital. (page 98)

The topical coverage corresponds with the following CFA Institute assigned reading:

41. Investing in Hedge Funds: A Survey

The candidate should be able to:

a. distinguish between hedge funds and mutual funds in terms of leverage, use of derivatives, disclosure requirements and practices, lockup periods, and fee structures. (page 117)
b. describe hedge fund strategies. (page 118)
c. explain possible biases in reported hedge fund performance. (page 120)
d. describe factor models for hedge fund returns. (page 121)
e. describe sources of non-normality in hedge fund returns and implications for performance appraisal. (page 122)
f. describe motivations for hedge fund replication strategies. (page 123)
g. explain difficulties in applying traditional portfolio analysis to hedge funds. (page 124)
h. compare funds of funds to single manager hedge funds. (page 125)

STUDY SESSION 14

The topical coverage corresponds with the following CFA Institute assigned reading:

42. Fundamentals of Credit Analysis

The candidate should be able to:

a. describe credit risk and credit-related risks affecting corporate bonds. (page 136)
b. describe seniority rankings of corporate debt and explain the potential violation of the priority of claims in a bankruptcy proceeding. (page 137)
c. distinguish between corporate issuer credit ratings and issue credit ratings and describe the rating agency practice of "notching". (page 138)
d. explain risks in relying on ratings from credit rating agencies. (page 139)
e. explain the components of traditional credit analysis. (page 140)
f. calculate and interpret financial ratios used in credit analysis. (page 142)
g. evaluate the credit quality of a corporate bond issuer and a bond of that issuer, given key financial ratios for the issuer and the industry. (page 146)
h. describe factors that influence the level and volatility of yield spreads. (page 148)
i. calculate the return impact of spread changes. (page 148)
j. explain special considerations when evaluating the credit of high yield, sovereign, and municipal debt issuers and issues. (page 150)

The topical coverage corresponds with the following CFA Institute assigned reading:

43. Term Structure and Volatility of Interest Rates

The candidate should be able to:

a. explain parallel and nonparallel shifts in the yield curve. (page 166)
b. describe factors that drive U.S. Treasury security returns, and evaluate the importance of each factor. (page 167)
c. explain various universes of Treasury securities that are used to construct the theoretical spot rate curve, and evaluate their advantages and disadvantages. (page 169)
d. explain the swap rate curve (LIBOR curve) and why market participants have used the swap rate curve rather than a government bond yield curve as a benchmark. (page 171)
e. explain the pure expectations, liquidity, and preferred habitat theories of the term structure of interest rates and the implications of each for the shape of the yield curve. (page 172)
f. calculate and interpret the yield curve risk of a security or a portfolio by using key rate duration. (page 177)
g. calculate and interpret yield volatility, distinguish between historical yield volatility and implied yield volatility, and explain how to forecast yield volatility. (page 179)

The topical coverage corresponds with the following CFA Institute assigned reading:

44. Valuing Bonds with Embedded Options

The candidate should be able to:

a. evaluate, using relative value analysis, whether a security is undervalued, fairly valued, or overvalued. (page 192)
b. evaluate the importance of benchmark interest rates in interpreting spread measures. (page 197)
c. describe the backward induction valuation methodology within the binomial interest rate tree framework. (page 198)

d. calculate the value of a callable bond from an interest rate tree. (page 198)
e. explain the relations among the values of a callable (putable) bond, the corresponding option-free bond, and the embedded option. (page 199)
f. explain the effect of volatility on the arbitrage-free value of an option. (page 200)
g. interpret an option-adjusted spread with respect to a nominal spread and to benchmark interest rates. (page 202)
h. explain how effective duration and effective convexity are calculated using the binomial model. (page 204)
i. calculate the value of a putable bond, using an interest rate tree. (page 206)
j. describe and evaluate a convertible bond and its various component values. (page 208)
k. compare the risk-return characteristics of a convertible bond with the risk-return characteristics of ownership of the underlying common stock. (page 213)

STUDY SESSION 15

The topical coverage corresponds with the following CFA Institute assigned reading:

45. **Mortgage-Backed Sector of the Bond Market**

The candidate should be able to:

a. describe a mortgage loan, and explain the cash flow characteristics of a fixed-rate, level payment, and fully amortized mortgage loan. (page 227)
b. explain investment characteristics, payment characteristics, and risks of mortgage passthrough securities. (page 229)
c. calculate the prepayment amount on a mortgage passthrough security for a month, given the single monthly mortality rate. (page 233)
d. compare the conditional prepayment rate (CPR) with the Public Securities Association (PSA) prepayment benchmark. (page 231)
e. explain why the average life of a mortgage-backed security is more relevant than the security's maturity. (page 235)
f. explain factors that affect prepayments and the types of prepayment risks. (page 234)
g. explain how a collateralized mortgage obligation (CMO) is created and how it provides a better matching of assets and liabilities for institutional investors. (page 236)
h. distinguish among the sequential pay tranche, the accrual tranche, the planned amortization class tranche, and the support tranche in a CMO. (page 236)
i. evaluate the risk characteristics and relative performance of each type of CMO tranche, given changes in the interest rate environment. (page 243)
j. explain investment characteristics of stripped mortgage-backed securities. (page 244)
k. compare agency and nonagency mortgage-backed securities. (page 245)
l. compare credit risk analysis of commercial and residential nonagency mortgage-backed securities. (page 247)
m. describe the basic structure of a commercial mortgage-backed security (CMBS), and explain the ways in which a CMBS investor may realize call protection at the loan level and by means of the CMBS structure. (page 248)

The topical coverage corresponds with the following CFA Institute assigned reading:

46. Asset-Backed Sector of the Bond Market

The candidate should be able to:

a. describe the basic structural features of and parties to a securitization transaction. (page 258)
b. explain and contrast prepayment tranching and credit tranching. (page 259)
c. distinguish between the payment structure and collateral structure of a securitization backed by amortizing assets and non-amortizing assets. (page 260)
d. distinguish among various types of external and internal credit enhancements. (page 261)
e. describe cash flow and prepayment characteristics for securities backed by home equity loans, manufactured housing loans, automobile loans, student loans, SBA loans, and credit card receivables. (page 264)
f. describe collateralized debt obligations (CDOs), including cash and synthetic CDOs. (page 270)
g. distinguish among the primary motivations for creating a collateralized debt obligation (arbitrage and balance sheet transactions). (page 272)

The topical coverage corresponds with the following CFA Institute assigned reading:

47. Valuing Mortgage-Backed and Asset-Backed Securities

The candidate should be able to:

a. explain the calculation, use, and limitations of the cash flow yield, nominal spread, and zero-volatility spread for a mortgage-backed security and an asset-backed security. (page 283)
b. describe the Monte Carlo simulation model for valuing a mortgage-backed security. (page 285)
c. describe path dependency in passthrough securities and the implications for valuation models. (page 286)
d. explain how the option-adjusted spread is calculated using the Monte Carlo simulation model and how this spread measure is interpreted. (page 286)
e. evaluate a mortgage-backed security using option-adjusted spread analysis. (page 290)
f. explain why effective durations reported by various dealers and vendors may differ. (page 291)
g. analyze the interest rate risk of a security, given the security's effective duration. (page 292)
h. explain cash flow, coupon curve, and empirical measures of duration, and describe limitations of each in relation to mortgage-backed securities. (page 293)
i. determine whether the nominal spread, zero-volatility spread, or option-adjusted spread should be used to evaluate a specific fixed income security. (page 295)

The following is a review of the Alternative Investments principles designed to address the learning outcome statements set forth by CFA Institute. This topic is also covered in:

Private Real Estate Investments

Study Session 13

Exam Focus

This topic review concentrates on valuation of real estate. The focus is on the three valuation approaches used for appraisal purposes, especially the income approach. Make sure you can calculate the value of a property using the direct capitalization method and the discounted cash flow method. Make certain you understand the relationship between the capitalization rate and the discount rate. Finally, understand the investment characteristics and risks involved with real estate investments.

LOS 38.a: Classify and describe basic forms of real estate investments.

CFA® Program Curriculum, Volume 5, page 7

Forms of Real Estate

There are four basic forms of real estate investment that can be described in terms of a two-dimensional quadrant. In the first dimension, the investment can be described in terms of public or private markets. In the private market, ownership usually involves a direct investment like purchasing property or lending money to a purchaser. Direct investments can be solely owned or indirectly owned through partnerships or **commingled real estate funds** (**CREF**). The public market does not involve direct investment; rather, ownership involves securities that serve as claims on the underlying assets. Public real estate investment includes ownership of a **real estate investment trust** (**REIT**), a **real estate operating company** (**REOC**), and mortgage-backed securities.

The second dimension describes whether an investment involves debt or equity. An equity investor has an ownership interest in real estate or securities of an entity that owns real estate. Equity investors control decisions such as borrowing money, property management, and the exit strategy.

A debt investor is a lender that owns a mortgage or mortgage securities. Usually, the mortgage is collateralized (secured) by the underlying real estate. In this case, the lender has a superior claim over an equity investor in the event of default. Since the lender must be repaid first, the value of an equity investor's interest is equal to the value of the property less the outstanding debt.

Each of the basic forms has its own risk, expected returns, regulations, legal issues, and market structure.

Private real estate investments are usually larger than public investments because real estate is indivisible and illiquid. Public real estate investments allow the property to remain undivided while allowing investors divided ownership. As a result, public real estate investments are more liquid and enable investors to diversify by participating in more properties.

Real estate must be actively managed. Private real estate investment requires property management expertise on the part of the owner or a property management company. In the case of a REIT or REOC, the real estate is professionally managed; thus, investors need no property management expertise.

Equity investors usually require a higher rate of return than mortgage lenders because of higher risk. As previously discussed, lenders have a superior claim in the event of default. As financial leverage (use of debt financing) increases, return requirements of both lenders and equity investors increase as a result of higher risk.

Typically, lenders expect to receive returns from promised cash flows and do not participate in the appreciation of the underlying property. Equity investors expect to receive an income stream as a result of renting the property and the appreciation of value over time.

Figure 1 summarizes the basic forms of real estate investment and can be used to identify the investment that best meets an investor's objectives.

Figure 1: Basic Forms of Real Estate Investment

	Debt	*Equity*
Private	Mortgages	Direct investments such as sole ownership, partnerships, and other forms of commingled funds
Public	Mortgage-backed securities	Shares of REITs and REOCs

LOS 38.b: Describe the characteristics, the classification, and basic segments of real estate.

CFA® Program Curriculum, Volume 5, page 9

Real Estate Characteristics

Real estate investment differs from other asset classes, like stocks and bonds, and can complicate measurement and performance assessment.

- **Heterogeneity.** Bonds from a particular issue are alike, as are stocks of a specific company. However, no two properties are exactly the same because of location, size, age, construction materials, tenants, and lease terms.
- **High unit value.** Because real estate is indivisible, the unit value is significantly higher than stocks and bonds, which makes it difficult to construct a diversified portfolio.

- **Active management.** Investors in stocks and bonds are not necessarily involved in the day-to-day management of the companies. Private real estate investment requires active property management by the owner or a property management company. Property management involves maintenance, negotiating leases, and collection of rents. In either case, property management costs must be considered.
- **High transaction costs.** Buying and selling real estate is costly because it involves appraisers, lawyers, brokers, and construction personnel.
- **Depreciation and desirability.** Buildings wear out over time. Also, buildings may become less desirable because of location, design, or obsolescence.
- **Cost and availability of debt capital.** Because of the high costs to acquire and develop real estate, property values are impacted by the level of interest rates and availability of debt capital. Real estate values are usually lower when interest rates are high and debt capital is scarce.
- **Lack of liquidity.** Real estate is illiquid. It takes time to market and complete the sale of property.
- **Difficulty in determining price.** Stocks and bonds of public firms usually trade in active markets. However, because of heterogeneity and low transaction volume, appraisals are usually necessary to assess real estate values. Even then, appraised values are often based on similar, not identical, properties. The combination of limited market participants and lack of knowledge of the local markets makes it difficult for an outsider to value property. As a result, the market is less efficient. However, investors with superior information and skill may have an advantage in exploiting the market inefficiencies.

The market for REITs has expanded to overcome many of the problems involved with direct investment. Shares of a REIT are actively traded and are more likely to reflect market value. In addition, investing in a REIT can provide exposure to a diversified real estate portfolio. Finally, investors don't need property management expertise because the REIT manages the properties.

Property Classifications

Real estate is commonly classified as residential or non-residential. Residential real estate includes single-family (owner-occupied) homes and multi-family properties, such as apartments. Residential real estate purchased with the intent to produce income is usually considered commercial real estate property.

Non-residential real estate includes commercial properties, other than multi-family properties, and other properties such as farmland and timberland.

Commercial real estate is usually classified by its end use and includes multi-family, office, industrial/warehouse, retail, hospitality, and other types of properties such as parking facilities, restaurants, and recreational properties. A *mixed-use development* is a property that serves more than one end user.

Some commercial properties require more management attention than others. For example, of all the commercial property types, hotels require the most day-to-day attention and are more like operating a business. Because of higher operational risk, investors require higher rates of return on management-intensive properties.

Farmland and timberland are unique categories (separate from commercial real estate classification) because each can produce a saleable commodity as well as have the potential for capital appreciation.

LOS 38.c: Explain the role in a portfolio, the major economic value determinants, investment characteristics, and principal risks of private real estate.

LOS 38.l: Explain the role in a portfolio, the major economic value determinants, investment characteristics, principal risks, and due diligence of private real estate debt investment.

CFA® Program Curriculum, Volume 5, page 13

Reasons to Invest in Real Estate

Current income. Investors may expect to earn income from collecting rents and after paying operating expenses, financing costs, and taxes.

Capital appreciation. Investors usually expect property values to increase over time, which forms part of their total return.

Inflation hedge. During inflation, investors expect both rents and property values to rise.

Diversification. Real estate, especially private equity investment, is less than perfectly correlated with the returns of stocks and bonds. Thus, adding private real estate investment to a portfolio can reduce risk relative to the expected return.

Tax benefits. In some countries, real estate investors receive favorable tax treatment. For example, in the United States, the depreciable life of real estate is usually shorter than the actual life. As a result, depreciation expense is higher, and taxable income is lower resulting in lower income taxes. Also, REITs do not pay taxes in some countries, which allow investors to escape double taxation (e.g., taxation at the corporate level and the individual level).

Principal Risks

Business conditions. Numerous economic factors—such as gross domestic product (GDP), employment, household income, interest rates, and inflation—affect the rental market.

New property lead time. Market conditions can change significantly while approvals are obtained, while the property is completed, and when the property is fully leased. During the lead time, if market conditions weaken, the resultant lower demand affects rents and vacancy resulting in lower returns.

Cost and availability of capital. Real estate must compete with other investments for capital. As previously discussed, demand for real estate is reduced when debt capital is scarce and interest rates are high. Conversely, demand is higher when debt capital is easily obtained and interest rates are low. Thus, real estate prices can be affected by capital market forces without changes in demand from tenants.

Unexpected inflation. Some leases provide inflation protection by allowing owners to increase rent or pass through expenses because of inflation. Real estate values may not keep up with inflation when markets are weak and vacancy rates are high.

Demographic factors. The demand for real estate is affected by the size and age distribution of the local market population, the distribution of socioeconomic groups, and new household formation rates.

Lack of liquidity. Because of the size and complexity of most real estate transactions, buyers and lenders usually perform due diligence, which takes time and is costly. A quick sale will typically require a significant discount.

Environmental issues. Real estate values can be significantly reduced when a property has been contaminated by a prior owner or adjacent property owner.

Availability of information. A lack of information when performing property analysis increases risk. The availability of data depends on the country, but generally more information is available as real estate investments become more global.

Management expertise. Property managers and asset managers must make important operational decisions—such as negotiating leases, property maintenance, marketing, and renovating the property—when necessary.

Leverage. The use of debt (leverage) to finance a real estate purchase is measured by the loan-to-value (LTV) ratio. Higher LTV results in higher leverage and, thus, higher risk because lenders have a superior claim in the event of default. With leverage, a small decrease in net operating income (NOI) negatively magnifies the amount of cash flow available to equity investors after debt service.

Other factors. Other risk factors, such as unobserved property defects, natural disasters, and acts of terrorism, may be unidentified at the time of purchase.

In some cases, risks that can be identified can be hedged using insurance. In other cases, risk can be shifted to the tenants. For example, a lease agreement could require the tenant to reimburse any unexpected operating expenses.

The Role of Real Estate in a Portfolio

Real estate investment has both bond-like and stock-like characteristics. Leases are contractual agreements that usually call for periodic rental payments, similar to the coupon payments of a bond. When a lease expires, there is uncertainty regarding renewal and future rental rates. This uncertainty is affected by the availability of competing space, tenant profitability, and the state of the overall economy, just as stock prices are affected by the same factors. As a result, the risk/return profile of real estate as an asset class, is usually between the risk/return profiles of stocks and bonds.

Role of Leverage in Real Estate Investment

So far, our discussion of valuation has ignored debt financing. Earlier we determined that the level of interest rates and the availability of debt capital impact real estate prices. However, the percentage of debt and equity used by an investor to finance real estate does not affect the property's value.

Investors use debt financing (leverage) to increase returns. As long as the investment return is greater than the interest paid to lenders, there is positive leverage and returns are magnified. Of course, leverage can also work in reverse. Because of the greater uncertainty involved with debt financing, risk is higher since lenders have a superior claim to cash flow.

LOS 38.d: Describe commercial property types, including their distinctive investment characteristics.

CFA® Program Curriculum, Volume 5, page 19

Commercial Property Types

The basic property types used to create a low-risk portfolio include office, industrial/warehouse, retail, and multi-family. Some investors include hospitality properties (hotels and motels) even though the properties are considered riskier since leases are not involved and performance is highly correlated with the business cycle.

It is important to know that with all property types, location is critical in determining value.

Office. Demand is heavily dependent on job growth, especially in industries that are heavy users of office space like finance and insurance. The average length of office leases varies globally.

In a *gross lease*, the owner is responsible for the operating expenses, and in a *net lease*, the tenant is responsible. In a net lease, the tenant bears the risk if the actual operating expenses are greater than expected. As a result, rent under a net lease is lower than a gross lease.

Some leases combine features from both gross and net leases. For example, the owner might pay the operating expenses in the first year of the lease. Thereafter, any increase in the expenses is passed through to the tenant. In a multi-tenant building, the expenses are usually prorated based on square footage.

Understanding how leases are structured is imperative in analyzing real estate investments.

Industrial. Demand is heavily dependent on the overall economy. Demand is also affected by import/export activity of the economy. Net leases are common.

Retail. Demand is heavily dependent on consumer spending. Consumer spending is affected by the overall economy, job growth, population growth, and savings rates. Retail lease terms vary by the quality of the property as well as the size and importance of the tenant. For example, an anchor tenant may receive favorable lease terms to attract them to the property. In turn, the anchor tenant will draw other tenants to the property.

Retail tenants are often required to pay additional rent once sales reach a certain level. This unique feature is known as a *percentage lease* or *percentage rent*. Accordingly, the lease will specify a minimum amount of rent to be paid without regard to sales. The minimum rent also serves as the starting point for calculating the percentage rent.

For example, assume a retail lease specifies minimum rent of $20 per square foot plus 5% of sales over $400 per square foot. If sales were $400 per square foot, the minimum rent and percentage rent would be equivalent ($400 sales per square foot × 5% = $20 per square foot). In this case, $400 is known as the natural breakpoint. If sales are $500 per square foot, rent per square foot is equal to $25 [$20 minimum rent + $5 percentage rent ($500 – $400) × 5%]. Alternatively, rent per square foot is equal to $500 sales per square foot × 5% = $25 because of the natural breakpoint.

Multi-family. Demand depends on population growth, especially in the age demographic that typically rents apartments. The age demographic can vary by country, type of property, and locale. Demand is also affected by the cost of buying versus the cost of renting, which is measured by the ratio of home prices to rents. As home prices rise, there is a shift toward renting. An increase in interest rates will also make buying more expensive.

LOS 38.e: Compare the income, cost, and sales comparison approaches to valuing real estate properties.

CFA® Program Curriculum, Volume 5, page 22

Real Estate Appraisals

Since commercial real estate transactions are infrequent, appraisals are used to estimate value or assess changes in value over time in order to measure performance. In most cases, the focus of an appraisal is *market value*; that is, the most probable sales price a typical investor is willing to pay. Other definitions of value include *investment value*, the value or worth that considers a particular investor's motivations; *value in use*, the value to a particular user such as a manufacturer that is using the property as a part of its business; and *assessed* value that is used by a taxing authority. For purposes of valuing collateral, lenders sometimes use a more conservative *mortgage lending value*.

Valuation Approaches

Appraisers use three different approaches to value real estate: the cost approach, the sales comparison approach, and the income approach.

The premise of the *cost approach* is that a buyer would not pay more for a property than it would cost to purchase land and construct a comparable building. Consequently, under the cost approach, value is derived by adding the value of the land to the current replacement cost of a new building less adjustments for estimated depreciation and obsolescence. Because of the difficulty in measuring depreciation and obsolescence, the cost approach is most useful when the subject property is relatively new. The cost approach is often used for unusual properties or properties where comparable transactions are limited.

The premise of the *sales comparison approach* is that a buyer would pay no more for a property than others are paying for similar properties. With the sales comparison approach, the sale prices of similar (comparable) properties are adjusted for differences with the subject property. The sales comparison approach is most useful when there are a number of properties similar to the subject that have recently sold, as is usually the case with single-family homes.

The premise of the *income approach* is that value is based on the expected rate of return required by a buyer to invest in the subject property. With the income approach, value is equal to the present value of the subject's future cash flows. The income approach is most useful in commercial real estate transactions.

Highest and Best Use

The concept of highest and best use is important in determining value. The highest and best use of a vacant site is not necessarily the use that results in the highest total value once a project is completed. Rather, the highest and best use of a vacant site is the use that produces the highest implied land value. The implied land value is equal to the value of the property once construction is completed less the cost of constructing the improvements, including profit to the developer to handle construction and lease-out.

Example: Highest and best use

An investor is considering a site to build either an apartment building or a shopping center. Once construction is complete, the apartment building would have an estimated value of €50 million and the shopping center would have an estimated value of €40 million. Construction costs, including developer profit, are estimated at €45 million for the apartment building and €34 million for the shopping center. Calculate the highest and best use of the site.

Answer:

The shopping center is the highest and best use for the site because the €6 million implied land value of the shopping center is higher than the €5 million implied land value of the apartment building as follows:

	Apartment Building	*Shopping Center*
Value when completed	€50,000,000	€40,000,000
Less: Construction costs	45,000,000	34,000,000
Implied land value	€5,000,000	€6,000,000

Note the highest and best use is not based on the highest value when the projects are completed but, rather, the highest implied land value.

LOS 38.f: Estimate and interpret the inputs (for example, net operating income, capitalization rate, and discount rate) to the direct capitalization and discounted cash flow valuation methods.

LOS 38.g: Calculate the value of a property using the direct capitalization and discounted cash flow methods.

CFA® Program Curriculum, Volume 5, page 27

Income Approach

The income approach includes two different valuation methods: the direct capitalization method and the discounted cash flow method. With the *direct capitalization method*, value is based on capitalizing the first year NOI of the property using a capitalization rate. With the *discounted cash flow method*, value is based on the present value of the property's future cash flows using an appropriate discount rate.

Value is based on NOI under both methods. As shown in Figure 2, NOI is the amount of income remaining after subtracting vacancy and collection losses, and operating expenses (e.g, insurance, property taxes, utilities, maintenance, and repairs) from potential gross income. NOI is calculated before subtracting financing costs and income taxes.

Figure 2: Net Operating Income

Rental income if fully occupied
\+ Other income
= Potential gross income
– Vacancy and collection loss
= Effective gross income
– Operating expense
= Net operating income

Example: Net operating income

Calculate net operating income (NOI) using the following information:

Property type	Office building
Property size	200,000 square feet
Gross rental income	€25 per square foot
Other income	€75,000
Vacancy and collection loss	5% of gross rental income
Property taxes and insurance	€350,000
Utilities and maintenance	€875,000
Interest expense	€400,000
Income tax rate	40%

Answer:

Gross rental income	€5,000,000 [200,000 SF × €25]
Other income	75,000
Potential gross income	€5,075,000
Vacancy and collection losses	(253,750)[5,075,000 × 5%]
Operating expenses	(1,225,000)[350,000 + 875,000]
Net operating income	€3,596,250

Note that interest expense and income taxes are not considered operating expenses.

The Capitalization Rate

The **capitalization rate**, or cap rate, and the discount rate are not the same rate although they are related. The discount rate is the required rate of return; that is, the risk-free rate plus a risk premium.

The cap rate is applied to first-year NOI, and the discount rate is applied to first-year and future NOI. So, if NOI and value is expected to grow at a constant rate, the cap rate is lower than the discount rate as follows:

$$\text{cap rate} = \text{discount rate} - \text{growth rate}$$

Using the previous formula, we can say the growth rate is implicitly included in the cap rate.

The cap rate can be defined as the current yield on the investment as follows:

$$\text{cap rate} = \frac{NOI_1}{\text{value}}$$

Since the cap rate is based on first-year NOI, it is sometimes called the *going-in cap rate.*

By rearranging the previous formula, we can now solve for value as follows:

$$\text{value} = V_0 = \frac{NOI_1}{\text{cap rate}}$$

If the cap rate is unknown, it can be derived from recent comparable transactions as follows:

$$\text{cap rate} = \frac{\text{NOI}_1}{\text{comparable sales price}}$$

It is important to observe several comparable transactions when deriving the cap rate. Implicit in the cap rate derived from comparable transactions are investors' expectations of income growth and risk. In this case, the cap rate is similar to the reciprocal of the price-earnings multiple for equity securities.

Example: Valuation using the direct capitalization method

Assume that net operating income for an office building is expected to be $175,000, and the cap rate is 8%. Estimate the market value of the property using the direct capitalization method.

Answer:

The estimated market value is:

$$V_0 = \frac{\text{NOI}_1}{\text{cap rate}} = \frac{\$175{,}000}{8\%} = \$2{,}187{,}500$$

When tenants are required to pay all expenses, the cap rate can be applied to rent instead of NOI. Dividing rent by comparable sales is called the *all risks yield* (ARY). In this case, the ARY is the cap rate and will differ from the discount rate if an investor expects growth in rents and value.

$$\text{value} = V_0 = \frac{\text{rent}_1}{\text{ARY}}$$

If rents are expected to increase at a constant rate each year, the internal rate of return (IRR) can be approximated by summing the cap rate and growth rate.

Stabilized NOI

Recall the cap rate is applied to first-year NOI. If NOI is not representative of the NOI of similar properties because of a temporary issue, the subject property's NOI should be stabilized. For example, assume a property is temporarily experiencing high vacancy during a major renovation. In this case, the first-year NOI should be stabilized; NOI should be calculated as if the renovation is complete. Once the stabilized NOI is capitalized, the loss in value, as a result of the temporary decline in NOI, is subtracted in arriving at the value of the property.

Example: Valuation during renovation

On January 1 of this year, renovation began on a shopping center. This year, NOI is forecasted at €6 million. Absent renovations, NOI would have been €10 million. After this year, NOI is expected to increase 4% annually. Assuming all renovations are completed by the seller at their expense, estimate the value of the shopping center as of the beginning of this year assuming investors require a 12% rate of return.

Answer:

The value of the shopping center after renovation is:

$$\frac{\text{stabilized NOI}}{\text{cap rate}} = \frac{10{,}000{,}000}{(12\% - 4\%)} = €125{,}000{,}000$$

Using the financial calculator, the present value of the temporary decline in NOI during renovation is:

N = 1; I/Y = 12, PMT = 0; FV = 4,000,000; CPT → PV = €3,571,429

(In the previous computation, we are assuming that all rent is received at the end of the year for simplicity).

The total value of the shopping center is:

Value after renovations	€125,000,000
Loss in value during renovations	(3,571,429)
Total value	€121,428,571

The gross income multiplier, another form of direct capitalization, is the ratio of the sales price to the property's expected gross income in the year after purchase. The gross income multiplier can be derived from comparable transactions just like we did earlier with cap rates.

$$\text{gross income multiplier} = \frac{\text{sales price}}{\text{gross income}}$$

Once we obtain the gross income multiplier, value is estimated as a multiple of a subject property's estimated gross income as follows:

value = gross income × gross income multiplier

A shortfall of the gross income multiplier is that it ignores vacancy rates and operating expenses. Thus, if the subject property's vacancy rate and operating expenses are higher than those of the comparable transactions, an investor will pay more for the same rent.

Discounted Cash Flow Method

Recall from our earlier discussion, we determined the growth rate is implicitly included in the cap rate as follows:

cap rate = discount rate – growth rate

Rearranging the above formula we get:

discount rate = cap rate + growth rate

So, we can say the investor's rate of return includes the return on first-year NOI (measured by the cap rate) and the growth in income and value over time (measured by the growth rate).

$$\text{value} = V_0 = \frac{NOI_1}{(r-g)} = \frac{NOI_1}{\text{cap rate}}$$

where:
r = rate required by equity investors for similar properties
g = growth rate of NOI (assumed to be constant)
r – g = cap rate

Professor's Note: This equation should look very familiar to you because it's just a modified version of the constant growth dividend discount model, also known as the Gordon growth model, from the equity valuation portion of the curriculum.

If no growth is expected in NOI, then the cap rate and the discount rate are the same. In this case, value is calculated just like any perpetuity.

Terminal Cap Rate

Using the discounted cash flow (DCF) method, investors usually project NOI for a specific holding period and the property value at the end of the holding period rather than projecting NOI into infinity. Unfortunately, estimating the property value at the end of the holding period, known as the *terminal value* (also know as *reversion* or *resale*), is challenging. However, since the terminal value is just the present value of the NOI received by the next investor, we can use the direct capitalization method to estimate the value of the property when sold. In this case, we need to estimate the future NOI and a future cap rate, known as the *terminal* or *residual cap rate*.

The terminal cap rate is not necessarily the same as the going-in cap rate. The terminal cap rate could be higher if interest rates are expected to increase in the future or if the growth rate is projected to be lower because the property would then be older and might be less competitive. Also, uncertainty about future NOI may result in a higher terminal cap rate. The terminal cap rate could be lower if interest rates are expected to be lower or if rental income growth is projected to be higher. These relationships are easily mastered using the formula presented earlier (cap rate = discount rate – growth rate).

Since the terminal value occurs in the future, it must be discounted to present. Thus, the value of the property is equal to the present value of NOI over the holding period and the present value of the terminal value.

Example: Valuation with terminal value

Because of existing leases, the NOI of a warehouse is expected to be $1 million per year over the next four years. Beginning in the fifth year, NOI is expected to increase to $1.2 million and grow at 3% annually thereafter. Assuming investors require a 13% return, calculate the value of the property today assuming the warehouse is sold after four years.

Answer:

Using the financial calculator, the present value of the NOI over the holding period is:

N = 4; I/Y = 13, PMT = 1,000,000; FV = 0; CPT → PV = $2,974,471

The terminal value after four years is:

$$V_4 = \frac{NOI_5}{\text{cap rate}} = \frac{\$1,200,000}{(13\% - 3\%)} = \$12,000,000$$

The present value of the terminal value is:

N = 4; I/Y = 13, PMT = 0; FV = 12,000,000; CPT → PV = $7,359,825

The total value of the warehouse today is:

PV of forecast NOI	$2,974,471
PV of terminal value	7,359,825
Total value	$10,334,296

Note: We can combine the present value calculations as follows:

N = 4; I/Y = 13, PMT = 1,000,000; FV = 12,000,000; CPT → PV = $10,334,296

Valuation with Different Lease Structures

Lease structures can vary by country. For example, in the U.K., it is common for tenants to pay all expenses. In this case, the cap rate is known as the ARY as discussed earlier. Adjustments must be made when the contract rent (passing or term rent) and the current market rent (open market rent) differ. Once the lease expires, rent will likely be adjusted to the current market rent. In the U.K. the property is said to have *reversionary potential* when the contract rent expires.

One way of dealing with the problem is known as the *term and reversion approach* whereby the contract (term) rent and the reversion are appraised separately using different cap rates. The reversion cap rate is derived from comparable, fully let, properties. Because the reversion occurs in the future, it must be discounted to present. The discount rate applied to the contract rent will likely be lower than the reversion rate because the contract rent is less risky (the existing tenants are not likely to default on a below-market lease).

Example: Term and Reversion Valuation Approach

A single-tenant office building was leased six years ago at £200,000 per year. The next rent review occurs in two years. The estimated rental value (ERV) in two years based on current market conditions is £300,000 per year. The all risks yield (cap rate) for comparable fully let properties is 7%. Because of lower risk, the appropriate rate to discount the term rent is 6%. Estimate the value of the office building.

Answer:

Using the financial calculator, the present value of the term rent is:

N = 2; I/Y = 6, PMT = 200,000; FV = 0; CPT → PV = £366,679

The value of reversion to ERV is:

$$V_2 = \frac{ERV_3}{\text{ERV cap rate}} = \frac{300{,}000}{7\%} = £4{,}285{,}714$$

The present value of the reversion to ERV is:

N = 2; I/Y = 7, PMT = 0; FV = 4,285,714; CPT → PV = £3,743,309

The total value of the office building today is:

PV of term rent	£366,679
PV of reversion to ERV	£3,743,309
Total value	£4,109,988

Except for the differences in terminology and the use of different cap rates for the term rent and reversion to current market rents, the term and reversion approach is similar to the valuation example using a terminal value.

A variation of the term and reversion approach is the *layer method*. With the layer method, one source (layer) of income is the contract (term) rent that is assumed to continue in perpetuity. The second layer is the increase in rent that occurs when the lease expires and the rent is reviewed. A cap rate similar to the ARY is applied to the term rent because the term rent is less risky. A higher cap rate is applied to the incremental income that occurs as a result of the rent review.

Example: Layer method

Let's return to the example of the term and reversion valuation approach. Assume the contract (term) rent is discounted at 7%, and the incremental rent is discounted at 8%.

Answer:

The value of term rent (bottom layer) into perpetuity is:

$$\frac{\text{term rent}}{\text{term rent cap rate}} = \frac{200{,}000}{7\%} = £2{,}857{,}143$$

The value of incremental rent into perpetuity (at time t = 2) is:

$$\frac{\text{ERV}}{\text{ERV cap rate}} = \frac{(300{,}000 - 200{,}000)}{8\%} = £1{,}250{,}000$$

Using the financial calculator, the present value of the incremental rent (top layer) into perpetuity is:

N = 2; I/Y = 8, PMT = 0; FV = 1,250,000; CPT → PV = £1,071,674

The total value of the office building today is:

PV of term rent	£2,857,143
PV of incremental rent	1,071,674
Total value	£3,928,817

Using the term and reversion approach and the layer method, different cap rates were applied to the term rent and the current market rent after review. Alternatively, a single discount rate, known as the *equivalent yield*, could have been used. The equivalent yield is an average, although not a simple average, of the two separate cap rates.

Using the discounted cash flow method requires the following estimates and assumptions, especially for properties with many tenants and complicated lease structures:

- *Project income from existing leases.* It is necessary to track the start and end dates and the various components of each lease, such as base rent, index adjustments, and expense reimbursements from tenants.
- *Lease renewal assumptions.* May require estimating the probability of renewal.
- *Operating expense assumptions.* Operating expenses can be classified as fixed, variable, or a hybrid of the two. Variable expenses vary with occupancy, while fixed expenses do not. Fixed expenses can change because of inflation.
- *Capital expenditure assumptions.* Expenditures for capital improvements, such as roof replacement, renovation, and tenant finish-out, are lumpy; that is, they do not occur evenly over time. Consequently, some appraisers average the capital expenditures and deduct a portion each year instead of deducting the entire amount when paid.
- *Vacancy assumptions.* It is necessary to estimate how long before currently vacant space is leased.

- *Estimate resale price.* A holding period that extends beyond the existing leases should be chosen. This will make it easier to estimate the resale price because all leases will reflect current market rents.
- *Appropriate discount rate.* The discount rate is not directly observable, but some analysts use buyer surveys as a guide. The discount rate should be higher than the mortgage rate because of more risk and should reflect the riskiness of the investment relative to other alternatives.

Example: Allocation of operating expenses

Total operating expenses for a multi-tenant office building are 30% fixed and 70% variable. If the 100,000 square foot building was fully occupied, operating expenses would total $6 per square foot. The building is currently 90% occupied. If the total operating expenses are allocated to the occupied space, calculate the operating expense per occupied square foot.

Answer:

If the building is fully occupied, total operating expenses would be $600,000 (100,000 SF × $6 per SF). Fixed and variable operating expenses would be:

Fixed	$180,000 (600,000 × 30%)
Variable	420,000 (600,000 × 70%)
Total	$600,000

Thus, variable operating expenses are $4.20 per square foot ($420,000 / 100,000 SF) if the building is fully occupied. Since the building is 90% occupied, total operating expenses are:

Fixed	$180,000
Variable	378,000 (100,000 SF × 90% × $4.20 per SF)
Total	$558,000

So, operating expenses per occupied square foot are $6.20 (558,000 total operating expenses / 90,000 occupied SF).

LOS 38.h: Compare the direct capitalization and discounted cash flow methods.

CFA® Program Curriculum, Volume 5, page 43

Under the direct capitalization method, a cap rate or income multiplier is applied to first-year NOI. Implicit in the cap rate or multiplier are expected increases in growth.

Under the discounted cash flow (DCF) method, the future cash flows, including the capital expenditures and terminal value, are projected over the holding period and discounted to present at the discount rate. Future growth of NOI is explicit in the DCF method.

Because of the inputs required, the DCF method is more complex than the direct capitalization method, as it focuses on NOI over the entire holding period and not just NOI in the first year. DCF does not rely on comparable transactions as long as an appropriate discount rate is chosen. Choosing the appropriate discount rate and terminal cap rate are crucial as small differences in the rates can significantly affect value.

Following are some common errors made using the DCF method:

- The discount rate does not adequately capture risk.
- Income growth exceeds expense growth.
- The terminal cap rate and the going-in cap rate are not consistent.
- The terminal cap rate is applied to NOI that is atypical.
- The cyclicality of real estate markets is ignored.

LOS 38.i: Calculate the value of a property using the cost and sales comparison approaches.

CFA® Program Curriculum, Volume 5, page 45

Cost Approach

The premise behind the cost approach is that a buyer is unlikely to pay more for a property than it would cost to purchase land and build a comparable building. The cost approach involves estimating the market value of the land, estimating the replacement cost of the building, and adjusting for depreciation and obsolescence. The cost approach is often used for unusual properties or properties where comparable transactions are limited.

Professor's Note: Depreciation for appraisal purposes is not the same as depreciation used for financial reporting or tax reporting purposes. Financial depreciation and tax depreciation involve the allocation of original cost over time. For appraisal purposes, depreciation represents an actual decline in value.

Following are the steps involved with applying the cost approach.

Step 1: **Estimate the market value of the land.** The value of the land is estimated separately, often using the sales comparison approach.

Step 2: **Estimate the building's replacement cost.** Replacement cost is based on current construction costs and standards and should include any builder/developer's profit.

Professor's Note: Replacement cost refers to the cost of a building having the same utility but constructed with modern building materials. Reproduction cost refers to the cost of reproducing an exact replica of the building using the same building materials, architectural design, and quality of construction. Replacement cost is usually more relevant for appraisal purposes because reproduction cost may be uneconomical.

Step 3: **Deduct depreciation including physical deterioration, functional obsolescence, locational obsolescence, and economic obsolescence.** *Physical deterioration* is related to the building's age and occurs as a result of normal wear and tear over time. Physical deterioration can be curable or incurable. An item is curable if the benefit of fixing the problem is at least as much as the cost to cure. For example, replacing the roof will likely increase the value of the building by at least as much as the cost of the roof. The cost of fixing curable items is subtracted from replacement cost.

An item is incurable if the problem is not economically feasible to remedy. For example, the cost of fixing a structural problem might exceed the benefit of the repair. Since an incurable defect would not be fixed, depreciation can be estimated based on the effective age of the property relative to its total economic life. For example, the physical depreciation of a property with an effective age of 30 years and a 50-year total economic life is 60% (30 year effective age / 50 year economic life). To avoid double counting, the age/life ratio is multiplied by and deducted from replacement cost minus the cost of fixing curable items.

Professor's Note: The effective age and the actual age can differ as a result of above-normal or below-normal wear and tear. Incurable items increase the effective age of the property.

Functional obsolescence is the loss in value resulting from defects in design that impairs a building's utility. For example, a building might have a bad floor plan. As a result of functional obsolescence, NOI is usually lower than it otherwise would be because of lower rent or higher operating expenses. Functional obsolescence can be estimated by capitalizing the decline in NOI.

Locational obsolescence occurs when the location is no longer optimal. For example, five years after a luxury apartment complex is completed, a prison is built down the street making the location of the apartment complex less desirable. As a result, lower rental rates will decrease the value of the complex. Care must be taken in deducting the loss in value because part of the loss is likely already reflected in the market value of the land.

Economic obsolescence occurs when new construction is not feasible under current economic conditions. This can occur when rental rates are not sufficient to support the property. Consequently, the replacement cost of the subject property exceeds the value of a new building if it was developed.

Example: The cost approach

Heavenly Towers is a 200,000 square foot high-rise apartment building located in the downtown area.

The building has an effective age of 10 years, while its total economic life is estimated at 40 years. The building has a structural problem that is not feasible to repair. The building also needs a new roof at a cost of €1,000,000. The new roof will increase the value of the building by €1,300,000.

The bedrooms in each apartment are too small and the floor plans are awkward. As a result of the poor design, rents are €400,000 a year lower than competing properties.

When Heavenly Towers was original built, it was located across the street from a park. Five years ago, the city converted the park to a sewage treatment plant. The negative impact on rents is estimated at €600,000 a year.

Due to recent construction of competing properties, vacancy rates have increased significantly resulting in a loss of an estimated value of €1,200,000.

The cost to replace Heavenly Towers is estimated at €400 per square foot plus builder profit of €5,000,000. The market value of the land is estimated at €20,000,000. An appropriate cap rate is 8%. Using the cost approach, estimate the value of Heavenly Towers.

Answer:

Replacement cost including builder profit [(200,000 SF × €400 per SF) + 5,000,000]	85,000,000
Curable physical deterioration – new roof	(1,000,000)
Replacement cost after curable physical deterioration	€84,000,000
Incurable physical deterioration – structural problem [(10-year effective age / 40 year life) × 84,000,000]	(21,000,000)
Incurable functional obsolescence – poor design [400,000 lower rent / 8% cap rate]	(5,000,000)
Locational obsolescence – sewage plant [600,000 lower rent / 8% cap rate]	(7,500,000)
Economic obsolescence – competing properties	(1,200,000)
Market value of land	20,000,000
Estimated value using the cost approach	€69,300,000

Because of the difficulty in measuring depreciation and obsolescence, the cost approach is most useful when the subject property is relatively new.

The cost approach is sometimes considered the upper limit of value since an investor would never pay more than the cost to build a comparable building. However, investors must consider that construction is time consuming and there may not be enough demand for another building of the same type. That said, market values that exceed the implied value of the cost approach are questionable.

Sales Comparison Approach

The premise of the sales comparison approach is that a buyer would pay no more for a property than others are paying for similar properties in the current market. Ideally, the comparable properties would be identical to the subject but, of course, this is impossible since all properties are different. Consequently, the sales prices of similar (comparable) properties are adjusted for differences with the subject property. The differences may relate to size, age, location, property condition, and market conditions at the time of sale. The values of comparable transactions are adjusted upward (downward) for undesirable (desirable) differences with the subject property. We do this to value the comparable as if it was similar to the subject property.

Example: Sales comparison approach

An appraiser has been asked to estimate the value of a warehouse and has collected the following information:

		Comparable Transactions		
Unit of Comparison	*Subject Property*	*1*	*2*	*3*
Size, in square feet	30,000	40,000	20,000	35,000
Age, in years	5	9	4	5
Physical condition	Average	Good	Average	Poor
Location	Prime	Prime	Secondary	Prime
Sale date, months ago		6	18	12
Sales price		$9,000,000	$4,500,000	$8,000,000

The appraiser's adjustments are based on the following:

- Each adjustment is based on the unadjusted sales price of the comparable.
- Properties depreciate at 2% per annum. Since comparable #1 is four years older than the subject, an upward adjustment of $720,000 is made [$9,000,000 × 2% × 4 years].
- *Condition adjustment*: Good: +5%, average: none; poor: –5%. Because comparable #1 is in better condition than the subject, a downward adjustment of $450,000 is made [$9,000,000 × 5%]. Similarly, an upward adjustment is made for comparable #3 to the tune of $400,000 [$8,000,000 × 5%].
- *Location adjustment*: Prime – none, secondary – 10%. Because both comparable #1 and the subject are in a prime location, no adjustment is made.
- Over the past 24 months, sales prices have been appreciating 0.5% per month. Because comparable #1 was sold six months ago, an upward adjustment of $270,000 is made [$9,000,000 × 0.5% × 6 months].

Answer:

Once the adjustments are made for all of the comparable transactions, the adjusted sales price per square foot of the comparable transactions are averaged and applied to the subject property as follows:

		Comparable Transactions		
Adjustments	*Subject Property*	*1*	*2*	*3*
Sales price		$9,000,000	$4,500,000	$8,000,000
Age		+720,000	–90,000	–
Condition		–450,000	–	+400,000
Location		–	+450,000	–
Sale date		+270,000	+405,000	+480,000
Adjusted sales price		$9,540,000	5,265,000	$8,880,000
Size in square feet	30,000	40,000	20,000	35,000
Adjusted sales price per SF		$238.50	$263.25	$253.71
Average sales price per SF	$251.82			
Estimated value	$7,554,600			

The sales comparison approach is most useful when there are a number of properties similar to the subject that have been recently sold, as is usually the case with single-family homes. When the market is weak, there tend to be fewer transactions. Even in an active market, there may be limited transactions of specialized property types, such as regional malls and hospitals. The sales comparison approach assumes purchasers are acting rationally; the prices paid are representative of the current market. However, there are times when purchasers become overly exuberant and market bubbles occur.

Reconciliation of Value

Because of different assumptions and availability of data, the three valuation approaches are likely to yield different value estimates. An important part of the appraisal process involves determining the final estimate of value by reconciling the differences in the three approaches.

An appraiser may provide more, or less, weight to an approach because of the property type or market conditions. For example, an appraiser might apply a higher weight to the value obtained with the sales comparison approach when the market is active with plenty of comparable properties. Alternatively, if the subject property is old and estimating depreciation is difficult, an appraiser might apply a lower weight to the cost method.

LOS 38.j: Describe due diligence in private equity real estate investment.

CFA® Program Curriculum, Volume 5, page 53

Real estate investors, both debt and equity, usually perform *due diligence* to confirm the facts and conditions that might affect the value of the transaction. Due diligence may include the following:

- Lease review and rental history.
- Confirm the operating expenses by examining bills.
- Review cash flow statements.
- Obtain an environmental report to identify the possibility of contamination.
- Perform a physical/engineering inspection to identify structural issues and check the condition of the building systems.
- Inspect the title and other legal documents for deficiencies.
- Have the property surveyed to confirm the boundaries and identify easements.
- Verify compliance with zoning laws, building codes, and environmental regulations.
- Verify payment of taxes, insurance, special assessments, and other expenditures.

Due diligence can be costly, but it lowers risk of unexpected legal and physical problems.

LOS 38.k: Discuss private equity real estate investment indices, including their construction and potential biases.

CFA® Program Curriculum, Volume 5, page 56

A number of real estate indices are used to track the performance of real estate including appraisal-based indices and transaction-based indices. Investors should be aware of how the indices are constructed as well as their limitations.

Appraisal-Based Indices

Because real estate transactions covering a specific property occur infrequently, indices have been developed based on appraised values. Appraisal-based indices combine valuations of individual properties that can be used to measure market movements. A popular index in the United States is the NCREIF Property Index (NPI). Members of NCREIF, mainly investment managers and pension fund sponsors, submit appraisal data quarterly, and NCREIF calculates the return as follows:

$$\text{return} = \frac{\text{NOI} - \text{capital expenditures} + (\text{end market value} - \text{beg market value})}{\text{beginning market value}}$$

The index is then value-weighted based on the returns of the separate properties. The return is known as a holding-period return and is equivalent to a single-period IRR.

Earlier, we found that the cap rate is equal to NOI divided by the beginning market value of the property. This is the current yield or income return of the property and is one component of the index equation. The remaining components of the equation produce the capital return. To have a positive capital return, the market value must increase by more than the capital expenditures.

The index allows investors to compare performance with other asset classes, and the quarterly returns can be used to measure risk (standard deviation). The index can also be used by investors to benchmark returns.

Appraisal-based indices tend to lag actual transactions because actual transactions occur before appraisals are performed. Thus, a change in price may not be reflected in appraised values until the next quarter or longer if a property is not appraised every quarter. Also, appraisal lag tends to smooth the index; that is, reduce its volatility, much like a moving average reduces volatility. Finally, appraisal lag results in lower correlation with other asset classes. Appraisal lag can be adjusted by unsmoothing the index or by using a transaction-based index.

Transaction-Based Indices

Transaction-based indices can be constructed using a repeat-sales index and a hedonic index.

A *repeat-sales index* relies on repeat sales of the same property. A change in market conditions can be measured once a property is sold twice. Accordingly, a regression is developed to allocate the change in value to each quarter.

A *hedonic index* requires only one sale. A regression is developed to control for differences in property characteristics such as size, age, location, and so forth.

LOS 38.m: Calculate and interpret financial ratios used to analyze and evaluate private real estate investments.

CFA® Program Curriculum, Volume 5, page 61

Lenders often use the **debt service coverage ratio (DSCR)** and the **loan-to-value (LTV)** ratio to determine the maximum loan amount on a specific property. The maximum loan amount is based on the measure that results in the lowest debt.

The DSCR is calculated as follows:

$$\text{DSCR} = \frac{\text{first-year NOI}}{\text{debt service}}$$

Debt service (loan payment) includes interest and principal, if required. Principal payments reduce the outstanding balance of the loan. An interest-only loan does not reduce the outstanding balance. The LTV ratio is calculated as follows:

$$\text{LTV} = \frac{\text{loan amount}}{\text{appraisal value}}$$

Example: Maximum loan amount

A real estate lender agreed to make a 10% interest-only loan on a property that just appraised for €1,200,000 as long as the debt service coverage ratio is at least 1.5 and the loan-to-value ratio does not exceed 80%. Calculate the maximum loan amount assuming the property's NOI is €135,000.

Answer:

Using the LTV ratio, the property will support a loan amount of €960,000 [1,200,000 value × 80% LTV ratio]. Using the DSCR, the property will support a debt service payment of €90,000 [135,000 NOI / 1.5]. Thus, the loan amount would be €900,000 [90,000 payment / 10% interest rate]. In this case, the maximum loan amount is the €900,000, which is the lower of the two amounts. At €900,000, the LTV is 75% [900,000 loan amount / 1,200,000 value] and the DSCR is 1.5 [135,000 NOI / 90,000 payment].

When debt is used to finance real estate, equity investors often calculate the **equity dividend rate**, also known as the cash-on-cash return, which measures the cash return on the amount of cash invested.

$$\text{equity dividend rate} = \frac{\text{first year cash flow}}{\text{equity}}$$

The equity dividend rate only covers one period. It is not the same as the IRR that measures the return over the entire holding period.

Example: Equity dividend maximum loan amount

Returning to the previous example, calculate the equity dividend rate (cash-on-cash return) assuming the property is purchased for the appraised value.

Answer:

The €1,200,000 property was financed with €900,000 debt and €300,000 equity. First-year cash flow is €45,000 (135,000 NOI – 90,000 debt service payment). Thus, the equity dividend rate is 15% (45,000 first year cash flow / 300,000 equity).

In order to calculate the IRR with leverage, we need to consider the cash flows over the entire holding period including the change in value of the original investment. Since the property was financed with debt, the cash flows that are received at the end of the holding period (i.e., net sales proceeds) are reduced by the outstanding mortgage balance.

Example: Leveraged IRR

Returning to the last example, calculate the IRR if the property is sold at the end of six years for €1,500,000.

Answer:

Over the holding period, annual cash flows of €45,000 are received and, at the end of six years, the sale proceeds of €1,500,000 are reduced by the outstanding mortgage balance of €900,000. Recall that the loan was interest only and, hence, the entire original mortgage amount of €900,000 was outstanding at the end of the holding period. Using the financial calculator, the leveraged IRR is 24.1% as follows:

N = 6; PV = (300,000), PMT = 45,000; FV = 600,000; CPT → I/Y = 24.1%

We can see the effects of leverage by calculating an unleveraged IRR. In this case, the initial cash outflow is higher because no debt is incurred. The annual cash flows are higher because there is no debt service, and the terminal cash flow is higher because no mortgage balance is repaid at the end of the holding period.

Returning to the last example, the unleveraged IRR is 14.2% as follows:

N = 6; PV = (1,200,000), PMT = 135,000; FV = 1,500,000; CPT → I/Y = 14.2%

Notice the leveraged IRR of 24.1% is higher than the unleveraged IRR of 14.2%. As a result, the equity investor benefits by financing the property with debt because of positive leverage. Remember, however, that leverage can also work in reverse.

Key Concepts

LOS 38.a

There are four basic forms of real estate investment; private equity (direct ownership), publicly traded equity (indirect ownership), private debt (direct mortgage lending), and publicly traded debt (mortgage-backed securities).

LOS 38.b

Real estate investments are heterogeneous, have high unit values, have high transaction costs, depreciate over time, are influenced by the cost and availability of debt capital, are illiquid, and are difficult to value.

Real estate is commonly classified as residential and non-residential. Income-producing properties (including income-producing residential properties) are considered commercial real estate.

LOS 38.c

Reasons to invest in real estate include current income, capital appreciation, inflation hedge, diversification, and tax benefits.

Risks include changing business conditions, long lead times to develop property, cost and availability of capital, unexpected inflation, demographic factors, illiquidity, environmental issues, property management expertise, and the effects of leverage.

Real estate is less than perfectly correlated with the returns of stocks and bonds; thus, adding real estate to a portfolio can reduce risk relative to the expected return.

LOS 38.d

Commercial property types, and the demand for each is driven by:

- Office—Job growth
- Industrial—The overall economy
- Retail—Consumer spending
- Multi-family—Population growth

LOS 38.e

Cost approach. Value is derived by adding the value of the land to the replacement cost of a new building less adjustments for estimated depreciation and obsolescence.

Sales comparison approach. The sale prices of similar (comparable) properties are adjusted for differences with the subject property.

Income approach. Value is equal to the present value of the subject's future cash flows over the holding period.

LOS 38.f

NOI is equal to potential gross income (rental income fully leased plus other income) less vacancy and collection losses and operating expenses.

The cap rate, discount rate, and growth rate are linked.

cap rate = discount rate (r) – growth rate (g)

If the cap rate is unknown, it can be derived from recent comparable transactions as follows:

$$\text{cap rate} = \frac{NOI_1}{\text{comparable sales price}}$$

The discount rate is the required rate of return of the investor.

discount rate = cap rate + growth rate

LOS 38.g

Direct capitalization method:

$$\text{value} = V_0 = \frac{NOI_1}{\text{cap rate}}$$

Discounted cash flow method:

Step 1 – Forecast the terminal value at the end of the holding period (use direct capitalization method if NOI growth is constant).

Step 2 – Discount the NOI over the holding period and the terminal value to present.

LOS 38.h

Under the direct capitalization method, a cap rate is applied to first-year NOI. Implicit in the cap rate is an expected increase in growth.

Under the DCF method, the future cash flows, including the capital expenditures and terminal value, are projected over the holding period and discounted to present at the discount rate. Future growth of NOI is explicit to the DCF method. Choosing the appropriate discount rate and terminal cap rate are crucial as small differences in the rates can significantly affect value.

LOS 38.i

Steps involved with applying the cost approach.

Step 1: Estimate the market value of the land.
Step 2: Estimate the building's replacement cost.
Step 3: Deduct physical deterioration (estimate incurable using effective age/economic life ratio), functional obsolescence, locational obsolescence, and economic obsolescence.

With the sales comparison approach, the sales prices of similar (comparable) properties are adjusted for differences with the subject property. The differences may relate to size, age, location, property condition, and market conditions at the time of sale. Once the adjustments are made, the adjusted sales price per square foot of the comparable transactions are averaged and applied to the subject property.

LOS 38.j
Investors perform due diligence to confirm the facts and conditions that might affect the value of the transaction. Due diligence can be costly, but it lowers risk of unexpected legal and physical problems. Due diligence involves reviewing leases, confirming expenses, performing inspections, surveying the property, examining legal documents, and verifying compliance.

LOS 38.k
Appraisal-based indices tend to lag transaction-based indices and appear to have lower volatility and lower correlation with other asset classes.

LOS 38.l
Investors use debt financing (leverage) to increase returns. As long as the investment return is greater than the interest paid to lenders, there is positive leverage and returns are magnified. Leverage results in higher risk.

LOS 38.m
Lenders often use the debt service coverage ratio and the loan-to-value ratio to determine the maximum loan amount on a specific property. Investors use ratios such as the equity dividend rate (cash-on-cash return), leveraged IRR, and unleveraged IRR to evaluate performance.

CONCEPT CHECKERS

1. Which form of investment is *most appropriate* for a first-time real estate investor that is concerned about liquidity and diversification?
   A. Direct ownership of a suburban office building.
   B. Shares of a real estate investment trust.
   C. An undivided participation interest in a commercial mortgage.

2. Which of the following real estate properties is *most likely* classified as commercial real estate?
   A. A residential apartment building.
   B. Timberland and farmland.
   C. An owner-occupied, single-family home.

3. A real estate investor is concerned about rising interest rates and decides to pay cash for a property instead of financing the transaction with debt. What is the *most likely* effect of this strategy?
   A. Inflation risk is eliminated.
   B. Risk of changing interest rates is eliminated.
   C. Risk is reduced because of lower leverage.

4. Which of the following *best describes* the primary economic driver of demand for multi-family real estate?
   A. Growth in savings rates.
   B. Job growth, especially in the finance and insurance industries.
   C. Population growth.

5. Which real estate valuation method is likely the *most appropriate* for a 40-year-old, owner-occupied single-family residence?
   A. Cost approach.
   B. Sales comparison approach.
   C. Income approach.

6. The Royal Oaks office building has annual net operating income of $130,000. A similar office building with net operating income of $200,000 recently sold for $2,500,000. Using the direct capitalization method, the market value of Royal Oaks is *closest* to:
   A. $1,200,000.
   B. $1,625,000.
   C. $2,500,000.

7. Using the discounted cash flow method, estimate the property value of a building with the following information:

NOI for next five years	$600,000
NOI in Year 6	$700,000
Holding period	5 years
Discount rate	10%
Terminal growth rate	2%

   A. $7,707,534.
   B. $8,350,729.
   C. $9,024,472.

8. Which of the following *most accurately* describes the relationship between a discount rate and a capitalization rate?
   A. The capitalization rate is the appropriate discount rate less NOI growth.
   B. The appropriate discount rate is the capitalization rate less NOI growth.
   C. The capitalization rate is the present value of the appropriate discount rate.

9. Using the cost approach, estimate the property value of the following:

Building size	50,000 square feet
Replacement cost	€75 per square foot
Actual age	10 years
Effective age	12 years
Total economic life	20 years
Economic obsolescence	€400,000
Land market value	€900,000

   A. €1,100,000
   B. €2,000,000
   C. €2,375,000

10. You just entered into a contract to purchase a recently renovated apartment building, and you are concerned that some of the contractors have not been paid. In performing your due diligence, which of the following procedures should be performed to alleviate your concern?
   A. Have the property surveyed.
   B. Have an environmental study performed.
   C. Search the public records for outstanding liens.

11. Which of the following statements about real estate indices is *most accurate*?
   A. Transaction-based indices tend to lag appraisal-based indices.
   B. Appraisal-based indices tend to lag transaction-based indices.
   C. Transaction-based indices appear to have lower correlation with other asset classes as compared to appraisal-based indices.

12. Which of the following statements about financial leverage is *most accurate*?
   A. Debt financing increases the appraised value of a property because interest expense is tax deductible.
   B. Increasing financial leverage reduces risk to the equity owner.
   C. For a property financed with debt, a change in NOI will result in a more than proportionate change in cash flow.

13. A lender will make a 10%, interest-only loan on a property as long as the debt service coverage ratio is at least 1.6 and the loan-to-value ratio does not exceed 80%. The maximum loan amount, assuming the property just appraised for $1,500,000 and NOI is $200,000, is *closest* to:
   A. $1,050,000.
   B. $1,200,000.
   C. $1,500,000.

Answers – Concept Checkers

1. **B** Of the three investment choices, REITs are the most liquid because the shares are actively traded. Also, REITs provide quick and easy diversification across many properties. Neither the direct investment nor the mortgage participation is liquid, and significant capital would be required to diversify the investments.

2. **A** Residential real estate (i.e., an apartment building) purchased with the intent to produce income is usually considered commercial real estate property. Timberland and farmland are unique categories of real estate.

3. **C** An all-cash transaction eliminates financial leverage and lowers risk. Inflation risk is typically lower with a real estate investment, but the risk is not totally eliminated. If interest rates rise, non-leveraged property values are still impacted. Investors require higher returns when rates rise. Resale prices also depend on the cost and availability of debt capital.

4. **C** Demand for multi-family properties depends on population growth, especially in the age demographic that typically rents apartments.

5. **B** The sales comparison approach is likely the best valuation approach because of the number of comparable transactions. The cost approach is not as appropriate because of the difficulty in estimating depreciation and obsolescence of an older property. The income approach is not appropriate because an owner-occupied property does not generate income.

6. **B** The cap rate of the comparable transaction is 8% (200,000 NOI / 2,500,000 sales price). The value of Royal Oaks is $1,625,000 (130,000 NOI / 8% cap rate).

7. **A** The terminal value at the end of five years is $8,750,000 [700,000 year 6 payment / (10% discount rate – 2% growth rate)]. The terminal value is discounted to present and added to the present value of the NOI during the holding period. You can combine both steps using the following keystrokes:

   N = 5; I/Y = 10; PMT = 600,000; FV = 8,750,000; CPT → PV = $7,707,534

8. **A** The capitalization rate is the discount rate (required rate of return on equity, *r*) less the constant growth rate in net operating income, *g* (i.e., cap rate = r – g).

9. **B**

Replacement cost	€3,750,000	[50,000 SF × €75 per SF]
Physical deterioration	(2,250,000)	[3,750,000 × (12 eff age / 20 life)]
Economic obsolescence	(400,000)	
Land value	900,000	
Total value	€2,000,000	

10. **C** The public records should be searched for outstanding liens filed by contractors involved in the renovation. An existing lien can result in legal problems for the purchaser and the lender. A survey will not identify outstanding liens. A survey confirms the property boundaries and identifies any easements.

11. **B** Appraisal-based indices tend to lag transaction-based indices because actual transactions occur before appraisals are performed (appraisals are based on transaction data). Appraisal-based indices, not transaction-based indices, appear to have lower correlations with other asset classes.

12. **C** Financial leverage magnifies the effect of changing NOI on cash flow because the interest expense owed to lenders is a fixed cost. The use of debt financing does not affect the value of property. Leverage increases (not decreases) risk.

13. **B** Using the DSCR, the property will support a debt service payment of $125,000 (200,000 NOI / 1.6); thus, the loan amount would be $1,250,000 ($125,000 payment / 10% interest rate). However, using the LTV ratio, the property will only support a loan amount of $1,200,000 (1,500,000 value × 80% LTV). Thus, the maximum loan amount is $1,200,000, which is the lower of the two amounts.

The following is a review of the Alternative Investments principles designed to address the learning outcome statements set forth by CFA Institute. This topic is also covered in:

Publicly Traded Real Estate Securities

Study Session 13

Exam Focus

For the exam, be able to describe the different types of publicly traded real estate securities, and understand the advantages and disadvantages of investing in real estate through publicly traded securities. Be able to explain the types of REITs, as well as their economic value determinants, investment characteristics, principal risks, and due diligence considerations. Understand the various approaches to REIT valuation, and be able to calculate the value of a REIT share.

LOS 39.a: Describe types of publicly traded real estate securities.

CFA® Program Curriculum, Volume 5, page 78

Publicly traded real estate securities can take several forms: real estate investment trusts (REITs), real estate operating companies (REOCs), and residential or commercial mortgage-backed securities (MBS).

We can categorize publicly traded real estate securities into two broad groups, debt and equity.

Equity

Publicly traded real estate equity securities represent ownership stakes in properties. Equity REITs and REOCs fall into this category.

Equity REITs (Real estate investment trusts): REITs are tax-advantaged companies (trusts) that are for the most part exempt from corporate income tax. Equity REITs are actively managed, own income-producing real estate, and seek to profit by growing cash flows, improving existing properties, and purchasing additional properties. REITs often specialize in a particular kind of property, while still diversifying holdings by geography and other factors.

REOCs (Real estate operating companies): REOCs are not tax-advantaged; rather, they are ordinary (i.e., taxable) corporations that own real estate. A business will form as a REOC if it is ineligible to organize as REIT. For example, the firm may intend to develop and sell real estate rather than generating cash from rental payments, or the firm may be based in a country that does not allow tax-advantaged REITs.

DEBT

MBS (mortgage-backed securities) and mortgage REITs fall into this category.

Residential or commercial mortgage-backed securities (MBS): Residential or commercial mortgage-backed securities are publicly traded asset-backed securitized debt obligations that receive cash flows from an underlying pool of mortgage loans. These loans may be for commercial properties (in the case of CMBS) or on residential properties (in the case of RMBS). Real estate debt securities represent a far larger aggregate market value than do publicly traded real estate equity securities.

Mortgage REITs: Mortgage REITs invest primarily in mortgages, mortgage securities, or loans that are secured by real estate.

LOS 39.b: Explain advantages and disadvantages of investing in real estate through publicly traded securities.

CFA® Program Curriculum, Volume 5, page 83

ADVANTAGES

Investments in REITs and REOCs offer a number of advantages compared to direct investments in physical real estate:

- **Superior liquidity.** Investors in publicly traded real estate securities enjoy far greater liquidity than do investors in physical real estate, because REIT and REOC shares trade daily on a stock exchange. The low liquidity of a direct real estate investment stems from the relatively high value of an individual real estate property and the unique nature of each property.
- **Lower minimum investment.** While a direct investment in a real estate property may require a multi-million dollar commitment, REIT or REOC shares trade for much smaller dollar amounts.
- **Limited liability.** The financial liability of a REIT investor is limited to the amount invested. Other types of investment in real estate, such as a general partnership interest, have potential liabilities greater than the investor's initial investment.
- **Access to premium properties.** Some prestigious properties, such as high-profile shopping malls or other prominent or landmark buildings, are difficult to invest in directly. Shares in REITs that have invested in these properties represent one way to take an ownership stake in these assets.
- **Active professional management.** While a direct investment in properties requires a degree of real estate investment expertise and property management skill, REIT and REOC investments do not. REITs and REOCs employ professional management to control expenses, maximize rents and occupancy rates, and sometimes to acquire additional properties.
- **Protections accorded to publicly traded securities.** REITs and REOCs must meet the same requirements applicable to other publicly traded companies, including rules related to financial reporting, disclosure, and governance. Investors benefit from these securities regulations and from having a board overseeing the management on behalf of investors. Additionally, having public investors monitor the actions of management and the board of directors leads to financial and operating efficiency.

- **Greater potential for diversification.** Because of the high cost of a single property, it is difficult to achieve adequate diversification though direct investments in real estate. Through REITs, however, an investor can diversify across property type and geographical location.

REIT-Specific Advantages

The following advantages apply to REITs, but not to REOCs:

- **Exemption from taxation.** As long as certain requirements are met, REITs enjoy favorable taxation, because a major part of REIT distributions are treated as a return of capital and are thus not taxable.
- **Predictable earnings.** The earnings of REITs tend to be relatively consistent over time, because REITs' rental income is fixed by contracts, unlike the income of companies in other industries.
- **High yield.** To maintain their tax-advantaged status, REITs are obligated to pay out most of their taxable income as dividends. Because of this high income payout ratio, the yields of REITs are higher than the yields on most other publicly traded equities.

DISADVANTAGES

Disadvantages of investing in real estate through publicly traded securities may include:

- **Taxes versus direct ownership.** Depending on local laws, investors that make direct investments in properties may be able to deduct losses on real estate from taxable income or replace one property for a similar property ("like-kind exchange" in the U.S.) without taxation on the gains. For investors in REITs or REOCs, these specific tax benefits are not available.
- **Lack of control.** REIT investors have comparatively little input into investment decisions compared to investors that make direct investments in real estate.
- **Costs of a publicly traded corporate structure.** There are clear benefits from maintaining a publicly traded REIT structure. However, there are also related costs, which may not be worthwhile for smaller REITs.
- **Price is determined by the stock market.** While the appraisal-based value of a REIT may be relatively stable, the market-determined price of a REIT share is likely to be much more volatile. While this relationship suggests a direct real estate investment is less risky, in reality much of this effect results from the underestimation of volatility that is associated with appraised values; appraisals tend to be infrequent and backward-looking, while the stock market is continuous and reflects forward-looking values.
- **Structural conflicts of interest.** When a REIT is structured as an UPREIT or a DOWNREIT there is the potential for conflict of interest. When the opportunity arises to sell properties or take on additional borrowing, a particular action may have different tax implications for REIT shareholders and for the general partners, which may tempt the general partners to act in their own interest, rather than in the interest of all stakeholders.

Professor's Note: An UPREIT is an "umbrella partnership" REIT structure, where the REIT is the general partner and holds a controlling interest in a partnership that owns and operates the properties. UPREITs are the most common REIT structure in the United States. In a DOWNREIT, the REIT has an ownership interest in more than one partnership and can own properties both at the partnership level and at the REIT level.

- **Limited potential for income growth.** REITs' high rates of income payout limit REITs' ability to generate future growth through reinvestment. This limits future income growth and may dampen the share price of REITs.
- **Forced equity issuance.** In order to maintain financial leverage, REITs frequently participate in bond markets to refinance maturing debt. When credit is difficult to obtain (e.g., during the 2008 credit crisis), a REIT may be forced to issue equity at a disadvantageous price.

The following disadvantage applies to REITs, but not to REOCs:

- **Lack of flexibility.** The rules that qualify REITs for favorable taxation also have a downside: REITs are prevented from making certain kinds of investments and from retaining most of their income. These limits may prevent REITS from being as profitable as they might otherwise be. REOCs, on the other hand, do not need to meet these requirements, and thus are free to retain income and devote those funds to property development when the REOC managers see attractive opportunities. REOCs are also not restricted in their use of leverage.

LOS 39.c: Explain economic value determinants, investment characteristics, principal risks, and due diligence considerations for real estate investment trust (REIT) shares.

CFA® Program Curriculum, Volume 5, page 88

Economic Value Determinants of REITs

National GDP growth is the largest driver of economic value for all REIT types. Overall growth in the economy means more jobs, more need for office space, more disposable income, more growth in shopping centers, more demand for hotel rooms from business and leisure travellers, and so on.

In addition to national GDP growth, there are four major economic factors that impact REITs, as shown in Figure 1.

Figure 1: Rank of Most Important Factors Affecting Economic Value for REIT Property Types

	Relative Importance of Factors Affecting REIT Economic Value			
REIT Type	*Population Growth*	*Job Creation*	*New Space Supply vs. Demand*	*Retail Sales Growth*
Shopping/Retail	3	2	3	1
Office	3	1	2	4
Residential	1	1	3	4
Healthcare	1	3	2	4
Industrial	2	4	3	1
Hotel	3	1	2	4
Storage	1	2	3	4

Note: 1 = most important, 4 = least important
Adapted from: Exhibit 6, Level II 2013 Volume 5, Alternative Asset Valuation and Fixed Income. John Wiley & Sons (P&T), p. 92.

Investment Characteristics of REITs

- **Exemption from corporate-level income taxes:** As mentioned earlier, the defining characteristic of REITs is that they are exempt from corporate taxation. However, in order to gain this status, REITs are required to distribute almost all of the REITs' otherwise-taxable income, and a sufficient portion of assets and income must relate to rental income-producing real estate.
- **High dividend yield:** To maintain their tax-exempt status, REITs' dividend yields are generally higher than yields on bonds or other equities.
- **Low income volatility:** REITs' revenue streams tend to be relatively stable. This characteristic is due to REITs' dependence on interest and rent as income sources.
- **Secondary equity offerings:** Since REITs distribute most earnings, they are likely to finance additional real estate acquisitions by selling additional shares. For this reason, REITs issue equity more frequently than do non-real estate companies.

Principal Risks of REITs

The most risky REITs are those that invest in property sectors where significant mismatches between supply and demand are likely (particularly health care, hotel, and office REITs), as well as those sectors where the occupancy rates are most likely to fluctuate within a short period of time (especially hotels). Other items to consider in assessing the riskiness of a REIT relate to the properties' financing, the leases that are in place, and the properties' locations and quality.

Due Diligence Considerations of REITs

- **Remaining lease terms:** An analyst should evaluate the length of remaining lease terms in conjunction with the overall state of the economy—short remaining lease terms provide an opportunity to raise rents in an expansionary economy, while long remaining lease terms are advantageous in a declining economy or softening rental market. Initial lease terms vary with the type of property—industrial and office buildings and shopping centers generally have long lease terms, while hotels and multi-family residential real estate have short lease terms.

- **Inflation protection:** The level of contractual hedging against rising general price levels should be evaluated—some amount of inflation protection will be enjoyed if leases have rent increases scheduled throughout the term of the lease or if rents are indexed to the rate of inflation.
- **In-place rents versus market rents:** An analyst should compare the rents that a REIT's tenants are currently paying (in-place rents) with current rents in the market. If in-place rents are high, the potential exists for cash flows to fall going forward.
- **Costs to re-lease space:** When a lease expires, expenses typically incurred include lost rent, any new lease incentives offered, the costs of tenant-demanded improvements, and broker commissions.
- **Tenant concentration in the portfolio:** Risk increases with tenant concentration; a REIT analyst should pay special attention to any tenants that make up a high percentage of space rented or rent paid.
- **Tenants' financial health:** Since the possibility of a major tenant's business failing poses a significant risk to a REIT, it is important to evaluate the financial position of the REIT's largest renters.
- **New competition:** An analyst should evaluate the amount of new space that is planned or under construction. New competition could impact the profitability of existing REIT properties.
- **Balance sheet analysis:** Due diligence should include an in-depth analysis of the REIT's balance sheet, with special focus on the amount of leverage, the cost of debt, and the debt's maturity.
- **Quality of management:** Senior management's performance record, qualifications, and tenure with the REIT should be considered.

LOS 39.d: Describe types of REITs.

CFA® Program Curriculum, Volume 5, page 89

SUBTYPES OF EQUITY REITS

The following paragraphs provide more details on several subtypes of equity REITs.

1. **Retail or Shopping Center REITs.** REITs in this category invest in shopping centers of various sizes and sometimes in individual buildings in prime shopping neighborhoods. Regional shopping malls are large enclosed centers where anchor tenants have very long fixed-rate leases, while smaller tenants often pay a "percentage lease," which consists of a fixed rental price (the "minimum lease"), plus a percentage of sales over a certain level. Community shopping centers, such as "big-box centers," consist of stores that surround parking lots. These stores commonly pay pre-determined rents that increase on a schedule. Lease rates and sales per square foot are important factors for analysts to consider when examining a shopping center REIT.

2. **Office REITs.** Office REITs own office properties that typically lease space to multiple business tenants. Leases are long (generally 5 to 25 years) and rents increase over time. In addition to rent, tenants pay a share of property taxes, operating expenses, and other common costs proportional to the size of their unit (i.e., they are net leases). Because of the length of time that it takes to build this type of property, there is often a supply-demand mismatch, resulting in variations in occupancy rates and rents over the economic cycle. In analyzing office REITs, analysts must consider properties' location, convenience and access to transportation, and the quality of the space including the condition of the building.

3. **Residential (Multi-Family) REITs.** This category of REITs invests in rental apartments. Demand for rental apartments tends to be stable; however, lease periods are short (usually one year), so rental income fluctuates over time as competing properties are constructed. Variables that will affect rental income include the overall strength of the local economy and any move-in inducements offered. Factors to consider when analysing a residential REIT include local demographic trends, availability of alternatives (i.e., home ownership), any rent controls imposed by the local government, and factors related to the portfolio properties themselves, such as the age of the properties and how appealing they are to renters in the local market compared to other competing properties. Additionally, because rents are typically based on a gross lease, the impact of rising costs must be considered (under a gross lease, operating costs are paid by the landlord). Examples include rising fuel or energy costs, taxes, and maintenance costs.

4. **Health Care REITs.** Health care REITs invest in hospitals, nursing homes, retirement homes, rehab centers, and medical office buildings. REITs in many countries are barred from operating this kind of business themselves. In order to participate in this property sector while maintaining their tax-free status, REITs rent properties to health care providers. Leases in this sector are usually net leases. Health care REITs are relatively unaffected by the overall economy. However, other factors are important, such as government funding of health care, demographic shifts, new construction versus demand, increases in the cost of insurance, and the potential for lawsuits by residents.

5. **Industrial REITs.** Industrial REITs own properties used in activities such as manufacturing, warehousing, and distribution. The value of industrial properties is relatively stable and less cyclical compared to the value of other types of properties, due to long leases (5 to 25 years) which smoothes rental income. In analysing industrial REITs, an analyst needs to closely examine the local market for industrial properties; new properties coming on to the market and the demand for such space by tenants will affect the value of existing properties. Location and availability of transportation links (airports, roads, and ports) are also important considerations for industrial REITs.

6. **Hotel REITs**. A hotel REIT (like a health care REIT) usually leases properties to management companies, so the REIT receives only passive rental income. Hotels are exposed to revenue volatility driven by changes in business and leisure travel, and the sector's cyclical nature is intensified by a lack of long-term leases. In analysing hotel REITs, analysts compare a number of statistics against industry averages (operating profit margins, occupancy rates, and average room rates). One key metric that is closely followed is RevPAR, the revenue per available room, which is calculated by multiplying the average occupancy rate by the average room rate. Other closely-watched variables are the level of margins, forward bookings, and food and beverage sales. Expenses related to maintaining the properties are also closely monitored. Because of the time lag associated with bringing new hotel properties on-line (up to three years), the cyclical nature of demand needs to be considered. Because of the uncertainty in income, the use of high amounts of leverage in financing hotel properties is risky.

7. **Storage REITs**. Properties owned by storage REITs rent self-storage lockers (also known as mini-warehouses) to individuals and small businesses. Space is rented to users on a monthly basis and under a gross lease. In analysing storage REITs, it is important to look at the local factors that drive demand for storage, such as housing sales, new business start-ups, demographic trends in the surrounding area, as well as any other competing facilities that are under construction. Seasonal demand should also be considered.

8. **Diversified REITs**. Diversified REITs own more than one category of REIT. While they are uncommon in North America, some investors in Europe and Asia are drawn to the diversified nature of these REITs. Because diversified REITs hold a range of property types, when analysing this class of REIT it is especially important to evaluate management's background in the kinds of real estate invested in.

Figure 2: Characteristics of REIT property subtypes

	Characteristic			
REIT Type	*Economic Value Determinant*	*Investment Characteristics*	*Principal Risks*	*Due Diligence Considerations*
Retail	• Retail sales growth • Job creation	• Stable revenue stream over the short term	• Depends on consumer spending	• Per-square-foot sales and rental rates
Office	• Job creation • New space supply vs. demand	• Long (5-25 yrs) lease terms • Stable year-to-year income	• Changes in office vacancy and rental rates	• New space under construction • Quality of office space (location, condition of building, and so on)
Residential	• Population growth • Job creation	• One-year leases • Stable demand	• Competition • Inducements • Regional economy • Inflation in operating costs	• Demographics and income trends • Age and competitive appeal • Cost of home ownership • Rent controls
Health care	• Population growth • New space supply vs. demand	• REITs lease facilities to health care providers. • Leases are usually net leases.	• Demographics • Government funding • Construction cycles • Financial condition of operators • Tenant litigation	• Operating trends • Government funding trends • Litigation settlements • Insurance costs • Competitors' new facilities vs demand
Industrial	• Retail sales growth • Population growth	• Less cyclical than some other REIT types • 5-25 year net leases • Change in income and values are slow	• Shifts in the composition of local and national industrial bases and trade	• Trends in tenants' requirements • Obsolescence of existing space • Need for new types of space • Proximity to transportation • Trends in local supply and demand
Hotel	• Job creation • New space supply vs. demand	• Variable income • Sector is cyclical because it is not protected by long-term leases	• Exposed to business-cycle • Changes in business and leisure travel • Exposure to travel disruptions	• Occupancy, room rates, and operating profit margins vs. industry averages • Revenue per available room (RevPAR) • Trends in forward bookings • Maintenance expenditures • New construction in local markets • Financial leverage
Storage	• Population growth • Job creation	• Space is rented under gross leases and on a monthly basis	• Ease of entry can lead to overbuilding.	• Construction of new competitive facilities • Trends in housing sales • Demographic trends • New business start-up activity • Seasonal trends in demand for storage facilities that can be significant in some markets

LOS 39.e: Justify the use of net asset value per share (NAVPS) in REIT valuation and estimate NAVPS based on forecasted cash net operating income.

CFA® Program Curriculum, Volume 5, page 95

NAVPS is the (per-share) amount by which assets exceed liabilities, using current market values rather than accounting book values. NAVPS is generally considered the most appropriate measure of the fundamental value of REITs (and REOCs). If the market price of a REIT varies from NAVPS, this is seen as a sign of over- or undervaluation.

Estimating NAVPS Based on Forecasted Cash Net Operating Income

In the absence of a reliable appraisal, analysts will estimate the value of operating real estate by capitalizing the net operating income. This process first requires the calculation of a market required rate of return, known as the **capitalization rate** ("cap rate"), based on the prices of comparable recent transactions that have take place in the market.

$$\text{capitalization rate} = \frac{\text{net operating income}}{\text{property value}}$$

Note that the net operating income (NOI) refers to the *expected income in the coming year*. Once a cap rate for the market has been determined, this cap rate can be used to capitalize the NOI:

$$\text{property value} = \frac{\text{net operating income}}{\text{capitalization rate}}$$

In the example below, we show how NAVPS is calculated by capitalizing a rental stream. First, estimated first-year NOI is capitalized using a market cap rate. Next, we add the value of other tangible assets and subtract the value of liabilities to find total net asset value. Net asset value divided by the number of outstanding shares gives us NAVPS.

Example: Computing NAVPS

Vinny Cestone, CFA, is undertaking a valuation of the Anyco Shopping Center REIT, Inc. Given the following financial data for Anyco, estimate NAVPS based on forecasted cash net operating income.

Select Anyco Shopping Center REIT, Inc. Financial Information (in millions)

Last 12-months NOI	$80
Cash and equivalents	$20
Accounts receivable	$15
Total debt	$250
Other liabilities	$50
Non-cash rents	$2
Full-year adjustment for acquisitions	$1
Land held for future development	$10
Prepaid/Other assets (excluding intangibles)	$5
Estimate of next 12 months growth in NOI	1.25%
Cap rate based on recent comparable transactions	8.0%
Shares outstanding	15

Answer:

	Last 12-months NOI	$80
–	Non-cash rents[1]	$2
+	Full-year adjustment for acquisitions[2]	$1
=	Pro forma cash NOI for last 12 months	$79
+	Next 12 months growth in NOI (@1.25%/yr)[3]	$ 1
=	Estimated next 12 months cash NOI	$80
÷	Cap rate[4]	8.0%
=	Estimated value of operating real estate[5]	$1,000
+	Cash and equivalents[6]	$20
+	Land held for future development	$10
+	Accounts receivable	$15
+	Prepaid/other assets (excluding intangibles)	$5
=	Estimated gross asset value	$1,050
–	Total debt[7]	$250
–	Other liabilities	$50
=	Net asset value	$750
÷	Shares outstanding	15
=	Net asset value per share[8]	$50.00

Notes:
(1) Non-cash rent (difference between average contractual rent and cash rent paid) is removed.
(2) NOI is increased to represent full-year rent for properties acquired during the year.
(3) Cash NOI is expected to increase by 1.25% over the next year.
(4) Cap rate is based on recent transactions for comparable properties.
(5) Operating real estate value = expected next 12-month cash NOI / 8% capitalization rate.
(6) Add the book value of other assets: cash, accounts receivable, land for future development, prepaid expenses, and so on. Certain intangibles, such as goodwill, deferred financing expenses, and deferred tax assets, if given, are ignored.
(7) Debt and other liabilities are subtracted to get to net asset value.
(8) NAVPS = NAV / number of outstanding shares

LOS 39.f: Describe the use of funds from operations (FFO) and adjusted funds from operations (AFFO) in REIT valuation.

CFA® Program Curriculum, Volume 5, page 101

Analysts calculate and use two measures, FFO and AFFO.

1. **Funds from operations:** FFO adjusts reported earnings and is a popular measure of the continuing operating income of a REIT or REOC. FFO is calculated as follows:

	Accounting net earnings
+	Depreciation expense
+	Deferred tax expenses (i.e., deferred tax expenses)
–	Gains from sales of property and debt restructuring
+	Losses from sales of property and debt restructuring
=	Funds from operations

Depreciation is added back under the premise that accounting depreciation often exceeds economic depreciation for real estate. Deferred tax liabilities and associated periodic charges are also excluded, under the idea that this liability will probably not be paid for many years, if ever. Gains from sales of property and debt restructuring are excluded because these are not considered to be part of continuing income.

2. **Adjusted funds from operations:** AFFO is an extension of FFO that is intended to be a more useful representation of current economic income. AFFO is also known as *cash available for distribution* (CAD) or *funds available for distribution* (FAD). The calculation of AFFO generally involves beginning with FFO and then subtracting non-cash rent and maintenance-type capital expenditures and leasing costs (such as improvement allowances to tenants or capital expenditures for maintenance).

	FFO (funds from operations)
–	Non-cash (straight-line) rent adjustment
–	Recurring maintenance-type capital expenditures and leasing commissions
=	AFFO (adjusted funds from operations)

Straight-line rent refers not to the cash rent paid during the lease but rather to the average contractual rent over a lease period—the two figures differ by non-cash rent, which reflects contractually-increasing rental rates. Capital expenditures related to maintenance, as well expenses related to leasing the space in properties, are subtracted from FFO because they represent costs that must be expended in order to maintain the value of the properties.

AFFO is considered a better measure of economic income than FFO because AFFO considers the capital expenditures that are required to sustain the property's economic income. However, FFO is more frequently cited in practice, because AFFO relies more on estimates and is considered more subjective.

LOS 39.g: Compare the net asset value, relative value (price-to-FFO and price-to-AFFO), and discounted cash flow approaches to REIT valuation.

CFA® Program Curriculum, Volume 5, page 101

REITs and REOCs are valued using several different approaches.

Net asset value per share: The net asset value method of valuation can be used either to generate an absolute valuation or as part of a relative valuation approach. Note, however, that net asset value is an indication of a REIT's assets to a buyer in the private market, which can be quite different from the value public market investors would attach to the REIT. For this reason, there have historically been significant differences (i.e., premiums or discounts) between NAV estimates and the prices at which REITs actually trade.

Professor's Note: Relative valuation using NAVPS is essentially comparing NAVPS to the market price of a REIT (or REOC) share. If, in general, the market is trading at a premium to NAVPS, a value investor would select the investments with the lowest premium (everything else held constant).

Relative value (price-to-FFO and price-to-AFFO): There are three key factors that impact that price-to-FFO and price-to-AFFO of REITs and REOCs:

1. Expectations for growth of FFO or AFFO.
2. The level of risks inherent in the underlying real estate.
3. Risk related to the firm's leverage and access to capital.

Discounted cash flow approach: Dividend discount and discounted cash flow models of valuation are appropriate for use with REITs and REOCs, because these two investment structures typically pay dividends and thereby return a high proportion of their income to investors. DDM and DCF are used in private real estate in the same way that they are used to value stocks in general. For dividend discount models, an analyst will typically develop near-term, medium-term, and long-term growth forecasts and then use these values as the basis for two- or three-stage dividend discount models. To build a discounted cash flow model, analysts will generally create intermediate-term cash flow projections plus a terminal value that is developed using historical cash flow multiples.

Professor's Note: We discuss dividend discount models extensively in the study session on equity valuation. Similar to price multiples in equity valuation, price multiples here depend on growth rate and risk. The first factor (above) focuses on growth rate, while the second and third factors above focus on risk.

LOS 39.h: Calculate the value of a REIT share using net asset value, price-to-FFO and price-to-AFFO, and discounted cash flow approaches.

CFA® Program Curriculum, Volume 5, page 101

We will demonstrate the calculation of the value of a REIT share using net asset value, price-to-FFO and price-to-AFFO, and discounted cash flow approaches with an example.

Example: Calculating the value of a REIT share

Lucinda Crabtree, CFA, is an asset manager that is interested in diversifying the portfolio she manages through an investment in an office building REIT.

Crabtree wants to value the potential investment using four different approaches as of the end of 2013, as follows:

Approach 1: Net asset value
Approach 2: Price-to-FFO
Approach 3: Price-to-AFFO
Approach 4: Discounted cash flow

Selected REIT Financial Information

	All amounts in $million
Estimated 12 months cash net operating income (NOI)	$80
Funds from operations (FFO)	$70
Cash and equivalents	$65
Accounts receivable	$35
Debt and other liabilities	$400
Non-cash rents	$5
Recurring maintenance-type capital expenditures	$15
Shares outstanding	10 million shares
Expected annual dividend next year (2014)	$5.00
Dividend growth rate in 2015 and 2016	2%
Dividend growth rate (from 2017 into perpetuity)	1%
Assumed cap rate	8%
Office subsector average P/FFO multiple	10×
Office subsector average P/AFFO multiple	14×
Crabtree's applicable cost of equity capital	9%
Risk-free rate	2%

Approach 1: Value of a REIT share using net asset value approach

The value per share for this REIT using net asset value valuation is computed as follows:

Estimated cash NOI	80
Assumed cap rate	8%
Estimated value of operating real estate (80 / .08)	1,000
Plus: cash + accounts receivable	100
Less: debt and other liabilities	400
Net asset value	700
Shares outstanding	10
NAV / share	$70.00

The REIT share value using the net asset value approach is thus $70.

Approach 2: Value of a REIT share using price-to-FFO approach

The value per share for this REIT using price-to-FFO valuation is computed as follows:

Funds from operations (FFO)	$70
Shares outstanding (millions)	10
FFO / share = $70 million / 10 million shares	$7.00

Applying the office subsector average P/FFO multiple of 10× yields a value per share of:

$$\$7.00 \times 10 = \$70.00$$

The REIT share value using the price-to-FFO approach is thus $70.

Approach 3: Value of REIT share using price-to-AFFO approach

Funds from operations (FFO)	$70
Subtract: non-cash rents	$5
Subtract: recurring maintenance-type capital expenditures	$15
Equals: AFFO	$50
Shares outstanding (million)	10
AFFO / share = $50 million / 10 million shares	$5
Property subsector average P/AFFO multiple	14×

Applying the office subsector average P/AFFO multiple of 14× yields a value per share of $5 × 14 = $70.

The REIT share value using the price-to-AFFO approach is thus $70.

Approach 4: Value of REIT share using discounted cash flow approach

	2014	*2015*	*2016*	*2017*
Dividends per share	$5.00	$5.10	$5.20	$5.25

Present value in 2016 of dividends stream beginning in 2017 = $5.25 / (0.09 – 0.02) = $75.06

These dividends are discounted at a rate of 9%.

value of a REIT share

= PV(dividends for years 1 through n) + PV(terminal value at the end of year n)

$= PV_{2014\ dividend} + PV_{2015\ dividend} + PV_{2016\ dividend} + PV_{2017\ and\ later\ dividends\ (terminal\ value)}$

$= \$5.00 / (1.09) + \$5.10 / (1.09)^2 + \$5.20 / (1.09)^3 + \$75.06 / (1.09)^3$

= $70.85

The REIT share value using the discounted cash flow approach is thus $70.85.

Note that the calculated value of a REIT share is likely to vary, sometimes greatly, depending on which of these approaches is used.

KEY CONCEPTS

LOS 39.a

The main types of publicly traded real estate securities are:

- Real estate investment trusts (REITs) which are tax-advantaged companies that own income-producing real estate.
- Real estate operating companies (REOCs) which are non-tax-advantaged companies that own real estate.
- Mortgage-backed securities (MBS) which are investments in residential or commercial mortgages that are backed by real estate.

The main types of REITs are:

- Equity REITs which take ownership stakes in income-producing property.
- Mortgage REITs which invest primarily in mortgages, mortgage securities, or loans that use real estate as collateral.

LOS 39.b

Advantages of publicly traded real estate securities include:

- Superior liquidity.
- Lower minimum investment.
- Limited liability.
- Access to premium properties.
- Active professional management.
- Protections accorded to publicly traded securities.
- Greater potential for diversification.
- Exemption from taxation.
- Earnings predictability.
- High yield.

Disadvantages of publicly traded real estate securities include:

- Taxes versus direct ownership.
- Lack of control.
- Costs of a publicly traded corporate structure.
- Price is determined by the stock market.
- Structural conflicts of interest.
- Limited potential for income growth.
- Forced equity issuance.
- Lack of flexibility.

LOS 39.c:

Investment characteristics of REITs include:

- Exemption from corporate-level income taxes.
- High dividend yield.
- Low income volatility.
- Frequent secondary equity offerings.

The most risky types of REIT property sectors are those in which significant mismatches between supply and demand are likely to happen (particularly health care, hotel, and office REITs), as well as those sectors where the occupancy rates are most likely to vary over a short period of time (especially hotels).

REIT due diligence considerations:

- Remaining lease terms.
- Inflation protection.
- Occupancy rates and leasing activity.
- In-place rents versus market rents.
- Costs to re-lease space.
- Tenant concentration in the portfolio.
- Tenants' financial health.
- New supply versus demand.
- Balance sheet analysis.
- Quality of management.

LOS 39.d

Types of REITs include:

- Retail REITs, which own properties used as shopping centers.
- Office REITs, which provide space to multiple business tenants.
- Residential ("multi-family") REITs, which invest in rental apartments.
- Health care REITs, which lease properties to hospitals and nursing homes.
- Industrial REITs, which own properties used in manufacturing, warehousing, and distribution.
- Hotel REITs, which receive passive rental income from hotel management companies.
- Storage REITs, which rent self-storage lockers to individuals and small businesses.
- Diversified REITs, which own multiple types of real estate.

LOS 39.e

Net asset value per share (NAVPS) is the (per-share) amount by which a REIT's assets exceed its liabilities, using current market value rather than accounting or book values. The REIT or REOC portfolio of operating real estate investments can be valued by capitalizing net operating income:

$$\text{property value} = \frac{\text{net operating income}}{\text{capitalization rate}}$$

	Estimated cash NOI
÷	Assumed cap rate
=	Estimated value of operating real estate
+	Cash and accounts receivable
–	Debt and other liabilities
=	Net asset value
÷	Shares outstanding
=	NAV / share

LOS 39.f

	Accounting net earnings
+	Depreciation expense
+	Deferred tax expenses
–	Gains (losses) from sales of property and debt restructuring
=	Funds from operations

	FFO (funds from operations)
–	Non-cash (straight-line) rent adjustment
–	Recurring maintenance-type capital expenditures and leasing commissions
=	AFFO (adjusted funds from operations)

LOS 39.g

Approaches to REIT valuation:

- Net asset value per share: NAVPS is based on market values and is considered to be the fundamental measure of value for REITs and REOCs.
- Relative value: Market-based-multiple approaches including price-to-FFO and price-to-AFFO can be used to value REITs and REOCs.
- Discounted cash flow: Dividend discount models typically include two- or three-stages, based on near- and long-term growth forecasts. Discounted cash flow models use intermediate-term cash flow projections, plus a terminal value based on historical cash flow multiples.

LOS 39.h

Price-to-FFO approach:

	Funds from operations (FFO)
÷	Shares outstanding
=	FFO / share
×	Sector average P/FFO multiple
=	NAV / share

Price-to-AFFO approach:

	Funds from operations (FFO)
–	Non-cash rents
–	Recurring maintenance-type capital expenditures
=	AFFO
÷	Shares outstanding
=	AFFO / share
×	Property subsector average P/AFFO multiple
=	NAV / share

Discounted cash flow approach:

Value of a REIT share
= PV(dividends for years 1 through n) + PV(terminal value at the end of year n)

Concept Checkers

1. Which of the following *least accurately* identifies one of the principal types of publicly traded real estate securities?
   A. Commingled real estate fund (CREF).
   B. Shares of real estate operating companies (REOC).
   C. Residential and commercial mortgage-backed securities (MBS).

2. Which of the following statements *most accurately* describes one of the advantages of investing in REITs? REITs:
   A. can pass on tax losses to their investors as deductions from their taxable income.
   B. have lower price and return volatility than a comparable direct investment in properties.
   C. limit investor liability to only the amount of the investor's original capital investment.

3. From the choices given, choose the *most accurate* to complete the following sentence. After overall growth in the economy, the *most* important economic factor affecting a(n):
   A. hotel REIT is job creation.
   B. storage REIT is retail sales growth.
   C. office REIT is population growth.

4. Compared with other publicly traded shares, REITs are *most likely* to offer relatively low:
   A. yields.
   B. stability of income and returns.
   C. growth from reinvested operating cash flows.

5. Which of the following statements *least accurately* describes a feature of the DOWNREIT structure? A DOWNREIT:
   A. is the most common REIT structure in the United States.
   B. may own properties at both the REIT level and the partnership level.
   C. can form partnerships for each property acquisition it undertakes.

6. Which of the following statements about the use of net asset value per share (NAVPS) in REIT valuation is *most accurate*? NAVPS is:
   A. the difference between the accounting book values of a real estate company's assets and its liabilities, divided by shares outstanding.
   B. considered to be a superior measure of the net worth of a REIT's shares, compared with book value per share.
   C. exactly equal to the intrinsic value of REIT shares.

7. In the process of calculating adjusted funds from operations (AFFO) from funds from operations (FFO), an analyst is *most likely* to:
   A. add depreciation and amortization.
   B. subtract non-cash rent.
   C. add recurring maintenance-type capital expenditures and leasing commissions.

8. Which statement regarding approaches to REIT valuation is *least accurate*?
   A. AFFO includes a number of adjustments to FFO that result in AFFO approximating continuing cash earnings.
   B. P/AFFO is the most frequently used multiple in analyzing the REIT sector.
   C. Dividend discount models are appropriate for valuing REITs because REITs return most of their income to investors.

Use the following information for Questions 9 through 12.

Anna Ginzburg, CFA, is using the following information to analyze a potential investment in an industrial building.

Selected REIT Financial Information

	All amounts in $million
Estimated 12 months cash net operating income (NOI)	$40
Funds from operations (FFO)	$30
Cash and equivalents	$30
Accounts receivable	$20
Debt and other liabilities	$250
Non-cash rents	$5
Recurring maintenance-type capital expenditures	$10
Shares outstanding	10 million shares
Expected annual dividend next year (2014)	$3.00
Dividend growth rate in 2015 and 2016	4%
Dividend growth rate (from 2017 into perpetuity)	3%
Assumed cap rate	8%
Office subsector average P/FFO multiple	12×
Office subsector average P/AFFO multiple	20×
Ginzburg's cost of equity capital	11%
Risk-free rate	2%

9. The value of Ginzburg's potential investment using a net asset value (NAV) approach is *closest* to:
   A. $30.
   B. $35.
   C. $40.

10. The value of Ginzburg's potential investment using a price-to-FFO approach is *closest* to:
    A. $30.
    B. $35.
    C. $40.

11. The value of Ginzburg's potential investment using a price-to-AFFO approach is *closest* to:
    A. $30.
    B. $35.
    C. $40.

12. The value of Ginzburg's potential investment using a discounted cash flow approach is *closest* to:
    A. $30.
    B. $35.
    C. $40.

ANSWERS – CONCEPT CHECKERS

1. **A** A commingled real estate fund (CREF) is an example of a private real estate investment, not a publicly traded security. The three principal types of publicly traded real estate securities available globally are real estate investment trusts (REITs), real estate operating companies (REOCs), and residential and commercial mortgage-backed securities (MBS).

2. **C** REIT investors have no liability for the REITs in which they invest beyond the original amount invested. REITs and REOCs usually cannot pass on tax losses to their investors as deductions from taxable income. Because REIT prices and returns are determined by the stock market, the value of a REIT is more volatile that its appraised net asset value.

3. **A** After growth in the GDP, the most important factor driving demand for hotel rooms is job creation, because business and leisure travel are closely tied to the size of the workforce. More important to the value of a storage REIT than retail sales growth is population growth. More important to the value of an office REIT than population growth is job creation.

4. **C** When we compare REITs to other kinds of publicly traded shares, REITs offer above-average yields and stable income and returns. Due to their high income-to-payout ratios, REITs have relatively low potential to grow by reinvesting operating cash flows.

5. **A** Most REITs in the United States are structured as UPREITs, not DOWNREITs. The other two statements are true: a DOWNREIT may own properties at both the REIT level and at the partnership level, and may form partnerships for each property acquisition it undertakes.

6. **B** NAVPS is the difference between a REIT's assets and its liabilities, using current market values instead of accounting book values and dividing by the number of shares outstanding. NAVPS is a superior measure of the net worth of a REIT, compared to book value per share which is based on historical cost values. NAV is the largest component of the intrinsic value of a REIT; however, other factors, such as the value of non-asset-based income streams, the value added by management, and the value of any contingent liabilities, also contribute to intrinsic value.

7. **B** To calculate AFFO, we begin with FFO and then deduct non-cash rent, maintenance-type capital expenditures, and leasing commissions.

8. **B** FFO has some shortcomings, but because it is the most standardized method of measuring a REIT's earnings, P/FFO is the most commonly used multiple in analyzing REITs. AFFO is used as a convenient proxy for a "cash flow" multiple because AFFO is an approximation of cash earnings. Dividend discount models are appropriate methods for valuing REITs because REITs return a significant portion of their income to their investors and tend to be high-dividend payers.

9. **A** The value per share for this REIT using net asset value valuation is computed as follows:

Estimated cash NOI	40
Assumed cap rate	8%
Estimated value of operating real estate (40 / .08)	500
Plus: cash + accounts receivable	50
Less: debt and other liabilities	250
Net asset value	300
Shares outstanding	10
NAV / share	$30.00

The REIT share value using the net asset value approach is $30.

10. **B** The value per share for this REIT using price-to-FFO valuation is computed as follows:

Funds from operations (FFO)	$30
Shares outstanding (millions)	10
FFO / share = $30 million / 10 million shares	$3.00

Applying the office subsector average P/FFO multiple of 12× yields a value per share of:

$3.00 × 12 = $36.00

The REIT share value using the price-to-FFO approach is $36.

11. **A** The value per share for this REIT using a price-to-AFFO valuation is computed as follows:

Funds from operations (FFO)	$30
Subtract: non-cash rents	$5
Subtract: recurring maintenance-type capital expenditures	$10
Equals: AFFO	$15
Shares outstanding	10 million
AFFO / share = $15 million / 10 million shares	$1.50
Property subsector average P/AFFO multiple	20×

Applying the office subsector average P/AFFO multiple of 20× yields a value per share of $1.50 × 20 = $30.

The REIT share value using the price-to-AFFO approach is $30.

12. **B** The value per share for this REIT using a discounted cash flow valuation is computed as follows:

	2014	*2015*	*2016*	*2017*
Dividends per share:	\$3.00	\$3.12	\$3.24	\$3.34

Present value in 2016 of dividends stream beginning in 2017 = \$3.34 / (0.11 – 0.02) = \$37.13

Present value of all dividends, when discounted at a rate of 11%

$= PV_{2014\ dividend} + PV_{2015\ dividend} + PV_{2016\ dividend} + PV_{(terminal\ value)}$

$= \$3.00/(1.11) + \$3.12/(1.11)^2 + \$3.24/(1.11)^3 + \$37.13/(1.11)^3$

$= \$34.76$

The REIT share value using the discounted cash flow approach is \$34.76.

The following is a review of the Alternative Investments principles designed to address the learning outcome statements set forth by CFA Institute. This topic is also covered in:

PRIVATE EQUITY VALUATION

Study Session 13

EXAM FOCUS

This topic has a great deal of testable material, both conceptual and quantitative. For the exam, know the three sources of value creation in private equity. Know that, relative to buyouts, venture capital concerns companies that are immature and generally more risky. Understand that the drivers of return for buyouts are earnings growth, the increase in multiple upon exit, and the reduction in the debt; whereas for venture capital, it is the pre-money valuation, the investment, and potential subsequent equity dilution.

Be familiar with risks, costs, structure, and terms that are unique to private equity funds. Know how to calculate management fees, carried interest, NAV, DPI, RVPI, and TVPI of a private equity fund. Using both the NPV and IRR venture capital methods, be able to calculate ownership fraction, number of new shares issued, and the price per share for the new investment.

BACKGROUND: PRIVATE EQUITY

Private equity is of increasing importance in the global economy. Private equity firms make investments ranging from investments in early stage companies (called a venture capital investment) to investments in mature companies (generally in a buyout transaction).

The following diagram may help you understand the private equity investment process.

Figure 1: The Typical Private Equity Investment Transaction

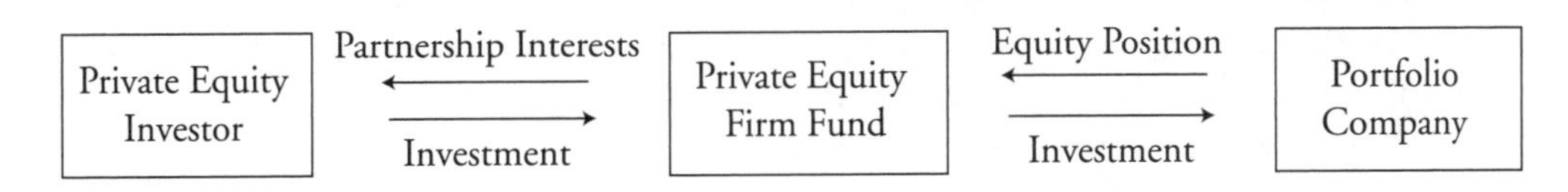

We will use the term *portfolio company* to denote the companies that private equity firms invest in. Portfolio companies are sometimes referred to as investee companies.

We will use the term *private equity firm* (PE firm) to denote the intermediary in the illustrated transaction.

We will use the term *private equity investor* to denote the outside investor who makes an investment in a fund offered by the PE firm.

In this review, we examine the perspective of both private equity firms evaluating investments in portfolio companies and the perspective of an outside investor who is evaluating an investment in a private equity firm.

LOS 40.a: Explain sources of value creation in private equity.

CFA® Program Curriculum, Volume 5, page 139

It is commonly believed that PE firms have the ability to add greater value to their portfolio companies than do publicly governed firms. The sources of this increased value are thought to come from the following:

1. The ability to re-engineer the porfolio company and operate it more efficiently.
2. The ability to obtain debt financing on more advantageous terms.
3. Superior alignment of interests between management and private equity ownership.

Re-engineering the Portfolio Company

In order to re-engineer their portfolio companies, many private equity firms have an in-house staff of experienced industry CEOs, CFOs, and other former senior executives. These executives can share their expertise and contacts with portfolio company management.

Obtaining Favorable Debt Financing

A second source of added value is from more favorable terms on debt financing. During 2006 and the first half of 2007, the availability of cheap credit with few covenants led many private equity firms to use debt for buyout transactions. In PE firms, debt is more heavily utilized and is quoted as a multiple of EBITDA (earnings before interest, taxes, depreciation, and amortization) as opposed to a multiple of equity, as for public firms.

The central proposition of the Modigliani-Miller theorems is that the use of debt versus equity is inconsequential for firm value. However, once the assumption of no taxes is removed from their model, the tax savings from the use of debt (i.e., the interest tax shield) increases firm value. The use of greater amounts of financial leverage may increase firm value in the case of private equity firms. Because these firms have a reputation for efficient management and timely payment of debt interest, this helps to allay concerns over their highly leveraged positions and helps maintain their access to the debt markets.

Professor's Note: The Modigliani-Miller theorems are discussed in detail in the corporate finance material, Study Session 8. In that corporate finance material, they are referred to as propositions.

The use of debt is thought to make private equity portfolio companies more efficient. According to this view, the requirement to make interest payments forces the portfolio companies to use free cash flow more efficiently because interest payments must be made on the debt.

Much of the debt financing for private equity firms comes from the syndicated loan market, but the debt is often repackaged and sold as collateralized loan obligations (CLOs). Private equity firms may also issue high-yield bonds which are repackaged as collateralized debt obligations (CDOs). These transactions have resulted in a large transfer of risk. However, the markets slowed beginning in 2007, creating less availability of financing for large buyouts.

Professor's Note: CLOs and CDOs are discussed in more detail in the topic review on asset backed securities and the bond market in Study Session 15.

A third source of value added for PE firms is the alignment of interests between private equity owners and the managers of the portfolio companies they own, as discussed in the next LOS.

LOS 40.b: Explain how private equity firms align their interests with those of the managers of portfolio companies.

CFA® Program Curriculum, Volume 5, page 140

In many private equity transactions, ownership and control are concentrated in the same hands. In buyout transactions, management often has a substantial stake in the company's equity. In many venture capital investments, the private equity firm offers advice and management expertise. The private equity firm can also gain increased control if the venture capital investee company does not meet specified targets.

In private equity firms, managers are able to focus more on long-term performance because, unlike public companies, private companies do not face the scrutiny of analysts, shareholders, and the broader market. This also allows the private equity firms to hire managers that are capable of substantial restructuring efforts.

Control Mechanisms

Private equity firms use a variety of mechanisms to align the interests of the managers of portfolio companies with the private equity firm's interests. The following contract terms are contained in the **term sheet** that specifies the terms of the private equity firm's investment.

Compensation: Managers of the portfolio companies receive compensation that is closely linked to the company's performance, and the compensation contract contains clauses that promote the achievement of the firm's goals.

Tag-along, drag-along clauses: Anytime an acquirer acquires control of the company, they must extend the acquisition offer to all shareholders, including firm management.

Board representation: The private equity firm is ensured control through board representation if the portfolio company experiences a major event such as a takeover, restructuring, initial public offering (IPO), bankruptcy, or liquidation.

Noncompete clauses: Company founders must agree to clauses that prevent them from competing against the firm within a prespecified period of time.

Priority in claims: Private equity firms receive their distributions before other owners, often in the form of preferred dividends and sometimes specified as a multiple of their original investment. They also have priority on the company's assets if the portfolio company is liquidated.

Required approvals: Changes of strategic importance (e.g., acquisitions, divestitures, and changes in the business plan) must be approved by the private equity firm.

Earn-outs: These are used predominantly in venture capital investments. Earn-outs tie the acquisition price paid by the private equity firm to the portfolio company's future performance over a specified time period.

By specifying the appropriate control mechanisms in the investment contract, private equity firms can make investments in companies of considerable risk.

LOS 40.c: Distinguish between the characteristics of buyout and venture capital investments.

CFA® Program Curriculum, Volume 5, page 142

Valuation Characteristics of Venture Capital vs. Buyout Investments

Venture capital and buyout are the two main forms of private equity investments. As previously noted, companies financed with venture capital are usually less mature than buyout targets. Venture capital firms usually have a specific industry focus, such as biotechnology, and emphasize revenue growth. When private equity firms make buyout purchases, the emphasis is on EBIT or EBITDA growth, and typically a portfolio of companies with stable earnings growth is purchased.

The following chart summarizes the key differences between venture capital and buyout investments.

Figure 2: Key Differences Between Venture Capital and Buyout Investments

Characteristic	*Venture Capital Investments*	*Buyout Investments*
Cash Flows	Low predictability with potentially unrealistic projections	Stable and predictable cash flows
Product Market	New product market with uncertain future	Strong market position with a possible niche position
Products	Product is based on new technology with uncertain prospects	Established products
Asset Base	Weak	Substantial base that can serve as collateral
Management Team	New team although individual members typically have a strong entrepreneurial record	Strong and experienced
Financial Leverage	Low debt use with a majority of equity financing	High amounts of debt with a large percentage of senior debt and substantial amounts of junior and mezzanine debt
Risk Assessment	Risk is difficult to estimate due to new technologies, markets, and company history	Risk can be estimated due to industry and company maturity
Exit	Exit via IPO or company sale is difficult to forecast	Exit is predictable
Operations	High cash burn rate required due to company and product immaturity	Potential exists for reduction in inefficiencies
Working Capital Required	Increasing requirements due to growth	Low requirements
Due Diligence Performed by Private Equity Firms	Private equity firms investigate technological and commercial prospects; investigation of financials is limited due to short history	Private equity firms perform extensive due diligence
Goal Setting	Goals are milestones set in business plan and growth strategy	Goals reference cash flows, strategic plan, and business plan
Private Equity Investment Returns	High returns come from a few highly successful investments with writeoffs from less successful investments	Low variability in the success of investments with failures being rare
Capital Market Presence	Generally not active in capital markets	Active in capital markets
Sales Transactions	Most companies are sold as a result of the relationship between venture capital firm and entrepreneurs	Companies are typically sold in an auction-type process
Ability to Grow Through Subsequent Funding	Companies are less scalable as subsequent funding is typically smaller	Strong performers can increase subsequent funding amounts
Source of General Partner's Variable Revenue	Carried interest is most common, transaction and monitoring fees are less common	Carried interest, transaction fees, and monitoring fees

Terms related to private equity, such as carried interest, and revenue of private equity general partners are discussed in greater detail in LOS 40.g.

Professor's Note: Many of these characteristics can be more easily remembered if you keep in mind that, relative to companies acquired through buyout, venture capital portfolio companies are immature companies with risky prospects and cash flows. They require a great deal of funding but may have limited access to financing, especially debt. The returns on venture capital come from a small number of highly successful investments.

General Valuation Issues for Private Equity

Public companies are bought and sold on regulated exchanges daily. Private companies, however, are bought by buyers with specific interests at specific points in time, with each potential buyer possibly having a different valuation for the company. Furthermore, valuing a private company is more difficult than valuing public companies because, as discussed previously, PE firms often transform and reengineer the portfolio company such that future cash flow estimates are difficult to obtain.

Private Equity Valuation Methodologies

There are six methodologies used to value private equity portfolio companies.

- **Discounted cash flow** (DCF) **analysis** is most appropriate for companies with a significant operating history because it requires an estimate of cash flows.
- A **relative value** or **market approach** applies a price multiple, such as the price-earnings ratio, against the company's earnings to get an estimate of the company's valuation. This approach requires predictable cash flows and a significant history.
- A third approach uses **real option analysis** and is applicable for immature companies with flexibility in their future strategies.

Professor's Note: Real options are covered in more detail in the topic review on capital budgeting in Study Session 8.

- The fourth approach uses the **replacement cost** of the business. It is generally not applicable to mature companies whose historical value added would be hard to estimate.
- The last two approaches, the **venture capital method** and the **leveraged buyout method**, are discussed at the end of this review.

Other Considerations

Other considerations for valuing private equity portfolio companies are control premiums, country risk, and marketability and illiquidity discounts. In buyouts, the private equity investors typically have complete control. In venture capital investments, however, these investors usually have a minority position, and their control of the companies depends on the alignment of their interests with that of controlling shareholders. When valuing companies in emerging markets, country risk premiums may be added, thereby increasing the discount rate applied to the company's cash flows. Illiquidity and marketability discounts refer to the ability and right to sell the company's shares, respectively.

Professor's Note: Country risk and premiums in emerging markets are covered in more detail in the topic review on return concepts in Study Session 10.

Price Multiples

To value private equity portfolio companies, many investors use market data from similar publicly traded companies, most commonly the price multiples from comparable public companies. However, it is often difficult to find public companies at the same stage of development, same line of business, same capital structure, and same risk. A decision must also be made as to whether trailing or future earnings are used. For these reasons, a relative value or market approach should be used carefully.

Discounted Cash Flow Analysis

Market data is also used with discounted cash flow (DCF) analysis, with beta and the cost of capital estimated from public companies while adjusting for differences in operating and financial leverage between the private and public comparables. In DCF analysis, an assumption must be made regarding the company's future value. Typically a terminal value (i.e., an exit value) is calculated using a price multiple of the company's EBITDA.

Professor's Note: Adjusting beta for differences in operating and financial leverage between comparables is covered in more detail in the topic review on return concepts in Study Session 10.

Given the uncertainty associated with private companies, a variety of valuation techniques is typically applied to a range of different potential scenarios.

Buyout Valuation Issues

Types of Buyouts

In a buyout transaction, the buyer acquires a controlling equity position in a target company. Buyouts include takeovers, management buyouts (MBOs), and leveraged buyouts (LBOs). This review focuses on LBOs, in which a high amount of debt is used to finance a substantial portion of the acquisition. The financing of a LBO typically involves senior debt, junk bonds, equity, and mezzanine finance. Mezzanine finance is a hybrid between debt and equity and can be structured to suit each particular transaction.

Leveraged Buyout (LBO)

The view of an LBO transaction, referred to as the LBO model, is not a form of valuation but rather a method of factoring in the company's capital structure and other parameters to determine the return the private equity firm should expect from the transaction. The objective is not to value the company but to determine the maximum price in negotiation that the private equity firm should pay for its stake.

LBO Model

The LBO model has three main inputs:

1. The target company's forecasted cash flows.
2. The expected returns to the providers of the financing.
3. The total amount of financing.

The cash flow forecasts are provided by the target's management but scrutinized by the private equity firm. The exit date (when the target company is sold) is evaluated at different dates to determine its influence on the projected returns. The value of the company at that time is forecast using a relative value or market approach.

Professor's Note: LOS order has been changed for the purposes of clarity.

LOS 40.d: Describe valuation issues in buyout and venture capital transactions.

CFA® Program Curriculum, Volume 5, page 144

Exit Value

The exit value can be viewed as:

investment cost + earnings growth + increase in price multiple + reduction in debt = exit value

As previously mentioned, private equity firms are known for their reengineering and improved corporate governance of target companies, which should result in operational efficiencies and higher earnings growth. As a result, the target company should see an increase in price multiples and increased ability to pay down its debt. Each of the three variables should be examined using scenario analysis to determine the plausibility of their forecasted values and the forecasted exit value. One purpose for calculating the exit value is to determine the investment's internal rate of return sensitivity in the exit year.

Example: Calculating payoff multiples and IRRs for equity investors

Suppose an LBO transaction is valued at $1,000 million and has the following characteristics (amounts are in millions of dollars):

- Exit occurs in five years at a projected multiple of 1.80 of the company's initial cost.
- It is financed with 60% debt and 40% equity.
- The $400 equity investment is composed of:
  - $310 in preference shares held by the private equity firm.
  - $80 in equity held by the private equity firm.
  - $10 in equity held by management equity participation (MEP).
- Preference shares are guaranteed a 14% compound annual return payable at exit.
- The equity of the private equity firm is promised 90% of the company's residual value at exit after creditors and preference shares are paid.
- Management equity receives the other 10% residual value.
- By exit, the company will have paid off $350 of the initial $600 in debt using operating cash flow.

Calculate the payoff for the company's claimants and the internal rate of return (IRR) and payoff multiple for the equity claimants.

Answer:

First calculate the exit value as: $1,000 × 1.8 = $1,800.

Next calculate the claimants' payoffs:

- *Debt*: The claim of debtholders is their initial investment minus the amount that has been paid down: $600 – $350 = $250.
- *Preference shares*: Earn a return of 14% so their claim is:
  $\$310 \times (1.14)^5 = \$596.88$.
- *Private equity firm*: Receives 90% of the residual exit value:
  0.90(1,800 – $250 – $596.88) = $857.81.
- *Management*: Receives 10% of the residual exit value:
  0.10(1,800 – $250 – $596.88) = $95.31.

The total investment by the private equity firm is $310 + $80 = $390.

The total payoff is $596.88 + $857.81 = $1454.69.

The payoff multiple for the private equity firm is: 1454.69 / 390 = 3.7.

Using your TI BA II Plus, the IRR is calculated as:
PV = –$390; FV = $1454.69; N = 5; CPT I/Y ⇒ 30.1%.

For the management equity, the IRR is:
PV = –$10; FV = $95.31; N = 5; CPT I/Y ⇒ 57.0%.

The payoff multiple for the management equity program (MEP) is: 95.31 / 10 = 9.5.

In the example, the equity held by the private equity firm and management experiences a significant increase in value. The IRR for each is attractive at 30.1% and 57.0%, respectively.

The components of the return are:

- The return on the preference shares for the private equity firm.
- The increased multiple upon exit.
- The reduction in the debt claim.

In most LBOs, most of the debt is senior debt that will amortize over time. In the preceding example, the debtholders' claim on assets was reduced from \$600 to \$250. The use of debt in this example is advantageous and magnifies the returns to the equityholders. However, the use of debt also increases risk to the equityholders. Use of debt becomes disadvantageous if a company experiences difficulties and cannot make the payments on the debt. In this case, the equityholders could lose control of the company if it is forced into bankruptcy.

VALUATION ISSUES IN VENTURE CAPITAL INVESTMENTS

Pre- and Post-Money Valuation

The two fundamental concepts in venture capital investments are pre-money (PRE) valuation and post-money (POST) valuation. A private equity firm makes an investment (INV) in an early-stage start-up company.

The post-money valuation of the investee company is:

$$PRE + INV = POST$$

The ownership proportion of the venture capital (VC) investor is:

$$= INV / POST$$

Example: Calculating post-money valuation and proportional ownership

A company is valued at \$3,000,000 prior to a capital infusion of \$1,000,000 by a VC investor.

Calculate the post-money valuation and the VC investor's proportional ownership.

Answer:

The post-money valuation is:

$$\$3,000,000 + \$1,000,000 = \$4,000,000$$

The ownership proportion of the VC investor is:

$$= \$1,000,000 / \$4,000,000 = 25\%$$

Appropriate Methods for Venture Capital Valuation

The pre-money valuation and investment will be negotiated between the investee company and the VC investor. Additionally, the VC investor should keep in mind that his ownership could be diluted in the future due to future financing, conversion of convertible debt into equity, and the issuance of stock options to management.

As discussed previously, it is difficult to forecast the cash flows for a VC portfolio company. Therefore, discounted cash flow analysis (the income approach) is not usually used as the primary valuation method for VC companies. It is also difficult to use a relative value or market approach. This is because a VC company is often unique, and there may be no comparable companies to estimate a benchmark price multiple from. A replacement cost approach may also be difficult to apply. Alternative methodologies include real option analysis and the venture capital method, which will be addressed later in this review.

To estimate the pre-money valuation, the VC investor typically examines the company's intellectual property and capital, the potential for the company's products, and its intangible assets. Sometimes a cap (e.g., $3,000,000) is placed on the pre-money valuation due to its uncertain value.

Valuation Issues: Buyout vs. Venture Capital

The following table highlights the different issues when valuing buyouts versus private equity.

Figure 3: Valuation Issues for Buyouts vs. Venture Capital Investments

Valuation Issue	*Buyout*	*Venture Capital*
Applicability of DCF Method	Frequently used to estimate value of equity	Less frequently used as cash flows are uncertain
Applicability of Relative Value Approach	Used to check the value from DCF analysis	Difficult to use because there may be no truly comparable companies
Use of Debt	High	Low as equity is dominant form of financing
Key Drivers of Equity Return	Earnings growth, increase in multiple upon exit, and reduction in the debt	Pre-money valuation, investment, and subsequent dilution

Professor's Note: Valuation methodologies for buyouts need to factor in the level and pattern of leverage over the investment term. Initially, debt levels are high but are expected to decrease to "normal" levels by the time of exit. We address this issue near the end of this topic review.

LOS 40.e: Explain alternative exit routes in private equity and their impact on value.

CFA® Program Curriculum, Volume 5, page 147

Types of Exit Routes

The exit value is a critical element in the return for the private equity firm and is considered carefully before the investment is undertaken. The means and timing of the exit strongly influence the exit value. There are four exit routes that private equity firms typically use: (1) an initial public offering (IPO), (2) secondary market sale, (3) management buyout (MBO), and (4) liquidation.

Initial Public Offering (IPO)

In an IPO, a company's equity is offered for public sale. An IPO usually results in the highest exit value due to increased liquidity, greater access to capital, and the potential to hire better quality managers. However, an IPO is less flexible, more costly, and a more cumbersome process than the other alternatives.

IPOs are most appropriate for companies with strong growth prospects and a significant operating history and size. The timing of an IPO is key. After the bursting of the U.S. tech bubble in 2000, the IPO market withered and venture capital firms had to find other means of exit.

Secondary Market Sale

In a secondary market sale, the company is sold to another investor or to another company interested in the purchase for strategic reasons (e.g., a company in the same industry wishes to expand its market share). Secondary market sales from one investor to another are quite frequent, especially in the case of buyouts. VC portfolio companies are sometimes exited via a buyout to another firm, but VC companies are usually too immature to support a large amount of debt. Secondary market sales result in the second highest company valuations after IPOs.

Management Buyout (MBO)

In an MBO, the company is sold to management, who utilize a large amount of leverage. Although management will have a strong interest in the subsequent success of the company, the resulting high leverage may limit management's flexibility.

Liquidation

Liquidation, the outright sale of the company's assets, is pursued when the company is deemed no longer viable and usually results in a low value. There is potential for negative publicity as a result of displaced employees and from the obvious implications of the company's failure to reach its objectives.

Exit Timing

The timing of the exit is also very important for company value, and the private equity firm should be flexible in this regard. For example, if a portfolio company cannot be sold due to weak capital markets, the private equity firm may want to consider buying another portfolio company at depressed prices, merging the two companies, and waiting until capital market conditions improve to sell both portfolio companies as one.

When an exit is anticipated in the next year or two, the exit valuation multiple can be forecasted without too much error. Beyond this time horizon, however, exit multiples become much more uncertain and stress testing should be performed on a wide range of possible values.

Professor's Note: Don't lose sight of the purpose of valuation: (1) to assess the ability of the portfolio company to generate cash flow and (2) to represent a benchmark for negotiations.

LOS 40.f: Explain private equity fund structures, terms, valuation, and due diligence in the context of an analysis of private equity fund returns.

CFA® Program Curriculum, Volume 5, page 149

Limited Partnership

The most common form of ownership structure for private equity funds is the limited partnership. In a limited partnership, the limited partners (LPs) provide funding and do not have an active role in the management of the investments. Their liability is limited to what they have invested (i.e., they cannot be held liable for any amount beyond their investment in the fund). The general partner (GP) in a limited partnership is liable for all the firm's debts and, thus, has unlimited liability. The GP is the manager of the fund.

Another form of private equity fund structure is the company limited by shares. It offers better legal protection to the partners, depending on the jurisdiction. Most fund structures are closed end, meaning that investors can only redeem the investment at specified time periods.

Private equity firms must both raise funds and manage the investment of those funds. The private equity firm usually spends a year or two raising funds. Funds are then drawn down for investment, after which returns are realized. Most private equity funds last 10 to 12 years but can have their life extended another 2 to 3 years.

Private Equity Fund Terms

As mentioned previously, private equity investments are often only available to qualified investors, the definition of which depends on the jurisdiction. In the United States, the individual must have at least $1 million in assets.

The terms in a fund prospectus are a result of negotiation between the GP and the LPs. If the fund is oversubscribed (i.e., has more prospective investors than needed), the GP has greater negotiating power.

The terms of the fund should be focused towards aligning the interests of the GP and LPs and specifying the compensation of the GP. The most important terms can be categorized into economic and corporate governance terms.

Economic Terms of a Private Equity Fund

Management fees: These are fees paid to the GP on an annual basis as a percent of paid-in capital invested and are commonly 2%.

Transaction fees: These are paid to the GP for fund investment banking services, such as arranging a merger. These fees are usually split evenly with the LPs and, when paid, are deducted from management fees.

Carried interest/performance fees: This is the GP's share of the fund profits and is usually 20% of profits (after management fees).

Ratchet: This specifies the allocation of equity between stockholders and management of the portfolio company and allows management to increase their allocation, depending on company performance.

Hurdle rate: This is the IRR that the fund must meet before the GP can receive carried interest. It usually varies from 7% to 10% and incentivizes the GP.

Target fund size: The stated total maximum size of the PE fund, specified as an absolute figure. It signals the GP's ability to manage and raise capital for a fund. It is a negative signal if actual funds ultimately raised are significantly lower than targeted.

Vintage: This is the year the fund was started and facilitates performance comparisons with other funds.

Term of the fund: As discussed previously, this is the life of the firm and is usually ten years.

Professor's Note: There are several "capital" terms used throughout this reading. Committed capital is the amount of funds promised by investors to private equity funds. Paid-in capital is the amount of funds actually received from investors (also referred to as invested capital in this reading).

Example: Calculating carried interest with a hurdle rate

Suppose a fund has committed capital of $100 million, carried interest of 20%, and a hurdle rate of 9%. The firm called 80% of its commitments in the beginning of Year 1. Of this, $50 million was invested in Company A and $30 million in Company B.

At the end of Year 2, a $7 million profit is realized on the exit from Company A. The investment in Company B is unchanged. The carried interest is calculated on a deal-by-deal basis (i.e., the IRR for determining carried interest is calculated for each deal upon exit).

Determine the theoretical carried interest and the actual carried interest.

Answer:

The theoretical carried interest is: 20% × $7,000,000 = $1,400,000.

The IRR for Company A is: PV = –$50; FV = $57; N = 2; CPT I/Y ⇒ 6.8%.

Because the 6.8% IRR is less than the hurdle rate of 9%, no carried interest is actually paid.

Corporate Governance Terms of a Private Equity Fund

The corporate governance terms in the prospectus provide the legal arrangements for the control of the fund and include the following:

Key man clause: If a key named executive leaves the fund or does not spend a sufficient amount of time at the fund, the GP may be prohibited from making additional investments until another key executive is selected.

Performance disclosure and confidentiality: This specifies the fund performance information that can be disclosed. Note that the performance information for underlying portfolio companies is typically not disclosed.

Clawback: If a fund is profitable early in its life, the GP receives compensation from the GP's contractually defined share of profits. Under a clawback provision, if the fund subsequently underperforms, the GP is required to pay back a portion of the early profits to the LPs. The clawback provision is usually settled at termination of the fund but can also be settled annually (also known as true-up).

Distribution waterfall: This provision specifies the method in which profits will flow to the LPs and when the GP receives carried interest. Two methods are commonly used. In a deal-by-deal method, carried interest can be distributed after each individual deal. The disadvantage of this method from the LPs' perspective is that one deal could earn $10 million and another could lose $10 million, but the GP will receive carried interest on the first deal, even though the LPs have not earned an overall positive return.

In the total return method, carried interest is calculated on the entire portfolio. There are two variants of the total return method: (1) carried interest can be paid only after the entire *committed* capital is returned to LPs; or (2) carried interest can be paid when the value of the portfolio exceeds *invested* capital by some minimum amount (typically 20%). Notice that the former uses committed capital whereas the latter uses only the capital actually invested.

Tag-along, drag-along clauses: Anytime an acquirer acquires control of the company, they must extend the acquisition offer to all shareholders, including firm management.

No-fault divorce: This clause allows a GP to be fired if a supermajority (usually 75% or more) of the LPs agree to do so.

Removal for cause: This provision allows for the firing of the GP or the termination of a fund given sufficient cause (e.g., a material breach of fund prospectus).

Investment restrictions: These specify leverage limits, a minimum amount of diversification, etc.

Co-investment: This provision allows the LPs to invest in other funds of the GP at low or no management fees. This provides the GP another source of funds. The provision also prevents the GP from using capital from different funds to invest in the same portfolio company. A conflict of interest would arise if the GP takes capital from one fund to invest in a troubled company that had received capital earlier from another fund.

Example: Applying distribution waterfalls methods

Suppose a fund has committed capital of $100 million and carried interest of 20%. An investment of $40 million is made. Later in the year, the fund exits the investment and earns a profit of $22 million.

Determine whether the GP receives any carried interest under the three distribution waterfall methods.

Answer:

In the deal-by-deal method, carried interest can be distributed after each individual deal, so carried interest of 20% × $22,000,000 = $4,400,000 is paid to the GP.

In the total return method #1, carried interest can be paid only after the portfolio value exceeds *committed* capital. Committed capital is $100 million and total proceeds from the exit are only $62 million, so no carried interest is paid.

In the total return method #2, carried interest can be paid when the value of the portfolio exceeds *invested* capital by some minimum amount (typically 20%).

Invested capital plus the 20% threshold is: $40,000,000 × 1.20 = $48 million.

The total proceeds from the exit are $62 million, so carried interest of $4,400,000 is paid to the GP.

Example: Applying clawback provision methods

Continuing with the previous example, assume in the second year, another investment of $25 million is exited and results in a loss of $4 million. Assume the deal-by-deal method and a clawback with annual true-up apply.

Determine whether the GP must return any former profits to the LPs.

Answer:

In the deal-by-deal method, the GP had received carried interest of $4,400,000.

With a subsequent loss of $4 million, the GP owes the LPs 20% of the loss:

20% × $4,000,000 = $800,000

Net Asset Value (NAV)

Because there is no ready secondary market for private equity investments, they are difficult to value. In a prospectus, however, the valuation is related to the fund's net asset value (NAV), which is the value of fund assets minus liabilities.

Ways to Determine NAV

The assets are valued by the GP in one of six ways:

1. At cost, adjusting for subsequent financing and devaluation.
2. At the minimum of cost or market value.
3. By revaluing a portfolio company anytime there is new financing.
4. At cost, with no adjustment until exit.
5. By using a discount factor for restricted securities (e.g., those that can only be sold to qualified investors).
6. Less frequently, by applying illiquidity discounts to values based on those of comparable publicly traded companies.

Issues in Calculating NAV

There are several issues with calculating NAV for a private equity fund:

- First, if the NAV is only adjusted when there are subsequent rounds of financing, then the NAV will be more stale when financings are infrequent.
- Second, there is no definitive method for calculating NAV for a private equity fund because the market value of portfolio companies is usually not certain until exit.

- Third, undrawn LP capital commitments are not included in the NAV calculation but are essentially liabilities for the LP. The value of the commitments depends on the cash flows generated from them, but these are quite uncertain. When a GP has trouble raising funds, this implies that the value of these commitments is low.
- Fourth, the investor should be aware that funds with different strategies and maturities may use different valuation methodologies. In the early stages, a venture capital investment is typically valued at cost. In the later stages, a method based on comparables may be used. Mature funds may use market comparables for their investments that are near exit. Asset price bubbles would inflate the value of these companies.
- Finally, it is usually the GP who values the fund. LPs are increasingly using third parties to value private equity funds.

Due Diligence of Private Equity Fund Investments

Before investing, outside investors should conduct a thorough due diligence of a private equity fund due to the following characteristics:

- First, private equity funds have returns that tend to persist. Hence, a fund's past performance is useful information. In other words, outperformers tend to keep outperforming and underperformers tend to keep underperforming or go out of business.
- Second, the return discrepancy between outperformers and underperformers is very large and can be as much as 20%.
- Third, private equity investments are usually illiquid, long-term investments. The duration of a private equity investment, however, is usually shorter than expected because when a portfolio company is exited, the funds are immediately returned to the fund investors.

LOS 40.g: Explain risks and costs of investing in private equity.

CFA® Program Curriculum, Volume 5, page 154

Post-Investment Investor Expectations

Once an investment is made by a private equity firm, the outside investors in the private equity fund expect to be apprised of the firm's performance. The following material now takes the perspective of this outside investor.

There are two important differences between investing in public equity and in a private equity fund. First, funds are committed in the private investments and later drawn down as capital is invested in portfolio companies. In a public firm, the committed capital is usually immediately deployed. Second, the returns on a private equity investment typically follow a J-Curve pattern through time. Initially, returns are negative but then turn positive as portfolio companies are sold at exit.

Private equity investments are usually regulated such that they are only available to "qualified" investors, usually defined as institutions and wealthy individuals. These regulations exist because of the high risks associated with private equity investing, which are disclosed in the private equity prospectus.

Risks of Investing in Private Equity

Classifying private equity risks broadly, the categories of private equity risk are general private equity risk (discussed in the following), risks specific to the investment strategy, industry risks, risks specific to the investment vehicle, and any regional or country risk.

General Risk Factors

The general private equity risk factors are as follows:

Liquidity risk: Because private equity investments are not publicly traded, it may be difficult to liquidate a position.

Unquoted investments risk: Because private equity investments do not have a publicly quoted price, they may be riskier than publicly traded securities.

Competitive environment risk: The competition for finding reasonably-priced private equity investments may be high.

Agency risk: The managers of private equity portfolio companies may not act in the best interests of the private equity firm and investors.

Capital risk: Increases in business and financial risks may result in a withdrawal of capital. Additionally, portfolio companies may find that subsequent rounds of financing are difficult to obtain.

Regulatory risk: The portfolio companies' products and services may be adversely affected by government regulation.

Tax risk: The tax treatment of investment returns may change over time.

Valuation risk: The valuation of private equity investments reflects subjective, not independent, judgment.

Diversification risk: Private equity investments may be poorly diversified, so investors should diversify across investment development stage, vintage, and strategy of private equity funds.

Market risk: Private equity is subject to long-term changes in interest rates, exchange rates, and other market risks. Short-term changes are usually not significant risk factors.

Costs of Private Equity Investing

The costs of investing in private equity are significantly higher than that with publicly traded securities and include the following:

Transaction costs: These costs include those from due diligence, bank financing, legal fees from acquisitions, and sales transactions in portfolio companies.

Investment vehicle fund setup costs: The legal and other costs of setting up the fund are usually amortized over the life of the fund.

Administrative costs: These are charged on a yearly basis and include custodian, transfer agent, and accounting costs.

Audit costs: These are fixed and charged annually.

Management and performance costs: These are typically higher than that for other investments and are commonly 2% for the management fee and a 20% fee for performance.

Dilution costs: As discussed previously, additional rounds of financing and stock options granted to portfolio company management will result in dilution. This is also true for options issued to the private equity firm.

Placement fees: Placement agents who raise funds for private equity firms may charge up-front fees as much as 2% or annual trailer fees as a percent of funds raised through limited partners.

Professor's Note: A trailer fee is the compensation paid by the fund manager to the person selling the fund to investors.

LOS 40.h: Interpret and compare financial performance of private equity funds from the perspective of an investor.

CFA® Program Curriculum, Volume 5, page 157

INTERNAL RATE OF RETURN (IRR)

The return metric recommended for private equity by the Global Investment Performance Standards (GIPS) is the IRR. The IRR is a cash-weighted (money-weighted) return measure. Although the private equity fund portfolio companies are actually illiquid, IRR assumes intermediate cash flows are reinvested at the IRR. Therefore, the IRR calculation should be interpreted cautiously.

Gross IRR

The IRR can be calculated gross or net of fees. Gross IRR reflects the fund's ability to generate a return from portfolio companies and is the relevant measure for the cash flows between the fund and portfolio companies.

Net IRR

Net IRR can differ substantially from Gross IRR because it is net of management fees, carried interest, and other compensation to the GP. Net IRR is the relevant measure for the cash flows between the fund and LPs and is therefore the relevant return metric for the LPs.

MULTIPLES

Multiples are also used to evaluate fund performance. Multiples are a popular tool of LPs due to their simplicity, ease of use, and ability to differentiate between realized and unrealized returns. Multiples, however, ignore the time value of money.

Quantitative Measures

The more popular multiples and those specified by GIPS include the following:

PIC (paid-in capital). This is the capital utilized by the GP. It can be specified in percentage terms as the paid-in capital to date divided by the committed capital. Alternatively, it can be specified in absolute terms as the cumulative capital utilized or called down.

DPI (distributed to paid-in capital). This measures the LP's realized return and is the cumulative distributions paid to the LPs divided by the cumulative invested capital. It is net of management fees and carried interest. DPI is also referred to as the cash-on-cash return.

RVPI (residual value to paid-in capital). This measures the LP's unrealized return and is the value of the LP's holdings in the fund divided by the cumulative invested capital. It is net of management fees and carried interest.

TVPI (total value to paid-in capital). This measures the LP's realized and unrealized return and is the sum of DPI and RVPI. It is net of management fees and carried interest.

Qualitative Measures

In addition to quantitative analysis of the fund, the investor should also analyze qualitative aspects of the fund, including the following:

- The realized investments, with an evaluation of successes and failures.
- The unrealized investments, with an evaluation of exit horizons and potential problems.
- Cash flow projections at the fund and portfolio company level.
- Fund valuation, NAV, and financial statements.

As an example, consider a fund that was started before the financial market collapse of 2007. If the RVPI is large relative to the DPI, this indicates that the firm has not successfully harvested many of its investments and that the fund may have an extended J-curve (it is taking longer than realized to earn a positive return on its investments). The investor should carefully examine the GP's valuations of the remaining portfolio companies, potential write-offs, and whether the routes for future exit have dried up.

Benchmarks

The benchmarking of private equity investments can be challenging. Private equity funds vary substantially from one to another; so before performance evaluation is performed, the investor should have a good understanding of the fund's structures, terms, valuation, and the results of due diligence. Because there are cyclical trends in IRR returns, the Net IRR should be benchmarked against a peer group of comparable private equity funds of the same vintage and strategy.

Professor's Note: The vintage refers to the year the fund was set up.

Note also that the private equity IRR is cash flow weighted whereas most other asset class index returns are time weighted. One solution to this problem has been to convert publicly traded equity benchmark returns to cash weighted returns using the cash flow patterns of private equity funds. This method, however, has some significant limitations.

Example: Comparing the financial performance of private equity funds

Two private equity funds, Fund A and Fund B, are being considered by an investor.

Financial Performance of Private Equity Fund A and Fund B

	Fund A	*Fund B*
Gross IRR	22.1%	2.4%
Net IRR	17.6%	–0.3%
Performance quartile	1	3
DPI	1.43	0.29
RVPI	1.52	1.03
TVPI	2.95	1.32
Maturity of fund	6 years	4 years

Interpret and compare the financial performance of private equity funds A and B.

Answer:

Examining its DPI, Fund A has distributed $1.43 in return for every dollar invested. Additionally, the RVPI implies that it will return $1.52 as other investments are harvested. Its Gross IRR of 22.1% is attractive, and after fees, the Net IRR is 17.6%. The fund ranks in the first quartile in its peer group of the same strategy and vintage.

At four years, Fund B is a less mature fund than Fund A. Fund B's DPI is 0.29, indicating that the realized returns for the fund are not substantial. Unrealized returns (RVPI) indicate that its investments not yet harvested should provide an additional return. The low Gross and Net IRRs indicate that the firm may still be affected by the J-curve, where a fund experiences initial losses before experiencing later profits. Currently, the firm is lagging its peers, as it ranks in the third quartile.

Note that in this illustrative example, we compared two funds of different maturities. As noted, a fund should be benchmarked against peers of the same vintage.

LOS 40.i: Calculate management fees, carried interest, net asset value, distributed to paid in (DPI), residual value to paid in (RVPI), and total value to paid in (TVPI) of a private equity fund.

CFA® Program Curriculum, Volume 5, page 159

In this section, we calculate the quantitative measures previously discussed using an example.

Example: Calculating performance measures

The GP for private equity Fund C charges a management fee of 2% and carried interest of 20%, using the first total return method. The total committed capital for the fund was $150 million. The statistics for years 2004–2009 are shown in the following table (in millions).

Cash Flows for Private Equity Fund C

	Capital Called Down	*Paid-in Capital*	*Management Fees*	*Operating Results*	*NAV before Distributions*	*Carried Interest*	*Distributions*	*NAV after Distributions*
2004	50	50	1.0	–10	39.0			39.0
2005	20	70	1.4	–25	32.6			32.6
2006	30	100	2.0	25	85.6			85.6
2007	20	120	2.4	50	153.2	0.6	20	132.6
2008	10	130	2.6	60	200.0	9.4	40	150.6
2009	10	140	2.8	110	267.8	13.6	80	174.2

Professor's Note: In the table, assume the capital called down, operating results, and distributions were given. The other statistics can be calculated.

Calculate the management fees, carried interest, NAV before distributions, NAV after distributions, distributed to paid in (DPI), residual value to paid in (RVPI), and total value to paid in (TVPI) of private equity Fund C.

Answer:

Paid-in capital: This is just the cumulative sum of the capital called down. For example, in 2005, it is the sum of the capital called down in 2004 and 2005: \$50 + \$20 = \$70.

Management fees: In each year, these are calculated as the percentage fee (here 2%) multiplied by the paid-in capital. For example, in 2005, it is 2% × \$70 = \$1.4.

Carried interest: Carried interest is not paid until the GP generates realized and unrealized returns (as reflected in the NAV before distributions) greater than the committed capital of \$150.

In 2007, the NAV before distributions exceeded the committed capital for the first time. In this first year, the carried interest is 20% multiplied by the NAV before distributions minus the committed capital: 20% × (\$153.2 – \$150) = \$0.6.

In subsequent years, it is calculated using the increase in the NAV before distributions. For example, in 2008, it is: 20% × (\$200 – \$153.2) = \$9.4.

NAV before distributions: These are calculated as:

= NAV after distributions in prior year + capital called down – management fees + operating results

For example in 2008, NAV before distributions is: \$132.6 + \$10 – \$2.6 + \$60 = \$200.

NAV after distributions: These are calculated as:

= NAV before distributions – carried interest – distributions

For example in 2008, NAV after distributions is: \$200 – \$9.40 – \$40 = \$150.60.

For DPI, RVPI, and TVPI, we will calculate these as of the most recent year (2009):

DPI: The DPI multiple is calculated as the cumulative distributions divided by the paid-in capital: ($20 + $40 + $80) / $140 = 1.0. This indicates that, in terms of distributed returns, the fund has returned every dollar invested.

RVPI: The RVPI multiple is calculated as the NAV after distributions (i.e., the net non-distributed value of the fund) divided by the paid-in capital: $174.2 / $140 = 1.24. This indicates that, although the distributed returns are not impressive for this fund, the fund has unrealized profits that should accrue to the LPs as investments are harvested.

TVPI: The TVPI multiple is the sum of the DPI and RVPI: 1.0 + 1.24 = 2.24. This indicates that on a realized and unrealized basis, the GP has more than doubled the investment of the LPs.

LOS 40.j: Calculate pre-money valuation, post-money valuation, ownership fraction, and price per share applying the venture capital method 1) with single and multiple financing rounds and 2) in terms of IRR.

CFA® Program Curriculum, Volume 5, page 163

Here, we describe the valuation of an investment in an existing company using the **venture capital** (VC) **method**.

At the time of a new investment in the company, the discounted present value of the estimated exit value, PV(exit value), is called the **post-money value** (after the investment is made). The value before the investment is made can be calculated as the post-money value minus the investment amount and is called the **pre-money value**.

POST = PV(exit value)

PRE = POST – INV

In order to determine the number of new shares issued to the venture capital firm (shares_{VC}) for an investment in an existing company, we need to determine the fraction of the company value (after the investment is made) that the investment represents. Based on the expected future value of the company (exit value) and the expected or required rate of return on the investment, we can do this in either of two ways with the same result.

The fraction of VC ownership (f) for the VC investment can be computed as:

The first method (**NPV method**):

$$f = \frac{\text{INV}}{\text{POST}}$$

where:
INV = amount of new investment for the venture capital investment.
POST = post-money value after the investment.

$$\text{POST} = \frac{\text{exit value}}{(1+r)^n}$$

The second method (**IRR method**):

$$f = \frac{\text{FV(INV)}}{\text{exit value}}$$

where:
FV(INV) = future value of the investment in round 1 at the expected exit date.
exit value = value of the company upon exit.

As long as the same compound rate is used to calculate the present value of the exit value and to calculate the future value of the VC investment, the fractional ownership required (f) is the same under either method.

Once we have calculated f, we can calculate the number of shares issued to the VC (shares_{VC}) based on the number of existing shares owned by the company founders prior to investment ($\text{shares}_{\text{Founders}}$).

$$\text{shares}_{VC} = \text{shares}_{\text{Founders}}\left(\frac{f}{1-f}\right)$$

The price per share at the time of the investment (price) is then simply the amount of the investment divided by the number of new shares issued.

$$\text{price} = \frac{\text{INV}}{\text{shares}_{VC}}$$

Example: Calculations using the NPV venture capital method and a single financing round

Ponder Technologies is a biotech company. Ponder's entrepreneur founders believe they can sell the company for $40 million in five years. They need $5 million in capital now, and the entrepreneurs currently hold 1 million shares.

The venture capital firm, VC Investors, decides that given the high risk of this company, a discount rate of 40% is appropriate.

Calculate the pre-money valuation, post-money valuation, ownership fraction, and price per share applying the NPV venture capital method with a single financing round.

Answer:

Step 1: The post-money (POST) valuation is the present value of the expected exit value (this assumes the investment was made in the company):

$$\text{POST} = \frac{40{,}000{,}000}{(1+0.40)^5} = 7{,}437{,}377$$

Step 2: The pre-money (PRE) valuation is what the company would hypothetically be worth without the investment:

PRE = 7,437,377 – 5,000,000 = 2,437,377

Step 3: To put $5 million in a company worth $7.4 million, the private equity firm must own 67.23% of the company:

$$f = \frac{5{,}000{,}000}{7{,}437{,}377} = 67.23\%$$

Note that under the IRR method, f is the same:

$$f = \frac{5 \text{ million}(1.40^5)}{40 \text{ million}} = 67.23\%$$

Step 4: If the entrepreneurs want 1 million shares, the private equity firm must get 2.05 million shares to get 67.23% ownership:

$$S_{VC} = 1{,}000{,}000\left[\frac{0.6723}{(1-0.6723)}\right] = 2{,}051{,}572$$

Step 5: Given a $5 million investment and 2.05 million shares, the stock price per share (P) must be:

$$P = \frac{5{,}000{,}000}{2{,}051{,}572} = \$2.44 \text{ per share}$$

Professor's Note: For the purpose of differentiating terms between multiple rounds of venture capital investment, we are using subscripts 1 and 2 in this section to denote first and second round, respectively. For multiple rounds of VC financing, we work backwards (from last round to first).

If there is a second round of VC financing (INV_2), we can calculate the new fractional ownership from the new investment (f_2) and the number of new shares required ($shares_{VC2}$) using the NPV method, as:

$$f_2 = \frac{INV_2}{POST_2}$$

Where $POST_2$ is the discounted present value of the company as of the time of the second financing round, its post-money value after the second round investment.

$$POST_2 = \frac{\text{exit value}}{(1+r_2)^{n2}}$$

and

$$PRE_2 = POST_2 - INV_2$$

$POST_1$ is the discounted present value of the company as of the time of the first financing round, its post-money value after the first round investment.

$$POST_1 = \frac{PRE_2}{(1+r_1)^{n1}}$$

As before, we can calculate the fractional ownership from the first round investment (f_1) using the NPV method, as:

$$f_1 = \frac{INV_1}{POST_1}$$

The new shares required to be issued to the VC in return for the first round financing amount (INV_1) and the price per share can then be calculated as:

$$shares_{VC1} = shares_{Founders}\left(\frac{f_1}{1-f_1}\right)$$

$$price_1 = \frac{INV_1}{shares_{VC1}}$$

The new shares required to be issued to the VC in return for the second round financing amount (INV_2) and the price per share can also be calculated as:

$$shares_{VC2} = (shares_{VC1} + shares_{Founders})\left(\frac{f_2}{1-f_2}\right)$$

$$price_2 = \frac{INV_2}{shares_{VC2}}$$

If the second round of financing is considered less risky than the first round (since the company has survived longer), a different, lower discount rate may be used in calculating the PV of the exit value at the time of the second round of financing. In the following example, we use a discount rate of 30% in calculating the company's value to reflect this fact.

Example: Calculating shares issued and share price for a second round financing

Suppose that instead of a single round of financing of $5 million, the company will need $3 million in the first round and a second round of financing (three years later) of $2 million to finance company expansion to the size expected at exit.

Use a discount rate of 40% for the first three years and 30% for the last two years. The company is still expected to be worth $40 million after five years, and founders will hold 1 million shares.

The value of the company at the time of the second round of financing (two years remaining to exit) is:

$$POST_2 = \frac{\text{exit value}}{(1+r_2)^{n2}} = \frac{40{,}000{,}000}{(1.30)^2} = 23{,}668{,}639$$

The fractional VC ownership required for the second round investment of $2 million is:

$$f_2 = \frac{INV_2}{POST_2} = \frac{2{,}000{,}000}{23{,}668{,}639} = 0.0845 \text{ or } 8.45\%$$

The value of the company before the second round financing would then be:

$$PRE_2 = POST_2 - INV_2 = 23{,}668{,}639 - 2{,}000{,}000 = 21{,}668{,}639$$

Value of the company at the first round of financing is:

$$POST_1 = \frac{PRE_2}{(1+r_1)^{n1}} = \frac{21{,}668{,}639}{(1.40)^3} = 7{,}896{,}734$$

The fractional VC ownership required for the first round investment of $3 million is:

$$f_1 = \frac{INV_1}{POST_1} = \frac{3{,}000{,}000}{7{,}896{,}734} = 0.38 \text{ or } 38\%$$

Number of shares issued at the time of first round of financing is:

$$shares_{VC1} = shares_{Founders}\left(\frac{f_1}{1-f_1}\right) = 1{,}000{,}000\left(\frac{0.38}{1-0.38}\right) = 612{,}903$$

The price per share at the time of first round of financing is:

$$price_1 = \frac{INV_1}{shares_{VC1}} = \frac{3{,}000{,}000}{612{,}903} = \$4.89$$

Number of shares issued to the VC firm at the time of the second round of financing is:

$$\text{shares}_{VC2} = (\text{shares}_{VC1} + \text{shares}_{Founders})\left(\frac{f_2}{1-f_2}\right)$$

$$= (612{,}903 + 1{,}000{,}000)\left(\frac{0.0845}{1-0.0845}\right) = 148{,}870$$

The price per share at the time of second round of financing is:

$$\text{price}_2 = \frac{\text{INV}_2}{\text{shares}_{VC2}} = \frac{2{,}000{,}000}{148{,}870} = \$13.43$$

After the second round, the first round investor's share dilutes from f_1 to $f_1(1 - f_2)$.

In this example, the dilution takes the investor's share from 38% to 0.38(1 – 0.0845) = 0.3479 or 34.79%.

LOS 40.k: Demonstrate alternative methods to account for risk in venture capital.

CFA® Program Curriculum, Volume 5, page 165

Our previous discussions have been highly dependent on the assumptions, and sensitivity analysis should be used to determine how changes in the input variables will affect company valuation. The discount rate used and the estimate of terminal value will strongly influence the current valuation.

Projections by entrepreneurs are typically overly optimistic and based on an assumption that the company will not fail. Instead of arguing over the validity of the projections with the entrepreneurs, most investors simply apply a high discount rate that reflects both the probability of failure and lack of diversification available in these investments.

Adjusting the Discount Rate

One approach to arriving at a more realistic valuation is to adjust the discount rate to reflect the risk that the company may fail in any given year. In the following formula, r^* is adjusted for the probability of failure, q:

$$r^* = \frac{1+r}{1-q} - 1$$

where:

r = discount rate unadjusted for probability of failure

Example: Adjusting the discount rate for the probability of failure

Assume a private equity investor has a discount rate of 30%. The investor believes, however, that the entrepreneur's projection of the company's success is overly optimistic and that the chance of the company failing in a given year is 25%.

Calculate a discount rate that factors in the company's probability of failure.

Answer:

$$r^* = \frac{1+0.30}{1-0.25} - 1 = 73.33\%$$

Alternatively, the investor could have deflated each future cash flow for the cumulative probability that the company will fail. The adjusted discount rate approach is more straightforward.

Adjusting the Terminal Value Using Scenario Analysis

A second approach to generating a realistic valuation is to adjust the terminal value for the probability of failure or poor results. Typically to obtain the terminal value, the future earnings are estimated and multiplied by an industry multiple. The problem is that almost by definition, early-stage companies are innovative with few true comparables. Price multiples also fluctuate a great deal so that the current multiple may not be indicative of what can be obtained in the future. We should therefore use scenario analysis to calculate an expected terminal value, reflecting the probability of different terminal values under different assumptions.

In theory, we should just determine the present value of future cash flows to get the current value. But estimating future cash flows is subject to error, and this method may not be any better than a price multiple approach.

Example: Using scenario analysis to arrive at an expected terminal value

In the previous valuation example, we were given a terminal value of $40 million. Assume that the scenario analysis is performed and examines three possible scenarios:

1. The expected earnings are $4 million and the expected price-earnings multiple is 10, resulting in the $40 million (as before).

2. The company is not as successful, and earnings are only $2 million. Growth is slower, so the expected price-earnings multiple is 5. The expected terminal value is $10 million.

3. The company fails, and its terminal value is $0.

If each scenario is equally likely, each possible value is weighted by one-third, and the expected terminal value is:

$$=\frac{1}{3}(\$40)+\frac{1}{3}(\$10)+\frac{1}{3}(\$0)=\$16.7 \text{ million}$$

The terminal value of $16.7 million is then used instead of the $40 million in the valuation analysis above. This is an alternative to adjusting the discount rate for the probability of failure.

In summary, VC valuation is highly dependent on the assumptions used and how risk is accounted for. Additionally, scenario and sensitivity analysis should be used to determine how changes in the input variables will affect the valuation of the company.

Note that the purpose of the valuation procedures discussed here is not to ascertain the exact value of the company. Rather, the purpose is to place some bounds on the value of the company before negotiations begin between the startup (investee) company and the private equity firm. The final price paid for the investee company will also be affected by the bargaining power of the respective parties.

Key Concepts

LOS 40.a

The sources of value creation in private equity are: (1) the ability to reengineer the company, (2) the ability to obtain debt financing on more favorable terms, and (3) superior alignment of interests between management and private equity ownership.

LOS 40.b

Private equity firms use the following mechanisms to align their interests with those of the managers of portfolio companies:

- Manager's *compensation* tied to the company's performance.
- *Tag-along, drag-along* clauses ensure that anytime an acquirer acquires control of the company, they must extend the acquisition offer to all shareholders, including firm management.
- *Board representation* by private equity firm.
- *Noncompete clauses* required for company founders.
- *Priority in claims.* PE firms have priority if the portfolio company is liquidated.
- *Required approval* by PE firm for changes of strategic importance.
- *Earn-outs.* Acquisition price paid is tied to portfolio company's future performance.

LOS 40.c

Relative to buyouts, venture capital portfolio companies are characterized by: unpredictable cash flows and product demand; weak asset base and newer management teams; less debt; unclear risk and exit; high demand for cash and working capital; less opportunity to perform due diligence; higher returns from a few highly successful companies; limited capital market presence; company sales that take place due to relationships; smaller subsequent funding; and general partner revenue primarily in the form of carried interest.

LOS 40.d

Valuation Issue	*Buyout*	*Venture Capital*
Applicability of DCF Method	Frequently used to estimate value of equity	Less frequently used as cash flows are uncertain
Applicability of Relative Value Approach	Used to check the value from DCF analysis	Difficult to use because there may be no true comparable companies
Use of Debt	High	Low as equity is dominant form of financing
Key Drivers of Equity Return	Earnings growth, increase in multiple upon exit, and reduction in the debt	Pre-money valuation, investment, and subsequent equity dilution

LOS 40.e

The means and timing of the exit strongly influence the exit value.

The four typical exit routes:

- Initial public offerings usually result in the highest exit value due to increased liquidity, greater access to capital, and the potential to hire better quality managers.
- Secondary market sales to other investors or firms result in the second highest company valuations after IPOs.
- In an MBO, the company is sold to management, who utilize a large amount of leverage.
- A liquidation is pursued when the company is deemed no longer viable and usually results in a low exit value.

LOS 40.f

The most common form of ownership structure for private equity funds is the limited partnership where limited partners (LPs) provide funding and have limited liability. The general partner (GP) manages the investment fund.

The economic terms in a private equity prospectus address the following issues: management fees; transaction fees; carried interest (the GP's share of the fund profits); ratchet (the allocation of equity between stockholders and management of the portfolio company); hurdle rate (the IRR that the GP must meet before receiving carried interest); target fund size; vintage year; and term of the fund.

The corporate governance terms in the prospectus address the following issues: key man clause (the provisions for the absence of a key named executive); performance disclosure and confidentiality (specifies the fund performance information that can be disclosed); clawback (the provision for when the GP must return profits); distribution waterfall (the method in which profits will flow to the LPs before the GP receives carried interest); tag-along, drag-along clauses (give management the right to sell their equity stake if the private equity firm sells its stake); no-fault divorce (specify when a GP can be fired); removal for cause (provisions for the firing of the GP or the termination of a fund); investment restrictions; and co-investment (allows the LPs to invest in other funds of the GP at low or no management fees).

Valuations are difficult for private equity funds because there is no ready secondary market for their investments. Additional issues with NAV calculations include the following: (1) the NAV will be stale if it is only adjusted when there are subsequent rounds of financing; (2) there is no definitive method for calculating NAV; (3) undrawn LP capital commitments are not included in the NAV calculation but are essentially liabilities for the LP; (4) different strategies and maturities may use different valuation methodologies; and (5) it is the GP who usually values the fund.

Investors should conduct due diligence before investing in a private equity fund due to the persistence in returns in private equity fund returns, the return discrepancies between outperformers and underperformers, and their illiquidity.

LOS 40.g

The general private equity risk factors are liquidity risk, unquoted investments risk, competitive environment risk, agency risk, capital risk, regulatory risk, tax risk, valuation risk, diversification risk, and market risk.

The costs of investing in private equity are significantly higher than those associated with publicly traded securities and include transactions costs, investment vehicle fund setup costs, administrative costs, audit costs, management and performance fee costs, dilution costs, and placement fees.

LOS 40.h

The Gross IRR reflects the fund's ability to generate a return from portfolio companies. The Net IRR is the relevant return metric for the LPs and is net of management fees, carried interest, and other compensation to the GP. The Net IRR should be benchmarked against a peer group of comparable private equity funds of the same vintage and strategy.

LOS 40.i

The following statistics are important for evaluating the performance of a PE fund:

- Management fees are calculated as the percentage fee multiplied by the total paid-in capital.
- The carried interest is calculated as the percentage carried interest multiplied by the increase in the NAV before distributions.
  - The NAV before distributions is calculated as:

$$= \text{NAV after distributions in prior year} + \text{capital called down} - \text{management fees} + \text{operating results}$$

  - The NAV after distributions is calculated as:

$$= \text{NAV before distributions} - \text{carried interest} - \text{distributions}$$

- The DPI multiple is the cumulative distributions divided by the paid-in capital.
- The RVPI multiple is the NAV after distributions divided by the paid-in capital.
- The TVPI multiple is the sum of the DPI and RVPI.

LOS 40.j

Under the NPV method, the proportion of the company (f) received for an investment in the company is calculated as the investment amount (INV) divided by the post-money (post-investment) value of the company. The post-money value of the company is calculated by discounting the estimated exit value for the company to its present value PV(exit value), as of the time the investment is made.

$$f = \frac{\text{INV}}{\text{POST}}$$

Alternatively, under the IRR method, we can calculate the fraction, *f*, as the future value of the VC investment at the time of exit (using the discount rate as a compound rate of return), divided by the value of the company at exit:

$$f = \frac{\text{FV(INV)}}{\text{exit value}}$$

Once we have calculated this post-money ownership share, we can calculate the number of shares issued to the venture capital investor for the investment ($\text{shares}_{\text{VC}}$) and the price per share as:

$$\text{shares}_{\text{VC}} = \text{shares}_{\text{Founders}}\left(\frac{f}{1-f}\right)$$

$$\text{price} = \frac{\text{INV}}{\text{shares}_{\text{VC}}}$$

If there is a second round of financing, we first calculate the fraction of the company (f_2) purchased for the second round of financing as:

$$f_2 = \frac{\text{INV}_2}{\text{POST}_2}$$

where:

$$\text{POST}_2 = \frac{\text{exit value}}{(1+r_2)^{n2}}$$

and

$$\text{PRE}_2 = \text{POST}_2 - \text{INV}_2$$

We then compute the fractional ownership from the first round of financing as:

$$f_1 = \frac{\text{INV}_1}{\text{POST}_1}$$

where:

$$\text{POST}_1 = \frac{\text{PRE}_2}{(1+r_1)^{n1}}$$

We can finally compute the number of shares issued and price per share in each round as:

$$\text{shares}_{\text{VC1}} = \text{shares}_{\text{Founders}}\left(\frac{f_1}{1-f_1}\right)$$

$$\text{price}_1 = \frac{\text{INV}_1}{\text{shares}_{\text{VC1}}}$$

$$\text{shares}_{\text{VC2}} = (\text{shares}_{\text{VC1}} + \text{shares}_{\text{Founders}})\left(\frac{f_2}{1-f_2}\right)$$

$$\text{price}_2 = \frac{\text{INV}_2}{\text{shares}_{\text{VC2}}}$$

LOS 40.k

The valuation of a venture capital investment is highly dependent on the assumptions used. The risk of the investment can be assessed using two methods.

- In the first approach, the discount rate is adjusted to reflect the risk that the company may fail in any given year:

  $$r^* = \frac{1+r}{1-q} - 1$$

  where:

  r^* = discount rate adjusted for probability of failure
  r = discount rate unadjusted for probability of failure
  q = probability of failure in a year

- In the second approach, scenario analysis is used to calculate an expected terminal value, reflecting different values under different assumptions.

Concept Checkers

1. Which of the following is *least likely* a source of value creation in private equity firms?
   A. The use of debt with few covenants.
   B. The overutilization of cheap equity financing in private equity firms.
   C. The ability to reengineer companies through the use of an experienced staff of former senior managers.

2. Which of the following is *least likely* to be contained in a private equity term sheet?
   A. Tag-along, drag-along clauses.
   B. Earn-outs that ensure portfolio company manager compensation.
   C. A clause that ensures private equity firm representation on the portfolio company board.

3. Which of the following is *more likely* to be associated with a venture capital investment as compared to a buyout investment?
   A. Valuation using a discounted cash flow model.
   B. High cash burn rate.
   C. Due diligence covering all aspects of the business.

4. Which of the following is *most likely* to be a key driver for the equity return in a buyout opportunity?
   A. The pre-money valuation.
   B. The reduction in debt's claim on assets.
   C. The potential subsequent equity dilution.

5. Which of the following exit routes typically results in the highest exit valuation?
   A. An initial public offering.
   B. A management buyout.
   C. A secondary market sale.

6. Which of the following *best* describes the competitive environment risk of investing in private equity?
   A. The competition for finding reasonably priced private equity investments may be high.
   B. The competition for funds from private equity investors has increased as financial markets have fallen in activity.
   C. The competitive environment in the product markets for portfolio companies has increased due to the economic slowdown.

7. Which of the following *best* describes the placement fee cost of investing in private equity?
   A. The general partner may charge the fund fees for finding prospective portfolio companies.
   B. Investment banking fees are paid when exiting a private equity portfolio company via an IPO.
   C. Placement agents who raise funds for private equity firms may charge up-front or annual trailer fees.

8. What is the most typical organizational structure of a private equity investment?
   A. An S-corporation.
   B. A limited partnership.
   C. A sole proprietorship.

9. A private equity general partner has invested in portfolio Company A that has been funded by private equity Fund A. Portfolio Company A is experiencing financial difficulty, so the general partner uses funds from a newly formed private equity fund, Fund B, to assist the company. Which of the following terms in the private equity prospectus has the general partner *most likely* violated?
   A. The co-investment clause.
   B. The no-fault divorce clause.
   C. The tag-along, drag-along clause.

10. Using the information in the table below, which of the following firms *likely* has the best corporate governance system?
   A. Firm A.
   B. Firm B.
   C. Firm C.

	Firm A	*Firm B*	*Firm C*
Key Man Clause	Yes	Yes	No
Management Fees	1.5%	2.0%	2.3%
Transaction Fees	The split between LPs and GP is 50/50	The split between LPs and GP is 50/50	GP share is 100%
Carried Interest	25%	20%	22%
Hurdle Rate	10%	8%	9%
Clawback Provision	Yes	Yes	No
Distribution Waterfall	Total return	Total return	Deal-by-deal
Removal for Cause Clause	Yes	No	No

11. Which of the following *best* describes the method that most private equity funds use to incorporate undrawn capital commitments into NAV calculations?
   A. The GP uses public comparables to determine their value.
   B. There is no straightforward method for calculating the value of the commitments.
   C. The GP estimates the net present value of the capital commitments using the historical record of previous allocations to the portfolio companies.

12. Which of the following measures the limited partner's unrealized return in a private equity fund?
   A. The DPI.
   B. The RVPI.
   C. The TVPI.

Professor's Note: From this point on, this set of Concept Checkers contains several multi-part questions where questions "nest" on each other—meaning that you need the answer to one question to complete the next. Note that it is unlikely you will encounter this situation on the exam. We recommend that after you complete a question, you check your answer to ensure that you begin the next question with the correct information.

Use the following information to answer Questions 13 through 21.

The GP for the private equity fund charges a management fee of 2% and carried interest of 20%, using the first total return method. The total committed capital for the fund was $200 million. The figures in the table are in millions.

	Capital Called Down	*Paid-in Capital*	*Management Fees*	*Operating Results*	*NAV Before Distributions*	*Carried Interest*	*Distributions*	*NAV After Distributions*
2004	60	60	1.2	–15	43.8	?		43.8
2005	20	80	1.6	–20	42.2	?		42.2
2006	10	90	1.8	30	80.4	?		80.4
2007	20	110	2.2	50	148.2	?	30	118.2
2008	25	135	2.7	70	210.5	?	50	158.4
2009	10	?	?	120	?	?	90	?

13. What is the paid-in capital for 2009?
    A. $125.
    B. $142.
    C. $145.

14. What are the management fees for 2009?
    A. $2.7.
    B. $2.9.
    C. $15.4.

15. In what year is carried interest first paid?
    A. 2007.
    B. 2008.
    C. 2009.

16. What is the NAV before distributions for 2009?
    A. $275.50.
    B. $285.50.
    C. $288.40.

17. What is the carried interest for 2009?
    A. $2.9.
    B. $15.0.
    C. $17.9.

18. What is the NAV after distributions for 2009?
    A. $180.50.
    B. $195.50.
    C. $270.50.

19. What is the DPI after 2009?
    A. 0.62.
    B. 0.83.
    C. 1.17.

20. What is the RVPI after 2009?
    A. 1.24.
    B. 1.35.
    C. 1.97.

21. What is the TVPI after 2009?
    A. 1.76.
    B. 2.41.
    C. 3.14.

Use the following information to answer Questions 22 through 26.

ScaleIt is a startup specializing in mobile applications. The company's founders believe they can sell the company for $50 million in four years. They need $7 million in capital now, and the founders wish to hold 1 million shares. The venture capital investor firm decides that, given the high risk of this company, a discount rate of 45% is appropriate. Use the NPV venture capital method, assuming a single financing round.

22. What is the post-money valuation?
    A. $4,310,922.
    B. $11,310,922.
    C. $50,000,000.

23. What is the pre-money valuation?
    A. $4,310,922.
    B. $7,310,922.
    C. $43,000,000.

24. What is the ownership fraction for the venture capital firm?
    A. 14.00%.
    B. 38.11%.
    C. 61.89%.

25. What is the number of shares for the venture capital firm?
    A. 615,846.
    B. 1,623,983.
    C. 2,603,078.

26. What is the stock price per share?
    A. $2.69.
    B. $4.31.
    C. $11.37.

Use the following information to answer Questions 27 through 32.

A company's founders believe that their company can be sold for $60 million in four years. The company needs $6 million in capital now and $3 million in three years. The entrepreneurs want to hold 1 million shares. The venture capital firm uses a discount rate of 50% over all four years.

27. What is the post-money valuation at the time of second-round financing?
    A. $17,777,778.
    B. $40,000,000.
    C. $57,000,000.

28. What is the post-money valuation at the time of first-round financing?
    A. $4,962,963.
    B. $9,851,259.
    C. $10,962,963.

29. What is the required fractional ownership for the second-round investors?
    A. 5.00%.
    B. 7.50%.
    C. 16.88%.

30. What is the fractional ownership for the first-round investors, after dilution by the second-round investors?
    A. 50.63%.
    B. 54.73%.
    C. 92.50%.

31. What is the stock price per share after the first round of financing?
    A. $4.96.
    B. $5.85.
    C. $6.00.

32. What is the stock price per share after the second round of financing?
    A. $5.77.
    B. $16.75.
    C. $37.00.

Use the following information to answer Questions 33 through 36.

The venture capital company's founders believe they can sell the company for $70 million in five years. They need $9 million in capital now, and the entrepreneurs wish to hold 1 million shares. The venture capital investor requires a return of 35%. Use the IRR venture capital method, assuming a single financing round.

33. What is the investor's ownership fraction?
    A. 12.86%.
    B. 42.35%.
    C. 57.65%.

34. What is the stock price per share?
 A. $2.39.
 B. $6.61.
 C. $12.25.

35. What is the post-money valuation?
 A. $6.61 million.
 B. $15.61 million.
 C. $70.00 million.

36. What is the pre-money valuation?
 A. $6.61 million.
 B. $9.00 million.
 C. $61.00 million.

37. A private equity investor has a discount rate of 30%. The investor believes, however, that the entrepreneur's projection of the company's success is overly optimistic and that the chance of the company failing in a given year is 20%. What is the discount rate that factors in the company's probability of failure?
 A. 50.0%.
 B. 62.5%.
 C. 71.4%.

Answers – Concept Checkers

1. **B** It is actually the overutilization of cheap *debt* financing in private equity firms that leads to value creation. Private equity firms carry more debt than public firms but have a reputation for paying it back.

2. **B** Earn-outs do not ensure portfolio company manager compensation. Earn-outs tie the acquisition price paid by private equity firms to the portfolio company's future performance. These are used predominantly in venture capital investments.

3. **B** Venture capital investments typically have significant cash burn rates. Discounted cash flow analysis is typically used for companies with substantial operating history and is, therefore, more likely to be associated with a buyout investment rather than a venture capital investment. Full due diligence is conducted for a buyout investment. Due diligence for typical venture capital investment is limited to technological feasibility and commercial potential due to limited operating results history.

4. **B** The pre-money valuation, investment, and potential subsequent equity dilution are issues for venture capital equity return. The key drivers of equity return for buyouts are earnings growth, the increase in multiple upon exit, and the reduction in the debt.

5. **A** Initial public offerings usually result in the highest exit value due to increased liquidity, greater access to capital, and the potential to hire better-quality managers.

6. **A** Competitive environment risk examines risk from the perspective of an investor who is considering an investment in private equity. It refers to the fact that the competition for finding reasonably priced private equity investments may be high.

7. **C** Placement fees are those charged by placement agents who raise funds for private equity firms. They may charge up-front fees as much as 2% or annual trailer fees as a percent of funds raised from limited partners.

8. **B** The most typical organizational structure of a private equity investment is a limited partnership. In a limited partnership, the limited partners provide funding and have limited liability. The general partner manages the investment fund.

9. **A** The clause in the private equity prospectus that the general partner has likely violated is the co-investment clause. The co-investment clause prevents the GP from using capital from different funds to invest in the same portfolio company. A conflict of interest arises here because portfolio Company A may be a poor use of the funds from Fund B investors.

10. **A** Firm A likely has the best corporate governance system. A large amount of the GP's compensation comes in the form of incentive-based compensation as the carried interest and hurdle rate necessary to obtain carried interest is the highest, but the compensation unrelated to performance (the management and transactions fees are the lowest). The clawback provision also incentivizes the GP because they have to return previously received profits.

    Furthermore, the key man clause and the removal for cause clause give the LPs the right to dismiss an underperforming GP. The total return distribution waterfall method is used instead of the deal-by-deal method, in which the GP can receive carried interest even in cases when the LPs have not earned a net positive return.

11. **B** There is no straightforward method for calculating the value of the commitments, which are essentially liabilities for the LP. The value of the commitments depends on the cash flows generated from them, but these are quite uncertain.

12. **B** The RVPI (residual value to paid-in capital) measures the limited partner's unrealized return in a private equity fund. It is the value of the LP's holdings in the fund divided by the cumulative invested capital. It is net of management fees and carried interest. The DPI (distributed to paid-in capital) measures the LP's realized return, and the TVPI (total value to paid-in capital) measures both the LP's realized and unrealized return.

13. **C** This is the cumulative sum of the capital called down, and in 2009 is: \$135 + \$10 = \$145.

14. **B** These are calculated as the percentage fee of 2% times the paid-in capital: 2% × \$145 = \$2.9.

15. **B** Carried interest is not paid until the NAV before distributions exceeds the committed capital of \$200 million, which is the year 2008.

16. **B** NAV before distributions is calculated as:

=	NAV after distributions in prior year	+	capital called down	–	management fees	+	operating results

For 2009, NAV before distributions is: \$158.4 + \$10 – \$2.9 + \$120 = \$285.50.

17. **B** It is calculated as the percentage carried interest times the increase in the NAV before distributions. In 2009, it is: 20% × (\$285.50 – \$210.50) = \$15.00.

18. **A** NAV after distributions is calculated as:

=	NAV before distributions	–	carried interest	–	distributions

In 2009, NAV after distributions is: \$285.50 – \$15.00 – \$90 = \$180.50.

19. **C** The DPI multiple is calculated as the cumulative distributions divided by the paid-in capital: (\$30 + \$50 + \$90) / \$145 = 1.17. The GP has distributed more than the paid-in capital.

20. **A** The RVPI multiple is calculated as the NAV after distributions divided by the paid-in capital: (\$180.50) / \$145 = 1.24. The net unrealized returns are more than the paid-in capital.

21. **B** The TVPI multiple is the sum of the DPI and RVPI: 1.17 + 1.24 = 2.41.

22. **B** The post-money valuation is the present value of the expected exit value:

$$\text{POST} = \frac{50{,}000{,}000}{(1+0.45)^4} = 11{,}310{,}922$$

23. **A** The pre-money valuation is what the company is worth before the investment:

PRE = 11,310,922 – 7,000,000 = 4,310,922

24. **C** To put up $7 million in a company worth $11.3 million, the venture capital firm must own 61.89% of the company:

$$f = \frac{7{,}000{,}000}{11{,}310{,}922} = 61.89\%$$

25. **B** If the entrepreneurs want 1 million shares, the venture capital firm must receive 1.6 million shares to get 61.89% ownership:

$$\text{Shares}_{VC} = 1{,}000{,}000\left[\frac{0.6189}{(1-0.6189)}\right] = 1{,}623{,}983$$

26. **B** Given a $7 million investment and 1.6 million shares, the stock price per share must be:

$$P = \frac{7{,}000{,}000}{1{,}623{,}983} = \$4.31 \text{ per share}$$

27. **B** Discount the terminal value of the company at exit back to the time of second round financing to obtain the post-money ($POST_2$) valuation:

$$POST_2 = \frac{60{,}000{,}000}{(1+0.5000)} = \$40{,}000{,}000$$

28. **C** First, calculate the second-round pre-money (PRE_2) valuation by netting the second-round investment (INV_2) from the post-money ($POST_2$) valuation:

$$PRE_2 = 40{,}000{,}000 - 3{,}000{,}000 = \$37{,}000{,}000$$

Next, discount the second-round pre-money valuation back to the time of the first-round financing to obtain the post-money ($POST_1$) valuation:

$$POST_1 = \frac{37{,}000{,}000}{(1+0.50)^3} = \$10{,}962{,}963$$

29. **B** The required fractional ownership for the second-round investors is:

$$f_2 = \frac{3{,}000{,}000}{40{,}000{,}000} = 7.50\%$$

30. **A** The required fractional ownership for the first-round investors is:

$$f_1 = \frac{6{,}000{,}000}{10{,}962{,}963} = 54.73\%$$

The first round investors will be later diluted by the second round investors to an ownership of: 54.73% × (1 – 0.0750) = 50.63%.

31. **A** First determine the number of shares the first-round venture capital investors ($Shares_{VC1}$) need to obtain their fractional ownership:

$$Share_{VC1} = 1{,}000{,}000\left[\frac{0.5473}{(1-0.5473)}\right] = 1{,}208{,}968$$

To obtain a 54.73% share of the company, the first-round investors must receive 1,208,968 shares.

Next, determine the stock price per share after the first round of financing (P_1):

$$P_1 = \frac{6{,}000{,}000}{1{,}208{,}968} = \$4.96$$

32. **B** First determine the number of shares the second-round venture capital investors ($Shares_{VC2}$) need to obtain their fractional ownership:

$$Shares_{VC2} = (1{,}000{,}000 + 1{,}208{,}968)\left[\frac{0.0750}{(1-0.0750)}\right] = 179{,}106$$

To obtain a 7.50% share of the company, the second-round investors must receive 179,106 shares.

Next, determine the stock price per share after the second round of financing (P_2):

$$P_2 = \frac{3{,}000{,}000}{179{,}106} = \$16.75$$

33. **C** First, calculate the investor's expected future wealth (W):

$$W = 9{,}000{,}000 \times (1 + 0.35)^5 = 40{,}356{,}301$$

Given this expected wealth, we determine the required fractional ownership (f) by calculating how much of the terminal value should be the investor's:

$$f = \frac{40{,}356{,}301}{70{,}000{,}000} = 57.65\%$$

34. **B** First, determine the number of shares the venture capital firm ($Shares_{VC}$) requires for its fractional ownership:

$$Shares_{VC} = 1{,}000{,}000\left[\frac{0.5765}{(1-0.5765)}\right] = 1{,}361{,}275$$

Next, determine the stock price per share (P):

$$P = \frac{9{,}000{,}000}{1{,}361{,}275} = \$6.61$$

35. **B** Divide the investment by the fractional ownership to obtain the post-money (POST) valuation:

$$\text{POST} = \frac{9{,}000{,}000}{0.5765} = 15.61 \text{ million}$$

36. **A** Determine the pre-money (PRE) valuation by netting the investment (INV) from the post-money (POST) valuation:

PRE = 15.61 million – 9 million = 6.61 million

37. **B** The discount rate that factors in the company's probability of failure is calculated as:

$$r^* = \frac{1+r}{1-q} - 1$$

$$r^* = \frac{1+0.30}{1-0.20} - 1 = 62.5\%$$

The following is a review of the Alternative Investments principles designed to address the learning outcome statements set forth by CFA Institute. This topic is also covered in:

INVESTING IN HEDGE FUNDS: A SURVEY[1]

Study Session 13

EXAM FOCUS

This topic review discusses hedge funds as an alternative asset class. Candidates should know the different hedge fund strategies and their risks. Pay special attention to biases in hedge fund performance reporting. Also, understand the concepts behind factor models and the motivations for replication strategies. Finally, understand the causes and impacts of non-normality in hedge fund returns on risk measurement and performance appraisal.

LOS 41.a: Distinguish between hedge funds and mutual funds in terms of leverage, use of derivatives, disclosure requirements and practices, lockup periods, and fee structures.

CFA® Program Curriculum, Volume 5, page 181

Hedge Funds vs. Mutual Funds

Hedge funds are a broad group of investment vehicles pursuing a wide variety of investment strategies. Compared to mutual funds, hedge funds are less regulated. This lower level of regulation allows less disclosure from hedge fund managers and fewer restrictions on the types of investments and the use of leverage. However, unlike mutual funds, hedge funds may offer their products only to qualified investors, and they require high minimum investment. Hedge funds also differ from mutual funds in that they may extensively use derivatives, leverage, short-selling, and multiple asset classes in their strategies.

Disclosure requirements for mutual funds include filing of prospectuses and reporting NAV daily and fund holdings semiannually. Hedge funds do not have these disclosure requirements, making performance appraisal difficult. Compared to the liquidity of mutual fund shares, hedge funds are less liquid. Additionally, many hedge funds impose *lockup* periods of 1–3 years. Lockup period means withdrawals are restricted during that period. Lockups can be hard or soft: in a hard lockup, withdrawals are not permitted, while in the case of a soft lockup, withdrawals are penalized with a redemption fee of 1–3%.

Mutual fund fee is typically an annual management fee equal to a percentage of assets under management (AUM). U.S. regulations require mutual fund fee structures to be symmetric: if fees are levied on gains, fund managers have to share in losses as well. Hedge funds are not subject to this requirement and typically charge performance

1. The terminology used throughout this topic review is industry convention as presented in Reading 47 of the 2012 CFA Level II exam curriculum.

or incentive fees in addition to management fees but do not share in losses. An asymmetrical fee is similar to owning a call option: the investment manager stands to gain when returns are high but does not share in losses. Such an arrangement gives hedge fund managers an incentive to take higher risk.

Hedge fund fees often have a high-water mark provision, wherein the manager cannot earn an incentive fee on the same dollar of investment return more than once. In the case of a negative return period, the manager will not earn an incentive fee until the investors have recouped that negative return in subsequent periods. Some funds also utilize a hurdle rate arrangement wherein managers do not earn an incentive fee until a minimum rate of return, known as a hurdle rate, is earned by the investors. Such a hurdle rate could be a fixed rate or a variable short-term rate.

LOS 41.b: Describe hedge fund strategies.

CFA® Program Curriculum, Volume 5, page 183

The Hedge Fund Universe

Hedge funds follow a wide variety of strategies:

1. **Arbitrage based:** This strategy attempts to profit from security mispricings while matching the characteristics of their short positions to those of their long positions. This hedging structure results in a lower standard deviation of net returns and the highest Sharpe ratios of all hedge fund strategies. Usually, these hedge funds are said to be short volatility—they experience gains in stable markets but experience losses in volatile markets. They make money slowly (during stable periods) but lose money rapidly (during market turbulence), which results in negative skewness and fat tails in their return distributions.

2. **Convertible bond arbitrage:** This strategy goes long a convertible bond and short the underlying equity. The convertible bond provides long exposure to a fixed-income security and a call option on the underlying stock. These funds perform well when stock volatility increases (the long call option gains value) and when credit spreads decline (the long fixed-income position gains value). These funds achieve market neutrality by matching the option delta of the long call position to the short stock position.

Professor's Note: Delta hedging using options is covered in the Derivatives section of the Level II curriculum.

3. **Equity market neutral:** This strategy seeks to hedge market exposure in equity investments through long and short positions with equal beta exposure. Though the long-term goal of this strategy is zero beta exposure, short-term deviations (to betas of +/–0.20) are common. While these strategies minimize beta risk, other equity factor exposures such as size (market capitalization), industry classification, and style (value or growth) may remain. Many of these funds utilize quantitative strategies. Quantitative strategies using longer holding period (months) may be based on factor

models with themes such as value, growth, or earnings momentum. Quantitative strategies using short holding periods (days) are called statistical arbitrage trading funds and engage in long-short trading of pairs of stocks with high returns correlations that have experienced short-term divergence.

4. **Event driven:** These strategies are driven by the outcome of specific expected events. One subset of event driven funds is distressed debt funds, which focus on debt securities of companies that are in or near bankruptcy, and take an active or passive role in the bankruptcy process. Distressed debt investing is typically a capital structure play whereby the investor goes long and short in different securities of the same issuer, such as long debt and short equity. Such strategies can also be pursued in the derivatives market with credit default swaps and options.

5. **Risk arbitrage:** Also known as **merger arbitrage**, this strategy attempts to profit on the eventual outcome of an announced merger. Typically, the fund takes a long position in the target's stock and a short position in the acquirer's stock. This strategy focuses on the difference between the announced merger price (in terms of acquirer's stock) and market price of the target. The price difference reflects the uncertainty of completion of the merger. Leverage is often used to magnify the small mispricings, which can result in a large loss if the expected outcome does not materialize. A risk arbitrage strategy is often compared to writing insurance against the failure of a merger: the strategy pays off if the merger is completed but incurs a large loss if the merger fails.

6. **Fixed-income arbitrage:** These strategies go long lower credit quality bonds and short higher quality bonds. The spread between the long and short provides income to the fund, as long as spreads remain stable or tighten and markets remain liquid. However, during times of volatility when spreads widen and/or liquidity dissipates, the fund may suffer large losses. Funds may also obtain the short exposure through the use of leverage.

7. **Medium volatility:** These strategies take both long and short positions in securities; however, the market exposures of the long and short positions in these strategies may differ, often resulting in a net long position. This partial hedge results in fund volatility below that of the underlying market.

8. **Global macro:** Make broad market bets on indices, currencies, commodities, and other asset classes based on expectations about specific markets and asset classes. Because of the larger universe from which these managers select securities, the intra fund category (within global macro fund category) correlations tend to be low.

9. **Long-short equity:** Similar to market neutral strategy but need not seek zero beta: a net beta of 0.3 to 0.6 is typical. Managers have the flexibility to adjust net beta exposure upwards when markets are rising and downwards when markets are falling.

10. **Managed futures:** These strategies employ quantitative models to speculate in futures (commodities, equities, currencies, interest rates, etc.). While the risk-return profile of this strategy is poor when considered in isolation, on a portfolio basis, managed futures provide the most diversification and hedging benefit of all the hedge fund strategies. Some typical hedge fund risks (e.g., liquidity, counterparty, and valuation risk) are negligible in these funds.

11. **Multistrategy:** Employ a combination of strategies. Similar to funds of funds but without the burden of a second layer of fees.

12. **Directional:** Makes active bets based on expectations of how security prices are going to move. Because no hedging is employed, these strategies experience the full volatility of the underlying markets.

13. **Dedicated short bias:** Focus exclusively on shorting equities, often resulting in a beta close to negative 1.00. The manager's security selection skill is the key factor driving performance.

14. **Emerging markets:** Invest in equity securities in emerging markets. Emerging markets are characterized by short-selling restrictions and limited availability of derivatives. Because short exposure is difficult or expensive to obtain in these markets, these funds have a distinct long bias.

LOS 41.c: Explain possible biases in reported hedge fund performance.

CFA® Program Curriculum, Volume 5, page 186

Because hedge funds are not subject to extensive disclosure requirements, performance analysis is problematic. Hedge fund databases and indices are based only on data from funds that choose to report performance. The composition of these indices and the methodologies of computing performance vary significantly among databases. While some databases compute index performance based on an equal weighting (indicating the performance of an average fund), other databases use size-weighted performance (indicating the overall performance of the hedge fund industry). Equally weighted databases require frequent rebalancing of portfolios tracking the index, though this would be difficult to implement in practice, given the illiquidity of hedge funds and their high minimum investment requirements.

Biases in Hedge Fund Indices

1. **Selection bias:** Because hedge fund performance reporting is voluntary, it is more likely that a high-performing fund (high return, low risk) will report performance than a poor-performing fund. Hence, the index return is higher than the overall returns of the hedge fund universe. Selection bias is also called self-reporting bias.

2. **Backfill bias:** When a fund begins reporting performance to an index provider, the provider will often fill in historical performance of the fund as reported. For example, if a fund starts reporting from June 2011 but submits the returns of the fund since inception in January 2008, the index may incorporate the fund's performance since January 2008. Studies have shown that such back-reported returns are significantly higher than the average of returns reported "live." Backfill bias is also known as incubation or instant history bias. One study estimated that backfill bias adds between 0.5% and 1.4% per year to reported hedge fund performance.[2]

3. **Survivorship bias:** Funds may also choose to stop reporting to index providers when they are liquidated or experience poor returns. When index providers remove such funds from the index, the removal results in survivorship bias: the index is composed of survivors only, resulting in average performance being overstated. Survivorship bias has been estimated to add between 0.6% and 3.6% to reported hedge fund performance.[3] Survivorship bias is greatest for equally weighted indices and indices that do not maintain a listing of deceased funds. Survivorship bias is lower for funds of funds, indices that continue to include the historical performance of funds that stop reporting, asset-weighted indices, and investible indices.

Style Indices as Inappropriate Benchmarks

Performance evaluation of individual hedge funds using style indices as benchmarks may be problematic because a fund's style exposures can change over time. Across funds within a specific style, there is considerable variation in algorithm and market exposures. Some styles (e.g., risk arbitrage) exhibit a high returns correlation between funds with that style (i.e., the funds are relatively homogenous), whereas for others the correlations are low (i.e., the funds are relatively heterogenous).

LOS 41.d: Describe factor models for hedge fund returns.

CFA® Program Curriculum, Volume 5, page 187

Factor Models

In order to understand the risks they are taking and the value they are receiving, hedge fund investors may seek to use regression analysis to quantify and separate the alpha return (value added) and beta return (market return) associated with a fund's return. As an alternative asset class, investors would prefer that hedge funds earn returns uncorrelated with stocks and bonds (low beta return). Funds that provide a large alpha justify the high cost of investing in hedge funds.

A hedge fund return factor model typically takes the following form:

$$\text{hedge fund return} = \text{alpha} + \text{risk-free rate} + \sum (\text{beta}_i \times \text{factor}_i)$$

---

2. Hamza, Olfa, Maher Kooli, and Mathieu Roberge, 2006. "Further Evidence on Hedge Fund Return Predictability." *Journal of Wealth Management*, Vol. 9, no. 3.
3. Malkiel, Burton G., and Atanu Saha, 2005. "Hedge Funds: Risk and Return." *Financial Analysts Journal*. Vol. 64, no. 6.

With this model, alpha is the return generated by the fund manager in excess of the risk-free rate plus the factor risk returns (i.e., beta return). Factors are exposures to traditional market sources.

It is important to include all relevant market factor exposures, otherwise the return attributable to alpha will be overestimated. Some factors commonly used include U.S. equity market indices (e.g., S&P 500, Russell 1000 and 2000), emerging market stock and bond indices, U.S. Treasury indices, the EAFE Index, and changes in yield spreads between high- and low-grade bonds. Studies have shown that these traditional risk factors explain 50–80% of hedge fund returns, indicating that hedge funds take a substantial amount of market risk.

Some hedge fund strategies such as market neutral or arbitrage funds exhibit lower exposures to traditional market factors, but they have exposures to other factors measured by exotic (or hedge fund) betas. These exposures may include equity market volatility; spreads between large- and small-cap stock returns; and spreads between value and growth stock returns, among others.

One of the issues with using a regression model to capture factor exposures is the static estimation of betas: betas are assumed to be constant throughout the sample period. Dynamic estimation techniques overcome this limitation and allow us to make a judgment on the market timing ability of the fund managers. Ideally, the manager should increase betas during rising markets and decrease betas during falling markets.

LOS 41.e: Describe sources of non-normality in hedge fund returns and implications for performance appraisal.

CFA® Program Curriculum, Volume 5, page 188

Performance Appraisal Issues

Traditional measures of performance evaluation (such as the Sharpe ratio) analyze the distribution of an asset's investment returns using mean and standard deviation. Standard deviation as a measure of risk, however, is misleading if the underlying distribution is non-normal.

Other traditional measures such as Jensen's alpha utilize a market model and assume that the factor exposures are constant and linearly related to returns. Hedge fund returns are neither normally distributed nor linearly related to traditional market risk exposures. When the underlying return distribution is non-normal, skewness and kurtosis present additional sources of risk. Along with a larger mean of returns and lower standard deviation of returns, investors prefer positive skewness and lower kurtosis. Unfortunately, hedge fund return distributions often have negative skewness and high kurtosis.

Professor's Note: The Sharpe ratio and the market model are discussed in the Portfolio Management section of the Level II curriculum.

These undesirable hedge fund traits result from long and short risk positions that are imperfectly matched. Some of the returns that hedge funds earn are simply rewards for taking those risks. For example, consider a merger arbitrage investment where the hedge fund takes highly leveraged positions in securities in anticipation of a successful merger. If the market price of the target is lower than the price implied by the merger announcement (in terms of acquirer's stock), a merger arbitrage fund may take a long position in the target stock and a corresponding short position in the acquirer's stock. If the merger occurs, the position pays off, resulting in positive returns for the fund. However, if the merger fails, a large loss for the fund will result. The return earned upon a successful merger is simply compensation for taking the risk associated with the uncertainty of completion of the merger. This leads to a negative skewness in the fund's returns.

Some hedge fund strategies such as short options, merger arbitrage, and fixed-income arbitrage are considered *short volatility* strategies. These strategies perform well during less-volatile market conditions but may suffer significant losses during turbulent times. Other strategies such as long options and managed futures perform well during high-volatility conditions and are considered to be *long volatility* strategies. When long volatility hedge funds are added to a portfolio of short volatility hedge funds, the portfolio volatility *level* will typically increase, but the portfolio returns will become more normally distributed (less negative skewness and lower kurtosis). This leads to an anomaly: the portfolio Sharpe ratio decreases (due to higher portfolio standard deviation), but its characteristics for an investor become more desirable (due to improved skewness and kurtosis).

LOS 41.f: Describe motivations for hedge fund replication strategies.

CFA® Program Curriculum, Volume 5, page 191

As discussed earlier, factor models can be used to quantify a hedge fund's factor exposures. If the majority of hedge fund return variance can be explained using traditional stock-market and bond-market indices, then hedge funds can be replicated using index funds and swaps products.

Replicating strategies are either static or dynamic. In a static strategy, the factor exposures are estimated using regression analysis, and corresponding investments in index funds and derivatives are used to replicate these exposures. In a dynamic strategy, the factor exposures are re-estimated periodically and the replicating portfolio rebalanced accordingly.

Motivations for Hedge Fund Replication Strategies

There are three primary motivations for using a replication strategy:

1. **Lower cost**: Portfolios that replicate hedge funds using traditional market securities are easier to manage than hedge funds. If hedge fund performance can be replicated using available market products, then high hedge fund management costs are avoided.

2. **Lack of alpha**: The factor model of hedge fund returns distinguishes return achieved from taking market risk (i.e., beta return) from value added by the hedge fund manager (i.e., alpha return). If it is determined that hedge fund managers are not delivering positive alpha return, a replicating strategy may be more attractive.

3. **Liquidity and transparency**: As mentioned earlier, lock-up provisions reduce liquidity for hedge funds. Additionally, the lax regulatory environment leads to lower transparency for hedge fund investors. Replicating strategies are not subject to these shortcomings.

LOS 41.g: Explain difficulties in applying traditional portfolio analysis to hedge funds.

CFA® Program Curriculum, Volume 5, page 192

Traditional portfolio analysis begins with the return, volatility, and correlation of each asset being considered, and it attempts to determine the allocation that minimizes portfolio risk for a given level of expected return. When we add hedge funds to an investment portfolio, we are attempting to reduce risk, increase expected return, or both. Unfortunately, hedge funds possess a number of characteristics that hampers the use of traditional portfolio analysis.

Professor's Note: Portfolio allocation using mean-variance optimization is discussed in the Portfolio Management section of Level II curriculum.

Difficult to develop expected return assumptions: A number of hedge fund characteristics contribute to difficulties in developing accurate expected returns for these assets, including selection bias, survivor bias, backfill bias, and stale pricing.

Professor's Note: Stale pricing in the context of hedge funds refers to the fact that some of the holdings of hedge funds are illiquid. For these assets, current market price may not be always available, necessitating the use of "most recent" price. Using such stale prices leads to underestimation of the standard deviation of measured returns.

Hedge fund performance can be dynamic: Hedge fund performance is not static: beta exposures, volatility, and correlations change over time. Furthermore, most hedge fund styles have negative asymmetrical beta exposures, meaning that correlations increase during market downturn and decrease during upturns. Some hedge fund strategies such as dedicated short bias and managed futures have exhibited attractive (positive) asymmetrical beta exposures, wherein betas increase during market upturns and decrease during downturns.

Standard deviation is an incomplete measure of risk: Hedge funds possess a number of features that may make methods that rely on standard deviation ineffective. Some hedge fund styles exhibit excess kurtosis or negative skewness; in fact, it is often hedge fund styles with the best standard deviation and Sharpe measures that most suffer from these higher-moment risk exposures. If mean-variance optimization is used to add hedge funds to a portfolio, adjustment for kurtosis and skewness should be included in the analysis in order to avoid an over-allocation to hedge funds.

LOS 41.h: Compare funds of funds to single manager hedge funds.

CFA® Program Curriculum, Volume 5, page 194

Funds of Funds

Funds of funds are intermediary funds that invest in a portfolio of single manager hedge funds. Funds of funds provide a number of advantages over single manager funds—due diligence, diversification, and lower minimum investment—that make these funds of funds attractive to smaller investors. Funds of funds typically invest in 15–20 single-strategy funds and may provide better liquidity terms to investors as compared to single manager hedge funds. However, these funds of funds add an additional layer of fees on top of fees payable to investee single manager funds. A common fee structure for funds of funds is a 1% management fee plus a 10% performance fee. These add-on fees make it difficult for funds of funds to generate positive alpha after fees.

Due to diversification, funds of funds tend to have performance similar to that of the average single manager hedge fund. They outperform the bottom single manager hedge funds but underperform top single manager hedge funds. Generally, funds of funds add value by reducing risk rather than by increasing return. Beckers et al. (2007)[4] found that funds of funds also tend to have lower traditional factor risk exposures than a typical single manager hedge fund. However, such exposures were typically poorly timed (lower beta exposure during rising marker and higher exposure during falling market). However, nontraditional factor exposures (exotic and hedge fund betas) were not examined in the study.

Other studies have separated alpha and beta return for funds of funds and found that some funds were able to generate alpha return (alpha funds), but most funds of funds simply generated beta return (beta funds).[5] Beta returns can be obtained relatively cheaply via traditional market sources. Hence, beta funds would be expected to lose market share over time as sophisticated investors channel money towards alpha funds.

Funds of funds generally have lower backfill bias, lower survivor bias, and lower mortality than do single manager hedge funds.

4. Beckers, Stan, Ross Curds, and Simon Weinberger, 2007. "Funds of Hedge Funds Take the Wrong Risks." *Journal of Portfolio Management,* Vol. 33, no. 3.
5. Hsieh, David A, 2006. "The Search for Alpha - Sources of Future Hedge Fund Returns." *CFA Institute Conference Proceedings Quarterly*, Vol. 23, no. 3.

KEY CONCEPTS

LOS 41.a

	Leverage	*Use of Derivatives*	*Disclosure Requirements*	*Lock-Up Periods*	*Fee Structure*	*Investors*	*Liquidity*
Hedge fund	May be high	May be high	Low	Long	Management & incentive (higher)	Qualified only	Low
Mutual fund	Low	Low—limited	High	Short or none	Management only (lower)	General public	High (daily liquidity)

LOS 41.b

Hedge funds pursue a variety of strategies differentiated by the types of securities they focus on, the amount of actual hedging involved, and the types of opportunities pursued. Strategies include arbitrage based, convertible bond arbitrage, equity market neutral, event driven, risk arbitrage, fixed-income arbitrage, medium volatility, global macro, long-short equity, managed futures, multistrategy, directional, dedicated short bias, and emerging markets.

LOS 41.c

Performance reported by hedge fund indices are subject to three biases:

- Selection bias: upward bias because funds that have performed well are more likely to report results.
- Backfill bias: upward bias resulting from backfilling of prior performance data for funds initiating reporting.
- Survivorship bias: upward bias from deletion of historical performance of funds ceasing to report.

All of these biases lead to better reported hedge fund performance.

LOS 41.d

Factor models attempt to disaggregate alpha and beta performance from reported hedge fund performance. Beta return is return from exposure to traditional market sources; alpha return is return in excess of risk-free rate and beta return. It is important to distinguish between alpha and beta returns because hedge fund managers are able to charge a higher fee to generate alpha return, while beta return could be obtained by an investor via traditional market sources cheaply.

LOS 41.e

Standard deviation as a measure of risk is unsuitable for hedge fund performance evaluation due to non-normality of hedge fund returns. Investors need to evaluate higher-order moments of the return distribution, specifically skewness and kurtosis. Negative skewness and high kurtosis are undesirable characteristics that are present in hedge fund returns.

LOS 41.f
Studies have found that the majority of hedge fund returns are due to exposure to traditional market risk factors. Hedge fund replication strategies take exposures to securities such as stock and bond indices, currencies, and commodities to achieve hedge fund–like returns (and diversification benefits) without the high costs associated with hedge fund investing.

LOS 41.g
Traditional portfolio analysis using hedge funds as an asset class is problematic due to estimation errors in expected return, standard deviation, and correlations. If mean-variance optimization is used to add hedge funds to a portfolio, adjustment for kurtosis and skewness should be included in the analysis in order to avoid an over-allocation to hedge funds.

LOS 41.h
Funds of funds are intermediary funds that invest in a portfolio of single manager hedge funds. Funds of funds provide due diligence, diversification, and a low minimum investment. Additionally, they provide higher liquidity than single manager funds but are subject to a second layer of fees.

CONCEPT CHECKERS

Use the following information for Questions 1 through 11.

Joe Dentice, CFA, is the managing director of Three Rivers, LLC, a consulting firm specializing in alternative investments. One of its clients, a large pension fund, had indicated a desire to invest a portion of plan assets in hedge funds. Dentice is preparing a presentation for the pension plan's board. He asks his assistant, Jeremy Laske, for some performance data of hedge funds. Laske obtains select performance data on five funds as shown in Exhibit 1. Return and standard deviation are based on monthly returns from 2006 to 2010 (five years) or since inception.

Summary Data on Select Hedge Funds

Fund	*Strategy*	*Inception Date*	*Assets Under Management*	*Fees*		*Annualized Returns*	*Standard Deviation*
				Management	*Incentive*		
Aquarius Ultra	Event driven	6/1/2006	$630 million	2%	15%	18%	21%
Beta Stable	Arbitrage	2/1/2004	$230 million	2%	20%	16.20%	23%
Venus	Fund of funds	5/15/2001	$150 million	2%	20%	17.5%	14%
Baltimore Select	Risk arbitrage	2/11/2006	$400 million	2%	18%	14%	16%
Sera Max	Fixed-income arbitrage	7/1/2003	$740 million	2%	20%	19%	28%

Laske includes the following statements in his presentation:

Statement 1: Hedge fund fees are asymmetrical and, hence, align investor and fund manager interests.

Statement 2: Hedge fund performance as reported by index providers suffers from biases. One of the biases is due to index providers including historical performance data of funds that initiate performance reporting.

Statement 3: Factor return models can be used to analyze hedge fund performance. In such a model, the return attributable to traditional market sources is called alpha.

Statement 4: Hedge fund returns are not distributed normally. Investors prefer positive skewness and high kurtosis.

Statement 5: Some hedge fund strategies, such as that employed by Sera Max, can be classified as short volatility. These strategies perform well during calm markets.

Statement 6: Funds of funds such as Venus generally produce higher returns than do top single manager funds. This is due to diversification and to the due diligence performed by the funds of funds managers. Funds of funds also tend to have lower risk than the average single manager fund.

Statement 7: Adding long volatility hedge fund strategies to a portfolio of short volatility strategies lowers portfolio volatility and results in a portfolio return distribution that is more normally distributed.

1. A strategy that seeks to ensure high correlation between long and short position returns is *most* consistent with:
   A. Sera Max.
   B. Beta Stable.
   C. Aquarius Ultra.

2. A distressed debt strategy would be *most likely* followed by:
   A. Baltimore Select.
   B. Aquarius Ultra.
   C. Sera Max.

3. The fund *most likely* to follow a strategy that is analogous to writing an insurance policy on the outcome of a specific event is:
   A. Baltimore Select.
   B. Beta Stable.
   C. Aquarius Ultra.

4. Laske's Statement 1 is *most likely*:
   A. correct.
   B. incorrect with respect to alignment of interest.
   C. incorrect with respect to asymmetry and alignment of interest.

5. The bias referred to by Laske's Statement 2 is *best* described as:
   A. incubation bias.
   B. survivorship bias.
   C. self-reporting bias.

6. Laske's Statement 3 is *most likely*:
   A. correct.
   B. incorrect with respect to the use of factor models.
   C. incorrect with respect to the definition of alpha.

7. Laske's Statement 4 is *most likely*:
   A. correct.
   B. incorrect with respect to investors' preference for kurtosis.
   C. incorrect with respect to investors' preference for positive skewness.

8. Laske's Statement 5 is *most likely*:
   A. correct.
   B. incorrect with respect to the performance of short volatility strategies in calm markets.
   C. incorrect with respect to the description of Sera Max's strategy as short volatility.

9. Laske's Statement 6 is *most likely*:
   A. correct.
   B. incorrect with respect to return performance.
   C. incorrect with respect to risk.

10. Laske's Statement 7 is *most likely*:
    A. correct.
    B. incorrect with respect to volatility.
    C. incorrect with respect to return distribution.

11. The *least likely* motivation for hedge fund replication is:
    A. reducing cost.
    B. overcoming non-normality of return distribution.
    C. reducing the illiquidity of the portfolio.

Answers – Concept Checkers

1. **B** Beta Stable follows an arbitrage-based strategy that tries to maintain long and short positions that are highly correlated in order to reduce the variability of net returns.

2. **B** Distressed debt strategy is a capital structure play that is typically followed by an event-driven hedge fund strategy.

3. **A** Risk arbitrage strategies, also known as merger arbitrage strategies, attempt to predict and profit from the outcome of corporate mergers. Because the strategy will lose money if the expected merger does not materialize, it can be compared to writing an insurance policy on the completion of an event.

4. **B** Hedge fund fees are asymmetrical and, hence, they do not align manager/investor interests. The managers receive incentive fees when performance is good but do not participate in the downside.

5. **A** Including past history of a fund's performance when the fund starts reporting leads to backfill bias. Backfill bias is also known as incubation or instant history bias. Survivorship bias occurs when index providers remove a fund's history when the fund ceases to report performance. Self-reporting bias, also known as selection bias, is a reference to the theory that fund managers with higher returns and lower volatility are more likely to report their performance to databases.

6. **C** Alpha is defined as return in excess of the risk-free rate and the return attributable to traditional market sources (beta return).

7. **B** Hedge fund return distributions are non-normal. Investors prefer positive skewness and lower kurtosis.

8. **A** Some hedge fund strategies are considered to be short volatility. Funds (such as Sera Max) that follow a fixed-income arbitrage have a short exposure to volatility, resulting in gains during calm markets but substantial losses during turbulent times when volatility increases.

9. **B** Funds of funds tend to have returns similar to the average single manager fund. They underperform the top managers and outperform the bottom managers. They tend to offer value primarily by reducing risk rather than by enhancing returns.

10. **B** When long volatility hedge funds are added to a portfolio of short volatility funds, the portfolio volatility level will typically *increase*, but the portfolio returns will be more normally distributed (less negative skewness and kurtosis).

11. **B** Reducing cost (fees of managers), transparency, liquidity, and lack of alpha are all motivations for hedge fund replication. However, the replication process strives to make the replicated return distribution as close as possible to the fund's return distribution rather than to change it.

SELF-TEST: ALTERNATIVE INVESTMENTS

Use the following information to answer Questions 1 through 6.

Eva Williams is an investment manager for Straughn Capital Management (SCM). Williams believes that it would be beneficial to add some real estate investments to SCM's existing portfolio. She has asked a local real estate broker, Steven Riley, to present some investment ideas to her. Riley is not certain which type of property might be most suitable for SCM, so he has prepared information regarding three different types of investment property. The first property is an undeveloped plot of land in an area that is not very heavily populated, but is on the fringe of a rapidly growing city. The second property is a hotel in the downtown district of the same city. The third property is a small shopping center in a well-developed, but declining section of the city.

While describing each of the properties, Riley makes the following statements:

Statement 1: The raw land is really a great opportunity. An investor is practically guaranteed steady price appreciation with any raw land deal given the way the city is growing. Another benefit is that if an investor buys the land and decides to sell it later, the investor will find that undeveloped land is very liquid. This is because the possible uses for undeveloped land are virtually unlimited.

Statement 2: Hotel properties do not require active management, so an investor in this type of property would not have to be very involved with the day-to-day operations. The current income from operations would be considerable, but hotels tend not to provide returns in the form of price appreciation. The current managers don't seem to be very efficient, but that is a secondary concern with this type of property. One considerable risk with hotels is potential competition from major chains that appear to have an interest in moving into the downtown area.

Statement 3: The community where the shopping center is located is not growing, so that may cause future rental income growth to slow. Also, median incomes are falling in that area, but that should not affect the value of the property because the property draws customers from a larger area. The center has a great mix of tenants and very low vacancy rates.

Riley also provides certain operating data for the hotel and the shopping center properties. The market value of the hotel is $2,500,000. Net operating income for the upcoming year is expected to be $275,000, and is expected to grow at a constant annual rate of 6% for the foreseeable future.

The shopping center would require an initial investment of $1,525,000 and is expected to generate after-tax cash flow of $330,000 for the next five years. In year six, a significant renovation would be required. This would result in after-tax cash flow of –$700,000 during that year. Following the renovation, after-tax cash flows would be $450,000 for years seven through twelve. Assume that there is no residual value for the shopping center after this time. Riley believes that a reasonable risk-adjusted after-tax return on this type of property would be 16%.

1. With respect to Statement 1, Riley's assertions regarding the price appreciation and the liquidity of raw land investments are:

	Price appreciation	Liquidity
A.	Correct	Incorrect
B.	Incorrect	Correct
C.	Incorrect	Incorrect

2. In Statement 2, Riley makes several generalizations about hotel investments. Which of Riley's statements is *most likely* to be true given the actual characteristics of hotels as investments?
   A. Competition is a primary risk for hotel investments.
   B. Hotels provide a return from income, but not price appreciation.
   C. Hotels do not require active management, so the investor would not have to be involved in the day-to-day operations.

3. Based on the information provided in Statement 3, which factors are *most likely* to have a negative impact on the market value of the shopping center property?
   A. Median incomes and vacancy rates.
   B. Community growth and vacancy rates.
   C. Community growth and median incomes.

4. What is the market capitalization rate for the hotel?
   A. 5%.
   B. 6%.
   C. 11%.

5. What is the required ROE for the hotel?
   A. 6%.
   B. 11%.
   C. 17%.

6. What are the Net Present Value (NPV) and Internal Rate of Return (IRR) for the shopping center?
   A. NPV = –$51,226, IRR = 15.21%.
   B. NPV = –$51,226, IRR is unreliable.
   C. NPV = $523,394, IRR = 23.19%.

SELF-TEST ANSWERS: ALTERNATIVE INVESTMENTS

1. C One of the principal characteristics of raw land investments is an appreciation in value. However, one of the primary risks is the unstable and unpredictable pattern of that appreciation. Riley's assertion that the price appreciation will be stable makes this part of the statement incorrect. Another principal characteristic of raw land is relatively low liquidity. Therefore, Riley's claim that this type of property is very liquid is also incorrect.

2. A Competition and competent management are two of the primary risks for hotel properties. Therefore, his assertion regarding competition is correct, but his assessment of the importance of competent managers is incorrect. Hotels typically require active management that would be likely to involve the investor on some level, maybe even in the day-to-day operations. Hotels typically provide a return from income AND price appreciation.

3. C Limited community growth and declining median incomes would tend to put downward pressure on the value of the property. A strong tenant mix and low vacancy rates would tend to increase the value of the property.

4. C Within the direct income capitalization framework, which is equivalent to the constant growth model, $MV_0 = NOI_1 / R_0$, where MV_0 is the current market value, NOI_1 is the net operating income for the coming year, and R_0 represents the market capitalization rate. Therefore, $R_0 = NOI_1 / MV_0 = \$275{,}000 / \$2{,}500{,}000 = 0.11$ or 11%.

5. C The market capitalization rate equals the difference between the required rate of return on equity minus the constant growth rate of net operating income ($R_0 = r - g$). So, $0.11 = r - 0.06$. Solving for r results in a required return on equity of $0.11 + 0.06 = 0.17$, or 17%.

6. **B** The NPV of the shopping center is –$51,226. In this case the IRR is unreliable for investment purposes because there is more than one sign change in the cash flow stream. The IRR should not be used when there is more than one sign change in the cash flow stream. The shopping center investment should be rejected because the NPV is negative. The NPV can be calculated as follows using the TI BA II Plus:

Procedure	*Keystrokes*	*Display*
Select cash flow worksheet	[CF]	CF0 (old contents)
Clear worksheet	[2nd] [CLR WORK]	CF0 = 0.00
Enter initial cash flow	1525000 [+/–] [ENTER]	CF0 = –1,525,000
Enter cash flows for years 1–5	↓ 330000 [ENTER]	C01 = 330,000
	↓ 5 [ENTER]	F01 = 5.00
Enter cash flow for year 6	↓ 700000 [+/–] [ENTER]	C02 = –700,000
	↓ 1 [ENTER]	F02 = 1
Enter cash flows for years 7–12	↓ 450000 [ENTER]	C03 = 450,000
	↓ 6 [ENTER]	F03 = 6
Access NPV portion of cash flow worksheet	[NPV]	I = 0.00
Enter interest rate per period	16 [ENTER]	I = 16
Compute net present value	↓ [CPT]	NPV = –51,226

The following is a review of the Fixed Income: Valuation concepts principles designed to address the learning outcome statements set forth by CFA Institute. This topic is also covered in:

FUNDAMENTALS OF CREDIT ANALYSIS

Study Session 14

EXAM FOCUS

This topic review introduces credit analysis, primarily for corporate bonds, but considerations for credit analysis of high yield, sovereign, and municipal bonds are also covered. Focus on credit ratings, credit spreads, and the impact on return when ratings and spreads change.

LOS 42.a: Describe credit risk and credit-related risks affecting corporate bonds.

CFA® Program Curriculum, Volume 5, page 216

Credit risk is the risk associated with losses stemming from the failure of a borrower to make timely and full payments of interest or principal. Credit risk has two components: *default risk* and *loss severity.*

- **Default risk** is the probability that a borrower (bond issuer) fails to pay interest or repay principal when due.
- **Loss severity,** or *loss given default,* refers to the value a bond investor will lose if the issuer defaults. Loss severity can be stated as a monetary amount or as a percentage of a bond's value (principal and unpaid interest).

The **expected loss** is equal to the default risk multiplied by the loss severity. Expected loss can be stated as a monetary value or as a percentage of a bond's value.

The **recovery rate** is the percentage of a bond's value an investor will receive if the issuer defaults. Loss severity as a percentage is equal to one minus the recovery rate.

Bonds with credit risk trade at higher yields than bonds thought to be free of credit risk. The difference in yield between a credit-risky bond and a credit-risk-free bond of similar maturity is called its **yield spread**. For example, if a 5-year corporate bond is trading at a spread of +250 basis points to Treasuries and the yield on 5-year Treasury notes is 4.0%, the yield on the corporate bond would be 4.0% + 2.5% = 6.5%.

Bond prices are inversely related to spreads: a wider spread implies a lower bond price and a narrower spread implies a higher price. The size of the spread reflects the creditworthiness of the issuer and the liquidity of the market for its bonds. **Spread risk** is the possibility that a bond's spread will widen due to one or both of these factors.

- **Credit migration risk** or **downgrade risk** is the possibility that spreads will increase because the issuer has become less creditworthy. As we will see later in this topic review, credit rating agencies assign ratings to bonds and issuers, and may upgrade or downgrade them over time.
- **Market liquidity risk** is the risk of receiving less than market value when selling a bond and is reflected in the size of the bid-ask spreads. Market liquidity risk is greater for the bonds of less creditworthy issuers and for the bonds of smaller issuers with relatively little publicly traded debt.

LOS 42.b: Describe seniority rankings of corporate debt and explain the potential violation of the priority of claims in a bankruptcy proceeding.

CFA® Program Curriculum, Volume 5, page 218

Each category of debt from the same issuer is ranked according to a **priority of claims** in the event of a default. A bond's priority of claims to the issuer's assets and cash flows is referred to as its **seniority ranking**.

Debt can be either **secured debt** or **unsecured debt**. Secured debt is backed by collateral, while unsecured debt or *debentures* represent a general claim to the issuer's assets and cash flows. Secured debt has higher priority of claims than unsecured debt.

Secured debt can be further distinguished as *first lien* or *first mortgage* (where a specific asset is pledged), *senior secured*, or *junior secured* debt. Unsecured debt is further divided into *senior*, *junior*, and *subordinated* gradations. The highest rank of unsecured debt is senior unsecured.

The general seniority rankings for debt repayment priority are the following:

- First lien or first mortgage.
- Senior secured debt.
- Junior secured debt.
- Senior unsecured debt.
- Senior subordinated debt.
- Subordinated debt.
- Junior subordinated debt.

All debt within the same category is said to rank **pari passu**, or have same priority of claims. All senior secured debt holders, for example, are treated alike in a corporate bankruptcy.

Recovery rates are highest for debt with the highest priority of claims and decrease with each lower rank of seniority. The lower the seniority ranking of a bond, the higher its credit risk. Investors require a higher yield to accept a lower seniority ranking.

In the event of a default or reorganization, senior lenders have claims on the assets before junior lenders and equity holders. A strict priority of claims, however, is not always applied in practice. Although in theory the priority of claims is absolute, in many cases lower-priority debt holders (and even equity investors) may get paid even if senior debt holders are not paid in full.

Bankruptcies can be costly and take a long time to settle. During bankruptcy proceedings, the value of a company's assets could deteriorate due to loss of customers and key employees, while legal expenses mount. A bankruptcy reorganization plan is confirmed by a vote among all classes of investors with less than 100% recovery rate. To avoid unnecessary delays, negotiation and compromise among various claimholders may result in a reorganization plan that does not strictly conform to the original priority of claims. By such a vote or by order of the bankruptcy court, the final plan may differ from absolute priority.

LOS 42.c: Distinguish between corporate issuer credit ratings and issue credit ratings and describe the rating agency practice of "notching".

CFA® Program Curriculum, Volume 5, page 226

Credit rating agencies assign ratings to categories of bonds with similar credit risk. Rating agencies rate both the issuer (i.e., the company issuing the bonds) and the debt issues, or the bonds themselves. Issuer credit ratings are called **corporate family ratings** (CFR), while issue-specific ratings are called **corporate credit ratings** (CCR). Issuer ratings are based on the overall creditworthiness of the company. The issuers are rated on their senior unsecured debt.

Figure 1 shows ratings scales used by Standard & Poor's, Moody's, and Fitch, three of the major credit rating agencies.

Figure 1: Credit Rating Categories

(a) Investment grade ratings

Moody's	*Standard &Poor's, Fitch*
Aaa	AAA
Aa1	AA+
Aa2	AA
Aa3	AA–
A1	A+
A2	A
A3	A–
Baa1	BBB+
Baa2	BBB
Baa3	BBB–

(b) Non-investment grade ratings

Moody's	*Standard &Poor's, Fitch*
Ba1	BB+
Ba2	BB
Ba3	BB–
B1	B+
B2	B
B3	B–
Caa1	CCC+
Caa2	CCC
Caa3	CCC–
Ca	CC
C	C
C	D

Triple A (AAA or Aaa) is the highest rating. Bonds with ratings of Baa3/BBB– or higher are considered **investment grade**. Bonds rated Ba1/BB+ or lower are considered **non-investment grade** and are often called *high yield bonds* or *junk bonds*.

Bonds in default are rated D by Standard & Poor's and Fitch and are included in Moody's lowest rating category, C. When a company defaults on one of its several outstanding bonds, provisions in bond indentures may trigger default on the remaining issues as well. Such a provision is called a *cross default provision*.

A borrower can have multiple debt issues that vary not only by maturities and coupons but also by credit rating. Issue credit ratings depend on the seniority of a bond issue and its covenants. **Notching** is the practice by rating agencies of assigning different ratings to bonds of the same issuer. Notching is based on several factors, including seniority of the bonds and its impact on potential loss severity.

An example of a factor that rating agencies consider when notching an issue credit rating is **structural subordination**. In a holding company structure, both the parent company and the subsidiaries may have outstanding debt. A subsidiary's debt covenants may restrict the transfer of cash or assets "upstream" to the parent company before the subsidiary's debt is serviced. In such a case, even though the parent company's bonds are not junior to the subsidiary's bonds, the subsidiary's bonds have a higher priority of claim to the subsidiary's cash flows. Thus the parent company's bonds are effectively subordinated to the subsidiary's bonds.

Notching is less common for highly rated issuers than for lower-rated issuers. For lower-rated issuers, higher default risk leads to significant differences between recovery rates of debt with different seniority rankings, leading to more notching.

LOS 42.d: Explain risks in relying on ratings from credit rating agencies.

CFA® Program Curriculum, Volume 5, page 227

Relying on ratings from credit rating agencies has some risks. Four specific risks are:

1. **Credit ratings are dynamic.** Credit ratings change over time. Rating agencies may update their default risk assessments during the life of a bond. Higher credit ratings tend to be more stable than lower credit ratings.

2. **Rating agencies are not perfect.** Ratings mistakes occur from time to time. For example, subprime mortgage securities were assigned much higher ratings than they deserved.

3. **Event risk is difficult to assess.** Risks that are specific to a company or industry are difficult to predict and incorporate into credit ratings. Litigation risk to tobacco companies is one example. Events that are difficult to anticipate, such as natural disasters, acquisitions, and equity buybacks using debt, are not easily captured in credit ratings.

4. **Credit ratings lag market pricing.** Market prices and credit spreads change much faster than credit ratings. Additionally, two bonds with same rating can trade at different yields. Market prices reflect expected losses, while credit ratings only assess default risk.

LOS 42.e: Explain the components of traditional credit analysis.

CFA® Program Curriculum, Volume 5, page 232

A common way to categorize the key components of credit analysis is by the **four Cs of credit analysis**: capacity, collateral, covenants, and character.

Capacity

Capacity refers to a corporate borrower's ability repay its debt obligations on time. Analysis of capacity is similar to the process used in equity analysis. Capacity analysis entails three levels of assessment: (1) industry structure, (2) industry fundamentals, and (3) company fundamentals.

Industry Structure

The first level of a credit analyst's assessment is industry structure. Industry structure can be described by Porter's five forces: rivalry among existing competitors, threat of new entrants, threat of substitute products, bargaining power of buyers, and bargaining power of suppliers.

Professor's Note: We describe industry analysis based on Porter's five forces in the Study Session on equity valuation.

Industry Fundamentals

The next level of a credit analyst's assessment is industry fundamentals, including the influence of macroeconomic factors on an industry's growth prospects and profitability. Industry fundamentals evaluation focuses on:

- **Industry cyclicality.** Cyclical industries tend to have more volatile earnings, revenues, and cash flows, which make them more risky than noncyclical industries.
- **Industry growth prospects.** Creditworthiness is poorer for the weaker companies in a slow-growing or declining industry.
- **Industry published statistics.** Industry statistics available from rating agencies, investment banks, industry periodicals, and government agencies can be a source for industry fundamentals and outlook.

Company Fundamentals

The last level of credit analysts' assessment is company fundamentals. A corporate borrower should be assessed on:

- **Competitive position.** Market share changes over time and cost structure relative to peers are some of the factors to analyze.
- **Operating history.** The performance of the company over different phases of business cycle, trends in margins and revenues, and current management's tenure.
- **Management's strategy and execution.** This includes the soundness of the strategy, the ability to execute the strategy, and the effects of management's decisions on bondholders.
- **Ratios and ratio analysis.** As we will discuss later in this topic review, leverage and coverage ratios are important tools for credit analysis.

Collateral

Collateral analysis is more important for less creditworthy companies. The market value of a company's assets can be difficult to observe directly. Issues to consider when assessing collateral values include:

- **Intangible assets.** Patents are considered high-quality intangible assets because they can be more easily sold to generate cash flows as compared to other intangibles. Goodwill is not considered a high-quality intangible asset and is usually written down when the company performance is poor.
- **Depreciation.** High depreciation expense relative to capital expenditures may signal that management is not investing sufficiently in the company. The quality of the company's assets may be poor, which may lead to reduced operating cash flow and potentially high loss severity.
- **Equity market capitalization.** A stock that trades below book value may indicate that company assets are of low quality.
- **Human and intellectual capital.** These are difficult to value, but a company may have intellectual property that can serve as collateral.

Covenants

Covenants are the terms and conditions the borrowers have agreed to as part of a bond issue. Covenants protect lenders while leaving some operating flexibility to the borrowers to run the company. There are two types of covenants: (1) *affirmative covenants* and (2) *negative covenants*.

Affirmative covenants require the borrower to take certain actions, such as paying interest, principal, and taxes; carrying insurance on pledged assets; and maintaining certain financial ratios within prescribed limits.

Negative covenants restrict the borrower from taking certain actions, such as incurring additional debt or directing cash flows to shareholders in the form of dividends and stock repurchases before servicing debt.

Covenants that are overly restrictive of an issuer's operating activities may reduce the issuer's ability to repay. On the other hand, covenants create a legally binding contractual framework for repayment of the debt obligation, which reduces uncertainty for the debt holders. A careful credit analysis should include an assessment of whether the covenants protect the interests of the bondholders without unduly constraining the borrower's operating activities.

Character

Character refers to management's integrity and its commitment to repay the loan. Factors such as management's business qualifications and operating record are important for evaluating character. Character analysis includes an assessment of:

- **Soundness of strategy**. Management's ability to develop a sound strategy.
- **Track record**. Management's past performance in executing its strategy and operating the company without bankruptcies, restructurings, or other distress situations that led to additional borrowing.
- **Accounting policies and tax strategies**. Use of inappropriate accounting policies and tax strategies, such as revenue recognition issues, policies leading to frequent restatements, and frequently changing auditors.
- **Fraud and malfeasance record**. Any record of fraud or other legal and regulatory problems.
- **Prior treatment of bondholders**. Benefits to equity holders at the expense of debt holders, through actions such as debt-financed acquisitions and special dividends, especially if they led to credit rating downgrades.

LOS 42.f: Calculate and interpret financial ratios used in credit analysis.

CFA® Program Curriculum, Volume 5, page 237

Ratio analysis is part of capacity analysis. Two primary categories of ratios for credit analysis are *leverage ratios* and *coverage ratios.* Credit analysts calculate company ratios to assess the viability of a company, to find trends over time, and to compare companies to industry averages and peers.

Profits and Cash Flows

Profits and cash flows are needed to service debt. Here we examine four profit and cash flow metrics commonly used in ratio analysis by credit analysts.

1. **Earnings before interest, taxes, depreciation, and amortization (EBITDA).** EBITDA is a commonly used measure that is calculated as operating income plus depreciation and amortization. A drawback to using this measure for credit analysis is that it does not adjust for capital expenditures and changes in working capital, which are necessary uses of funds for a going concern. Cash needed for these uses is not available to debt holders.

2. **Funds from operations (FFO).** Funds from operations are net income from continuing operations plus depreciation, amortization, deferred taxes, and noncash items. FFO is similar to cash flow from operations (CFO) except that FFO excludes changes in working capital.

3. **Free cash flow before dividends.** Free cash flow before dividends is net income plus depreciation and amortization minus capital expenditures minus increase in working capital. Free cash flow before dividends excludes non-recurring items.

4. **Free cash flow after dividends.** This is free cash flow before dividends minus the dividends. If free cash flow after dividends is greater than zero, it represents cash that could be used to pay down debt or allowed to accumulate on the balance sheet. Either outcome is a form of deleveraging, a positive indicator for creditworthiness.

Leverage Ratios

Analysts should adjust debt reported on the financial statements by including the firm's obligations such as underfunded pension plans (net pension liabilities) and off-balance-sheet liabilities such as operating leases.

The three most common measures of leverage used by credit analysts are the debt-to-capital ratio, the debt-to-EBITDA ratio, and the FFO-to-debt ratio.

1. **Debt/capital.** Capital is the sum of total debt and shareholders' equity. The debt-to-capital ratio is the percentage of the capital structure financed by debt. A lower ratio indicates less credit risk. If the financial statements list high values for intangible assets such as goodwill, an analyst should calculate a second debt-to-capital ratio adjusted for a writedown of these assets' after-tax value.

2. **Debt/EBITDA.** A higher ratio indicates higher leverage and higher credit risk. This ratio is more volatile for firms in cyclical industries or with high operating leverage because of their high variability of EBITDA.

3. **FFO/debt.** Because this ratio divides a cash flow measure by the value of debt, a higher ratio indicates lower credit risk.

Coverage Ratios

Coverage ratios measure the borrower's ability to generate cash flows to meet interest payments. The two most commonly used are EBITDA-to-interest and EBIT-to-interest.

1. **EBITDA/interest expense.** A higher ratio indicates lower credit risk. This ratio is used more often than the EBIT-to-interest expense ratio. Because depreciation and amortization are still included as part of the cash flow measure, this ratio will be higher than the EBIT version.

2. **EBIT/interest expense.** A higher ratio indicates lower credit risk. This ratio is the more conservative measure because depreciation and amortization are subtracted from earnings.

Example: Credit analysis with financial ratios (Part 1)

A credit analyst is assessing Saxor, a U.S. multimedia company with the following selected financial information:

In $ millions	*20X1*	*20X2*	*20X3*
Operating income	5,205	6,456	7,726
Revenue	36,149	38,063	40,893
Depreciation and amortization	1,631	1,713	1,841
Capital expenditures	1,753	2,110	3,559
Cash flow from operations	5,319	6,578	6,994
Total debt	12,701	12,480	13,977
Total equity	33,734	37,519	37,385
Dividends paid	648	653	756
Interest expense	300	330	360

Calculate the cash flows and ratios listed below. Free cash flow (FCF) is after dividends for all calculations.

	20X1	*20X2*	*20X3*
EBITDA			
FCF after dividends			
Operating margin			
Debt/EBITDA			
EBITDA/interest			
FCF/debt			
Debt/capital			

Answer:

EBITDA = operating income + depreciation and amortization:
20X1: 5,205 + 1,631 = $6,836 million
20X2: 6,456 + 1,713 = $8,169 million
20X3: 7,726 + 1,841 = $9,567 million

FCF = cash flow from operations – capital expenditures – dividends:
20X1: 5,319 – 1,753 – 648 = $2,918 million
20X2: 6,578 – 2,110 – 653 = $3,815 million
20X3: 6,994 – 3,559 – 756 = $2,679 million

Operating margin = operating income / revenue:
20X1: 5,205 / 36,149 = 14.4%
20X2: 6,456 / 38,063 = 17.0%
20X3: 7,726 / 40,893 = 18.9%

Debt/EBITDA:
20X1: 12,701 / 6,836 = 1.9x
20X2: 12,480 / 8,169 = 1.5x
20X3: 13,977 / 9,567 = 1.5x

EBITDA/interest:
20X1: 6,836 / 300 = 22.8x
20X2: 8,169 / 330 = 24.8x
20X3: 9,567 / 360 = 26.6x

FCF/debt:
20X1: 6,836 / 12,701 = 23.0%
20X2: 8,169 / 12,480 = 30.6%
20X3: 9,567 / 13,977 = 19.2%

Debt/capital:
20X1: 12,701 / (12,701 + 33,734) = 27.4%
20X2: 12,480 / (12,480 + 37,519) = 25.0%
20X3: 13,977 / (13,977 + 37,385) = 27.2%

	20X1	*20X2*	*20X3*
EBITDA	6,836	8,169	9,567
FCF after dividends	2,918	3,815	2,679
Operating margin	14.4%	17.0%	18.9%
Debt/EBITDA	1.9×	1.5×	1.5×
EBITDA/interest	22.8×	24.8×	26.6×
FCF/debt	23.0%	30.6%	19.2%
Debt/capital	27.4%	25.0%	27.2%

Example: Credit analysis with financial ratios (Part 2)

2. Coyote Media is also a multimedia company and is a rival of Saxor. Given the following ratios for Coyote over the same period, calculate the 3-year averages for both Saxor and Coyote and comment on which multimedia company is expected to have a better credit rating.

Coyote Media	*20X1*	*20X2*	*20X3*
Operating margin	18.0%	7.0%	9.5%
Debt/EBITDA	1.9×	3.0×	2.0×
EBITDA/interest	27.5×	12.7×	18.3×
FCF/debt	15.0%	28.0%	26.6%
Debt/capital	28.7%	41.2%	42.6%

Answer:

3-Year Averages	*Saxor*	*Coyote*
Operating margin	16.8%	11.5%
Debt/EBITDA	1.6x	2.3x
EBITDA/interest	24.7x	19.5x
FCF/debt	24.2%	23.2%
Debt/capital	26.5%	37.5%

All ratios support a higher credit rating for Saxor. Saxor has a better operating margin and better coverage for interest (EBITDA/interest) and for debt (FCF/debt). Lower leverage as measured by debt-to-capital and debt-to-EBITDA also favor Saxor.

LOS 42.g: Evaluate the credit quality of a corporate bond issuer and a bond of that issuer, given key financial ratios for the issuer and the industry.

CFA® Program Curriculum, Volume 5, page 240

Ratings agencies publish benchmark values for financial ratios that are associated with each ratings classification. Credit analysts can evaluate the potential for upgrades and downgrades based on subject company ratios relative to these benchmarks.

Example: Credit ratings based on ratios (Part 1)

A credit rating agency publishes the following benchmark ratios for bond issues of multimedia companies in each of the investment grade ratings, based on 3-year averages over the period 20X1 to 20X3:

Credit Ratings	*AAA*	*AA*	*A*	*BBB*
Operating margin	24.5%	16.5%	10.0%	7.5%
Debt/EBITDA	1.3x	1.8x	2.2x	2.5x
EBITDA/interest	25.0x	20.0x	17.5x	15.0x
FCF/debt	30.0%	24.0%	20.0%	17.0%
Debt/capital	25.0%	30.0%	35.0%	40.0%

Based on the ratios calculated in the previous example and the industry standards in the table above, what are the expected issuer credit ratings for Coyote and Saxor?

Answer:

3-Year Averages	*Saxor*	*Coyote*
Operating margin	16.8%	11.5%
Debt/EBITDA	1.6×	2.3×
EBITDA/interest	24.7×	19.5×
FCF/debt	24.3%	23.2%
Debt/capital	26.6%	37.5%

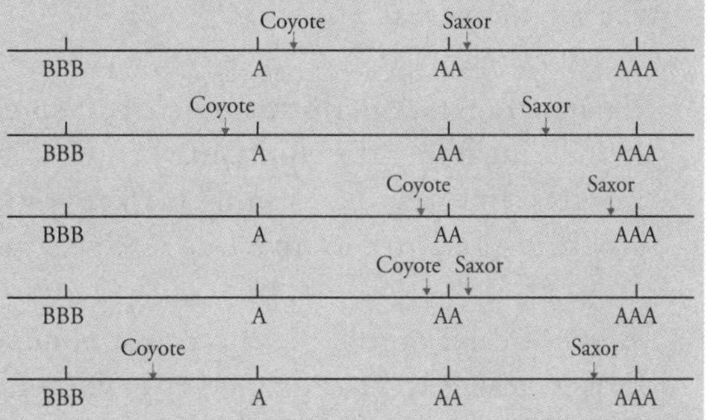

Based on the ratio averages, it is most likely that Saxor's issuer rating is AA and Coyote's issuer rating is A.

Example: Credit ratings based on ratios (Part 2)

Coyote Media decides to spin off its television division. The new company, CoyTV, will issue new debt and will not be a restricted subsidiary of Coyote Media. CoyTV is more profitable and generates higher and less volatile cash flows. Describe possible notching for the new CoyTV issue and the potential credit rating change to Coyote Media.

Answer:

Because CoyTV may be a better credit risk due to a better profit potential, the new issue may have a credit rating one notch above Coyote Media.

Coyote Media may now be less profitable and could have more volatile cash flows. This suggests an increase in credit risk that could lead to a credit rating downgrade.

LOS 42.h: Describe factors that influence the level and volatility of yield spreads.

CFA® Program Curriculum, Volume 5, page 253

We can think of the yield on an option-free corporate bond as the sum of the real risk-free interest rate, the expected inflation rate, a maturity premium, a liquidity premium, and a credit spread. The last two components are the yield spread:

yield spread = liquidity premium + credit spread

Yield spreads on corporate bonds are affected primarily by five interrelated factors:

1. **Credit cycle.** The market's perception of overall credit risk is cyclical. At the top of the credit cycle, the bond market perceives low aggregate credit risk and is generally bullish. Credit spreads narrow as the credit cycle improves. Credit spreads widen as the credit cycle deteriorates.

2. **Economic conditions.** Credit spreads narrow as the economy strengthens and investors expect firms' credit metrics to improve. Conversely, credit spreads widen as the economy weakens.

3. **Financial market performance.** Credit spreads narrow in strong-performing markets overall, including the equity market. Credit spreads widen in weak-performing markets. In steady-performing markets with low volatility of returns, credit spreads also tend to narrow as investors reach for yield.

4. **Broker-dealer capital.** Because most bonds trade over the counter, investors need broker-dealers to provide market-making capital for bond markets to function. Yield spreads are narrower when broker-dealers provide sufficient capital but can widen when market-making capital becomes scarce.

5. **General market demand and supply.** Credit spreads narrow in times of high demand for bonds. Credit spreads widen in times of low demand for bonds. Excess supply conditions, such as large issuances in a short period of time, can lead to widening spreads.

Yield spreads on lower-quality issues tend to be more volatile than spreads on higher-quality issues.

LOS 42.i: Calculate the return impact of spread changes.

CFA® Program Curriculum, Volume 5, page 255

The return impact of spread changes is a combination of two factors: (1) the magnitude of the spread change (Δspread) and (2) the price sensitivity of the bond to interest rate changes (i.e., the bond's modified duration).

For small spread changes, the return impact (percent change in bond price) can be approximated by:

$$\text{return impact} \approx -\text{ modified duration} \times \Delta\text{spread}$$

The negative sign in the equation reflects the inverse relationship between prices and yields. As spreads widen (the change in spread is positive), bond prices decrease and the impact on return is negative. As spreads narrow (the change in spread is negative), bond prices increase and the impact on return is positive.

For larger spread changes, incorporating convexity improves the accuracy of return impact measurement.

$$\text{return impact} \approx -\text{ modified duration} \times \Delta\text{spread} + \frac{1}{2}\text{convexity} \times (\Delta\text{spread})^2$$

Professor's Note: Make sure the value of convexity is scaled correctly. For option-free bonds, convexity should be on the same order of magnitude as modified duration squared. For example, if you are given that duration is 6.0 and convexity is 0.562, duration squared is 36.0 and the correctly scaled convexity is 56.2.

Longer maturity bonds have higher duration and consequently higher spread sensitivity; their prices and returns are more sensitive to changes in spread. The longer the maturity, the higher the uncertainty of the future creditworthiness of the debt issuer, implying higher credit spreads for longer maturity bonds. Longer maturity bonds also tend to have larger bid-ask spreads (i.e., higher transaction costs), implying investors in longer maturity bonds would require higher spreads.

Credit curves or *spread curves* show the relationship between spread and maturity. Because longer maturity bonds tend to have wider spreads, credit curves are typically upward sloping.

Bond performance is positively affected by narrowing credit spreads and negatively affected by widening credit spreads. To enhance bond portfolio performance, active bond managers need to forecast spread changes and expected credit losses for individual issues held and for the overall bond portfolio.

Example: Impact on return

An 8-year semiannual-pay corporate bond with a 5.75% coupon is priced at $108.32. This bond's duration and reported convexity are 6.4 and 0.5. The bond's credit spread narrows by 75 basis points due to a credit rating upgrade. Estimate the return impact with and without the convexity adjustment.

Answer:

return impact (without convexity adjustment) $\approx$ – modified duration × Δspread
$\approx$ – 6.4 × –0.0075
$\approx$ 0.0480
$\approx$ 0.048 or **4.80%**

return impact with convexity adjustment

$$\approx -\text{ modified duration} \times \Delta\text{spread} + \frac{1}{2}\text{convexity} \times (\Delta\text{spread})^2$$

$$\approx -6.4 \times -0.0075 + \frac{1}{2}(50.0) \times (-0.0075)^2$$

$$\approx 0.0480 + 0.0014$$

$$\approx 0.0494 \text{ or } \mathbf{4.94\%}$$

Notice that convexity needed to be corrected to match the scale of duration.

We can calculate the actual change in the bond's price from the information given to illustrate the need for the convexity adjustment.

Beginning yield to maturity:

N = 16; PMT = 5.75 / 2 = 2.875; FV = 100; PV = –108.32;
CPT → I/Y = 2.25 × 2 = 4.50

Yield to maturity after upgrade: 4.50 – 0.75 = 3.75%

Price after upgrade:

I/Y = 3.75 / 2 = 1.875; CPT → PV = –113.71

The calculated bond price of $113.71 is an increase of (113.71 / 108.32) – 1 = 4.98%. The return impact approximation is closer with the convexity adjustment.

LOS 42.j: Explain special considerations when evaluating the credit of high yield, sovereign, and municipal debt issuers and issues.

CFA® Program Curriculum, Volume 5, page 259

High Yield Debt

High yield or *non-investment grade* corporate bonds are rated below Baa3/BBB by credit rating agencies. These bonds are also called *junk bonds* because of their higher perceived credit risk.

Reasons for non-investment grade ratings may include:

- High leverage.
- Unproven operating history.
- Low or negative free cash flow.
- High sensitivity to business cycles.
- Low confidence in management.
- Unclear competitive advantages.
- Large off-balance-sheet liabilities.
- Industry in decline.

Because high yield bonds have higher default risk than investment grade bonds, credit analysts must pay more attention to loss severity. Special considerations for high yield bonds include their liquidity, financial projections, debt structure, corporate structure, and covenants.

Liquidity. Liquidity or availability of cash is critical for high yield issuers. High yield issuers have limited access to additional borrowings, and available funds tend to be more expensive. Bad company-specific news and difficult financial market conditions can quickly dry up the liquidity of debt markets. Many high yield issuers are privately owned and cannot access public equity markets for needed funds.

Analysts focus on six sources of liquidity (in order of reliability):

1. Balance sheet cash.

2. Working capital.

3. Operating cash flow (CFO).

4. Bank credit.

5. Equity issues.

6. Sales of assets.

For a high yield issuer with few or unreliable sources of liquidity, significant amounts of debt coming due within a short time frame may indicate potential default. Running out of cash with no access to external financing to refinance or service existing debt is the primary reason why high yield issuers default. For high yield financial firms that are highly levered and depend on funding long-term assets with short-term liabilities, liquidity is critical.

Financial projections. Projecting future earnings and cash flows, including stress scenarios and accounting for changes in capital expenditures and working capital, are important for revealing potential vulnerabilities to meet debt payments.

Debt structure. High yield issuers' capital structures often include different types of debt with several levels of seniority and hence varying levels of potential loss severity. Capital structures typically include secured bank debt, second lien debt, senior unsecured debt, subordinated debt, and preferred stock. Some of these, especially subordinated debt, may be convertible to common shares.

A credit analyst will need to calculate leverage for each level of the debt structure when an issuer has multiple layers of debt with a variety of expected recovery rates.

High yield issuers for whom secured bank debt is a high proportion of the capital structure are said to be *top heavy* and have less capacity for additional bank borrowings in financially stressful periods. Companies that have top-heavy capital structures are more likely to default and have lower recovery rates for unsecured debt issues.

Example: Debt structure and leverage

Two European high yield issuers in the same industry have the following financial information:

In € million	*A*	*B*
Cash	100.0	50.0
Interest expense	40.0	20.0
EBITDA	85.0	42.5
Secured bank debt	500.0	125.0
Senior unsecured debt	200.0	50.0
Convertible bonds	50.0	200.0

1. Calculate total leverage through each level of debt for both companies.

2. Calculate net leverage for both companies.

3. Comment on which company is more creditworthy for an unsecured debt investor.

Answer:

	A	*B*
Secured debt leverage: secured debt/EBITDA	500.0 / 85.0 = 5.9x	125.0 / 42.5 = 2.9x
Senior unsecured leverage: (secured + senior unsecured debt)/EBITDA	(500.0 + 200.0) / 85.0 = 8.2x	(125.0 + 50.0) / 42.5 = 4.1x
Total debt leverage: total debt/EBITDA	(500.0 + 200.0 + 50.0) / 85.0 = 8.8x	(125.0 + 50.0 + 200.0) / 42.5= 8.8x
Net leverage: (total debt – cash)/ EBITDA	(750.0 – 100.0) / 85.0 = 7.6x	(375.0 – 50.0) / 42.5 = 7.6x

Company B has a lower secured debt leverage ratio than Company A, while total and net leverage ratios are about the same. Company B is more creditworthy for unsecured debt holders because it is less top heavy and may have additional capacity to borrow from banks, which suggests a lower probability of default. If it does default, Company B may have a higher percentage of assets available to unsecured debt holders than Company A, especially if holders of convertible bonds have exercised their options.

Corporate structure. Many high-yield companies use a holding company structure. A parent company receives dividends from the earnings of subsidiaries as its primary source of operating income. Because of structural subordination, subsidiaries' dividends paid upstream to a parent company are subordinate to subsidiary's interest payments. These dividends can be insufficient to pay the debt obligations of the parent, thus reducing the recovery rate for debt holders of the parent company.

Despite structural subordination, a parent company's credit rating may be superior to subsidiaries' ratings because the parent can benefit from having access to multiple cash flows from diverse subsidiaries.

Some complex corporate structures have intermediate holding companies that carry their own debt and do not own 100% of their subsidiaries' stock. These companies are typically a result of mergers, acquisitions, or leveraged buyouts.

Default of one subsidiary may not necessarily result in cross default. Analysts need to scrutinize bonds' indentures and other legal documents to fully understand the impact of complex corporate structures. To analyze these companies, analysts should calculate leverage ratios at each level of debt issuance and on a consolidated basis.

Covenants. Important covenants for high yield debt include:

- **Change of control put.** This covenant gives debt holders the right to require the issuer to buy back debt (typically for par value or a value slightly above par) in the event of an acquisition. For investment grade bonds, a change of control put typically applies only if an acquisition of the borrower results in a rating downgrade to below investment grade.

- **Restricted payments.** The covenant protects lenders by limiting the amount of cash that may be paid to equity holders.
- **Limitations on liens.** The covenant limits the amount of secured debt that a borrower can carry. Unsecured debt holders prefer the issuer to have less secured debt, which increases the recovery amount available to them in the event of default.
- **Restricted versus unrestricted subsidiaries.** Issuers can classify subsidiaries as restricted or unrestricted. Restricted subsidiaries' cash flows and assets can be used to service the debt of the parent holding company. This benefits creditors of holding companies because their debt is pari passu with the debt of restricted subsidiaries, rather than be structurally subordinated. Restricted subsidiaries are typically the holding company's larger subsidiaries that have significant assets. Tax and regulatory issues can factor into the classification of subsidiary's restriction status. A subsidiary's restriction status is found in the bond indenture.

Bank covenants are often more restrictive than bond covenants, and when covenants are violated, banks can block additional loans until the violation is corrected. If a violation is not remedied, banks can trigger a default by accelerating the full repayment of a loan.

In terms of the factors that affect their return, high yield bonds may be viewed as a hybrid of investment grade bonds and equity. Compared to investment grade bonds, high yield bonds show greater price and spread volatility and are more highly correlated with the equity market.

High yield analysis can include some of the same techniques as equity market analysis, such as enterprise value. **Enterprise value** (EV) is equity market capitalization plus total debt minus excess cash. For high yield companies that are not publicly traded, comparable public company equity data can be used to estimate EV. Enterprise value analysis can indicate a firm's potential for additional leverage, or the potential credit damage that might result from a leveraged buyout. An analyst can compare firms based on the differences between their EV/EBITDA and debt/EBITDA ratios. Firms with a wider difference between these ratios have greater equity relative to their debt and therefore have less credit risk.

Sovereign Debt

Sovereign debt is issued by national governments. Sovereign credit analysis must assess both the government's ability to service debt and its willingness to do so. The assessment of willingness is important because bondholders usually have no legal recourse if a national government refuses to pay its debts.

A basic framework for evaluating and assigning a credit rating to sovereign debt includes five key areas:

1. **Institutional effectiveness** includes successful policymaking, absence of corruption, and commitment to honor debts.

2. **Economic prospects** include growth trends, demographics, income per capita, and size of government relative to the private economy.

3. **International investment position** includes the country's foreign reserves, its external debt, and the status of its currency in international markets.

4. **Fiscal flexibility** includes the government's willingness and ability to increase revenue or cut expenditures to ensure debt service, as well as trends in debt as a percentage of GDP.

5. **Monetary flexibility** includes the ability to use monetary policy for domestic economic objectives (this might be lacking with exchange rate targeting or membership in a monetary union) and the credibility and effectiveness of monetary policy.

Credit rating agencies assign each national government two ratings: (1) a local currency debt rating and (2) a foreign currency debt rating. The ratings are assigned separately because defaults on foreign currency denominated debt have historically exceeded those on local currency debt. Foreign currency debt typically has a higher default rate and a lower credit rating because the government must purchase foreign currency in the open market to make interest and principal payments, which exposes it to the risk of significant local currency depreciation. In contrast, local currency debt can be repaid by raising taxes, controlling domestic spending, or simply printing more money. Ratings can differ as much as two notches for local and foreign currency bonds.

Sovereign defaults can be caused by events such as war, political instability, severe devaluation of the currency, or large declines in the prices of the country's export commodities. Access to debt markets can be difficult for sovereigns in bad economic times.

Municipal Debt

Municipal bonds are issued by state and local governments or their agencies. Municipal bonds usually have lower default rates than corporate bonds with same credit ratings.

Most municipal bonds can be classified as *general obligation bonds* or *revenue bonds.* **General obligation** (GO) bonds are unsecured bonds backed by the full faith and credit of the issuing governmental entity, which is to say they are supported by its taxing power.

Unlike sovereigns, municipalities cannot use monetary policy to service their debt and usually must balance their operating budgets. Municipal governments' ability to service their general obligation debt depends ultimately on the local economy (i.e., the tax base). Economic factors to assess include employment, trends in per capita income and per capita debt, tax base dimensions (depth, breadth and stability), demographics, and ability to attract new jobs (location, infrastructure). Credit analysts must also observe revenue variability through economic cycles. Relying on highly variable taxes that are subject to economic cycles, such as capital gains and sales taxes, can signal higher credit risk. Municipalities may have long-term obligations such as underfunded pensions and post-retirement benefits. Inconsistent reporting requirements for municipalities are also an issue.

Revenue bonds finance specific projects. Revenue bonds often have higher credit risk than GO bonds because the project is the sole source of funds to service the debt. Analysis of revenue bonds combines analysis of the project, using techniques similar to those for analyzing corporate bonds, with analysis of the financing of the project.

A key metric for revenue bonds is the **debt service coverage ratio** (DSCR), which is the ratio of the project's net revenue to the required interest and principal payments on the bonds. Many revenue bonds include a covenant requiring a minimum debt service coverage ratio to protect the lenders' interests. Lenders prefer higher debt service coverage ratios, as this represents lower default risk (better creditworthiness).

KEY CONCEPTS

LOS 42.a

Credit risk refers to the possibility that a borrower fails to make the scheduled interest payments or return of principal. Credit risk is composed of default risk, which is the probability of default, and loss severity, which is the portion of the value of a bond or loan a lender or investor will lose if the borrower defaults. The expected loss is the probability of default multiplied by the loss severity.

Spread risk is the possibility that a bond loses value because its credit spread widens relative to its benchmark. Spread risk includes credit migration or downgrade risk and market liquidity risk.

LOS 42.b

Corporate debt is ranked by seniority or priority of claims. Secured debt is a direct claim on specific firm assets and has priority over unsecured debt. Secured or unsecured debt may be further ranked as senior or subordinated. Priority of claims may be summarized as follows:

- First mortgage or first lien.
- Second or subsequent lien.
- Senior secured debt.
- Senior subordinated debt.
- Senior unsecured debt.
- Subordinated debt.
- Junior subordinated debt.

LOS 42.c

Issuer credit ratings, or corporate family ratings, reflect a debt issuer's overall creditworthiness and typically apply to a firm's senior unsecured debt.

Issue credit ratings, or corporate credit ratings, reflect the credit risk of a specific debt issue. Notching refers to the practice of adjusting an issue credit rating upward or downward from the issuer credit rating to reflect the seniority and other provisions of a debt issue.

LOS 42.d

Lenders and bond investors should not rely exclusively on credit ratings from rating agencies for the following reasons:

- Credit ratings can change during the life of a debt issue.
- Rating agencies cannot always judge credit risk accurately.
- Firms are subject to risk of unforeseen events that credit ratings do not reflect.
- Market prices of bonds often adjust more rapidly than credit ratings.

LOS 42.e

Components of traditional credit analysis are known as the four Cs:

- Capacity: The borrower's ability to make timely payments on its debt.
- Collateral: The value of assets pledged against a debt issue or available to creditors if the issuer defaults.
- Covenants: Provisions of a bond issue that protect creditors by requiring or prohibiting actions by an issuer's management.
- Character: Assessment of an issuer's management, strategy, quality of earnings, and past treatment of bondholders.

LOS 42.f

Credit analysts use profitability, cash flow, and leverage and coverage ratios to assess debt issuers' capacity.

- Profitability refers to operating income and operating profit margin, with operating income typically defined as earnings before interest and taxes (EBIT).
- Cash flow may be measured as earnings before interest, taxes, depreciation, and amortization (EBITDA); funds from operations (FFO); free cash flow before dividends; or free cash flow after dividends.
- Leverage ratios include debt-to-capital, debt-to-EBITDA, and FFO-to-debt.
- Coverage ratios include EBIT-to-interest expense and EBITDA-to-interest expense.

LOS 42.g

Lower leverage, higher interest coverage, and greater free cash flow imply lower credit risk and a higher credit rating for a firm. When calculating leverage ratios, analysts should include in a firm's total debt its obligations such as underfunded pensions and off-balance-sheet financing.

For a specific debt issue, secured collateral implies lower credit risk compared to unsecured debt, and higher seniority implies lower credit risk compared to lower seniority.

LOS 42.h

Corporate bond yields comprise the real risk-free rate, expected inflation rate, credit spread, maturity premium, and liquidity premium. An issue's yield spread to its benchmark includes its credit spread and liquidity premium.

The level and volatility of yield spreads are affected by the credit and business cycles, the performance of financial markets as a whole, availability of capital from broker-dealers, and supply and demand for debt issues. Yield spreads tend to narrow when the credit cycle is improving, the economy is expanding, and financial markets and investor demand for new debt issues are strong. Yield spreads tend to widen when the credit cycle, the economy, and financial markets are weakening, and in periods when the supply of new debt issues is heavy or broker-dealer capital is insufficient for market making.

LOS 42.i

Analysts can use duration and convexity to estimate the impact on return (the percentage change in bond price) of a change in credit spread.

For small spread changes:

$$\text{return impact} \approx -\text{duration} \times \Delta\text{spread}$$

For larger spread changes:

$$\text{return impact} \approx -\text{duration} \times \Delta\text{spread} + \frac{1}{2}\text{convexity} \times (\Delta\text{spread})^2$$

LOS 42.j

High yield bonds are more likely to default than investment grade bonds, which increases the importance of estimating loss severity. Analysis of high yield debt should focus on liquidity, projected financial performance, the issuer's corporate and debt structures, and debt covenants.

Credit risk of sovereign debt includes the issuing country's ability and willingness to pay. Ability to pay is greater for debt issued in the country's own currency than for debt issued in a foreign currency. Willingness refers to the possibility that a country refuses to repay its debts.

Analysis of general obligation municipal debt is similar to analysis of sovereign debt, focusing on the strength of the local economy and its effect on tax revenues. Analysis of municipal revenue bonds is similar to analysis of corporate debt, focusing on the ability of a project to generate sufficient revenue to service the bonds.

Concept Checkers

1. Expected loss can decrease with an increase in a bond's:
   A. default risk.
   B. loss severity.
   C. recovery rate.

2. Absolute priority of claims in a bankruptcy might be violated because:
   A. of the *pari passu* principle.
   B. creditors negotiate a different outcome.
   C. available funds must be distributed equally among creditors.

3. "Notching" is *best* described as a difference between a(n):
   A. issuer credit rating and an issue credit rating.
   B. company credit rating and an industry average credit rating.
   C. investment grade credit rating and a non-investment grade credit rating.

4. Which of the following statements is *least likely* a limitation of relying on ratings from credit rating agencies?
   A. Credit ratings are dynamic.
   B. Firm-specific risks are difficult to rate.
   C. Credit ratings adjust quickly to changes in bond prices.

5. Ratio analysis is *most likely* used to assess a borrower's:
   A. capacity.
   B. character.
   C. collateral.

6. Higher credit risk is indicated by a higher:
   A. FFO/debt ratio.
   B. debt/EBITDA ratio.
   C. EBITDA/interest expense ratio.

7. Compared to other firms in the same industry, an issuer with a credit rating of AAA should have a lower:
   A. FFO/debt ratio.
   B. operating margin.
   C. debt/capital ratio.

8. Credit spreads tend to widen as:
   A. the credit cycle improves.
   B. economic conditions worsen.
   C. broker-dealers become more willing to provide capital.

9. Compared to shorter duration bonds, longer duration bonds:
   A. have smaller bid-ask spreads.
   B. are less sensitive to credit spreads.
   C. have less certainty regarding future creditworthiness.

10. One key difference between sovereign bonds and municipal bonds is that sovereign issuers:
    A. can print money.
    B. have governmental taxing power.
    C. are affected by economic conditions.

CHALLENGE PROBLEM

Woden, Inc., is a high yield bond issuer with a credit rating of Ba2/BB. Woden presents the following balance sheet for the most recent year (in millions of dollars):

Cash	10	Accounts payable	10
Accounts receivable	15	Short-term debt	5
Inventories	55	Current portion of long-term debt	3
Current assets	80	Current liabilities	18
Land	10	Long-term bank loans	30
Property, plant, and equipment, net	85	Secured bonds	10
Goodwill	25	Unsecured bonds	20
Non-current assets	120	Total long-term debt	60
Total assets	200	Net pension liability	22
		Total liabilities	100
		Paid-in capital	10
		Retained earnings	90
		Total shareholders' equity	100
		Total liabilities and equity	200

For the year, Woden's earnings before interest, taxes, depreciation, and amortization (EBITDA) were $45 million.

For firms in Woden's industry, credit rating standards for an investment grade (Baa3/BBB–) credit rating include a debt-to-EBITDA ratio less than 1.8× and a debt-to-capital ratio (based on all sources of financing) less than 40%. On a conference call with analysts, Woden's management states that they believe Woden should be upgraded to investment grade, based on its debt-to-EBITDA ratio of 1.5× and its debt-to-capital ratio of 34%.

Why might a credit analyst disagree with management's assessment?

Answers – Concept Checkers

1. **C** An increase in the recovery rate means that the loss severity has decreased, which decreases expected loss.

2. **B** A negotiated bankruptcy settlement does not always follow the absolute priority of claims.

3. **A** Notching refers to the credit rating agency practice of distinguishing between the credit rating of an issuer (generally for its senior unsecured debt) and the credit rating of particular debt issues from that issuer, which may differ from the issuer rating because of provisions such as seniority.

4. **C** Bond prices and credit spreads change much faster than credit ratings.

5. **A** Ratio analysis is used to assess a corporate borrower's capacity to repay its debt obligations on time.

6. **B** A higher debt/EBITDA ratio is sign of higher leverage and higher credit risk. Higher FFO/debt and EBITDA/interest expense ratios indicate lower credit risk.

7. **C** A low debt/capital ratio is an indicator of low leverage. An issuer rated AAA is likely to have a high operating margin and a high FFO/debt ratio compared to its industry group.

8. **B** Credit spreads widen as economic conditions worsen. Spreads narrow as the credit cycle improves and as broker-dealers provide more capital to bond markets.

9. **C** Longer duration bonds usually have longer maturities and carry more uncertainty of future creditworthiness.

10. **A** Sovereign entities can print money to repay debt, while municipal borrowers cannot. Both sovereign and municipal entities have taxing powers, and both are affected by economic conditions.

ANSWERS – CHALLENGE PROBLEM

The debt ratios calculated by management are based on the firm's short-term and long-term debt:

Total debt = 5 + 3 + 30 + 10 + 20 = 68

Debt/EBITDA = 68 / 45 = 1.5×

Debt/capital = 68 / 200 = 34%

A credit analyst, however, should add Woden's net pension liability to its total debt:

Debt + net pension liability = 68 + 22 = 90

Adjusted debt/EBITDA = 90 / 45 = 2.0×

Adjusted debt/capital = 90 / 200 = 45%

Additionally, a credit analyst may calculate what the debt-to-capital ratio would be if Woden wrote down the value of its balance sheet goodwill and reduced retained earnings by the same amount:

Adjusted capital = 200 – 25 = 175

Adjusted debt / adjusted capital = 90 / 175 = 51%

These adjustments suggest Woden does not meet the requirements for an investment grade credit rating.

The following is a review of the Fixed Income: Valuation Concepts principles designed to address the learning outcome statements set forth by CFA Institute. This topic is also covered in:

TERM STRUCTURE AND VOLATILITY OF INTEREST RATES

Study Session 14

EXAM FOCUS

This topic review provides important information on the construction, theoretical underpinnings, and implications of the term structure of interest rates. Interpreting the shape of the yield curve and implied forward rates in the context of one of the three term structure theories is a favorite exam topic. Make sure you understand all three theories and can discuss their implications. Also pay close attention to key rate duration, a useful bond portfolio management tool.

WARM-UP: YIELD CURVE SHAPES

Historically, the yield curve has taken on three fundamental shapes, as shown in Figure 1.

Figure 1: Yield Curve Shapes

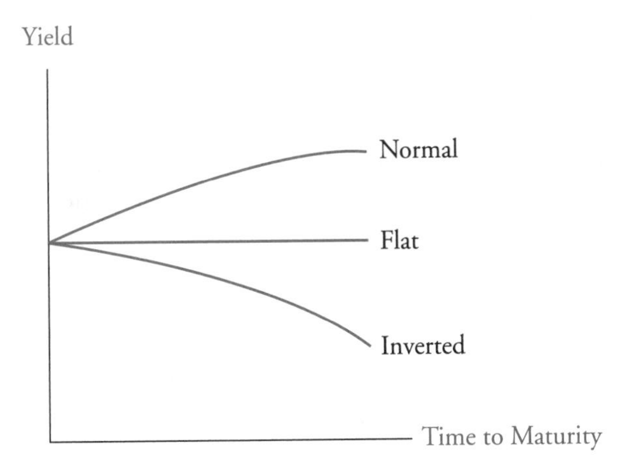

A *normal* yield curve is one in which long-term rates are greater than short-term rates, so the curve has a *positive slope*. A *flat* yield curve represents the situation where the yield on all maturities is essentially the same. An *inverted* yield curve reflects the condition where long-term rates are less than short-term rates, giving the yield curve a *negative slope*.

LOS 43.a: Explain parallel and nonparallel shifts in the yield curve.

CFA® Program Curriculum, Volume 5, page 286

When the yield curve undergoes a **parallel shift**, the yields on all maturities change in the same direction and by the same amount. As indicated in Figure 2, the slope of the yield curve remains unchanged following a parallel shift.

Figure 2: Parallel Yield Curve Shift

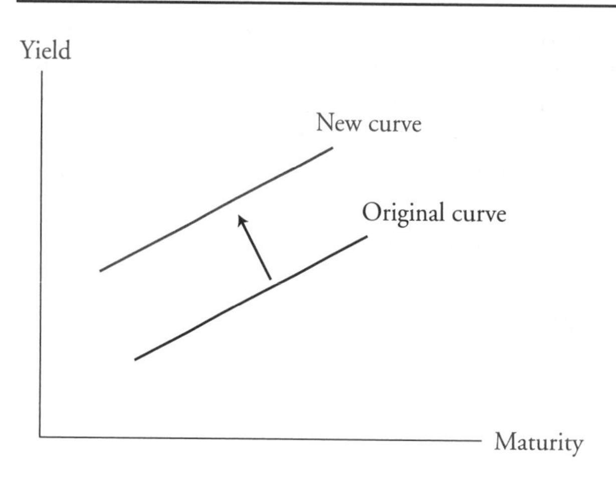

When the yield curve undergoes a **nonparallel shift**, the yields for the various maturities change by differing amounts. The slope of the yield curve after a nonparallel shift is not the same as it was prior to the shift. Nonparallel shifts fall into two general categories: twists and butterfly shifts.

Yield curve twists refer to yield curve changes when the slope becomes either flatter or steeper. A flattening of the yield curve means that the spread between short- and long-term rates has narrowed; the curve gets steeper when spreads widen.

As shown in Figure 3, the most common shifts tend to be either a downward shift and a steepened curve or an upward shift and a flattened curve.

Figure 3: Nonparallel Yield Curve Shifts—Twists

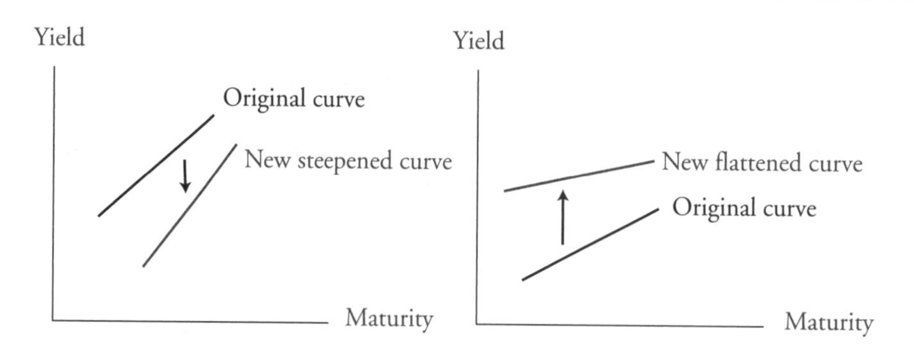

Yield curve butterfly shifts refer to changes in the degree of curvature. A positive butterfly means that the yield curve has become less curved. For example, if rates increase, the short and long maturity yields increase by more than the intermediate maturity yields, as shown in Figure 4. A negative butterfly means that there is more curvature to the yield curve. For example, if rates increase, intermediate term yields increase by more than the long and short maturity yields, as shown in Figure 4.

Figure 4: Nonparallel Yield Curve Shifts—Butterfly Shifts

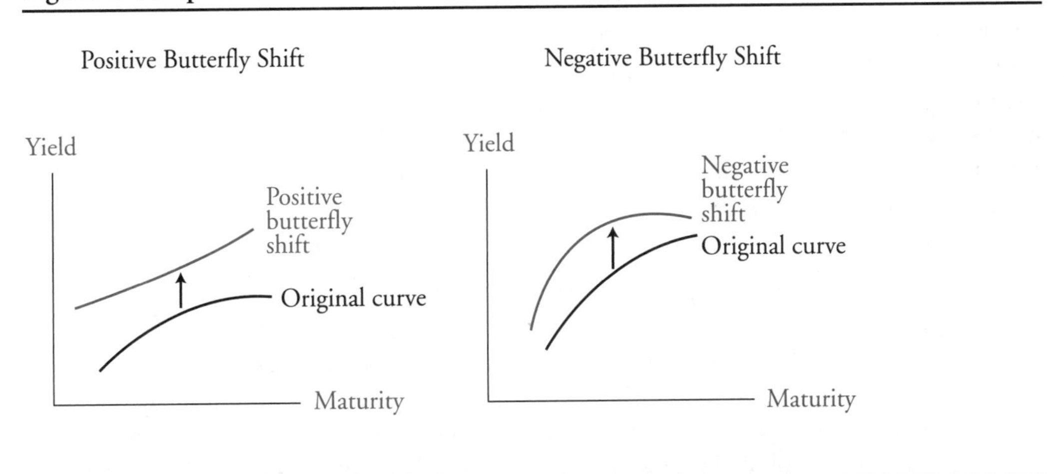

LOS 43.b: Describe factors that drive U.S. Treasury security returns, and evaluate the importance of each factor.

CFA® Program Curriculum, Volume 5, page 288

Research studies have identified three factors that explain historical Treasury security returns. Each one corresponds to the types of yield curve shifts discussed in the previous LOS.

1. Changes in the **level** of interest rates (parallel shifts in the yield curve).
2. Changes in the **slope** of the yield curve (twists in the yield curve).
3. Changes in the **curvature** of the yield curve (butterfly shifts).

Litterman and Scheinkman (1991)[1] used the R^2 from regression analysis to estimate the ability of these three variables to explain the total returns on 6-month through 18-year zero-coupon Treasury securities. The results indicated that, collectively, these three factors explained more than 95% of the total return variance.

- **Factor 1: Changes in the level of rates** made the greatest contribution, explaining almost 90% of the observed variation in total returns for all maturity levels.
- **Factor 2: Slope changes** explained, on average, 8.5% of the total returns' variance over all maturity levels.
- **Factor 3: Curvature changes** contributed relatively little toward the explanation of total returns, with an average proportion of total explained variance equal to 1.5%.

1. Robert Litterman and Jose Scheinkman, "Common Factors Affecting Bond Returns," *Journal of Fixed Income* (June 1991), pp. 54–61.

Professor's Note: As you probably remember from Study Session 3, R^2 measures the variability in the dependent variable (Treasury returns) explained by the independent variables (changes in yield curve level, slope, and curvature).

Recall from Level I that duration measures bond price sensitivity to *parallel* changes in interest rates. Because parallel changes in the level of interest rates (Factor 1) have a significant influence on Treasury returns, duration is a useful tool for quantifying interest rate risk. Later on in this topic review, we will discuss key rate duration, which is used to quantify bond price sensitivity to changes in the slope of the yield curve. Because changes in the shape of the yield curve (nonparallel shifts) also impact Treasury returns, key rate duration is useful to supplement the information provided by duration when measuring interest rate risk exposure.

WARM-UP: SPOT CURVES AND BOOTSTRAPPING

Suppose you want to know the required return on a fixed-income security with seven years to maturity in order to determine its correct price. Your first impulse may be to look at the current rate on a U.S. Treasury note (T-note) with seven years to maturity. However, this methodology ignores all other characteristics of the bonds except maturity.

For example, suppose that the 7-year Treasury security you are interested in pricing has a coupon rate of 9%. If you look at the universe of 7-year Treasury securities, you will find that there are several different issues, each with different coupon rates. Which one is correct? Unfortunately, the answer is that none of them are correct. In order to accurately price a fixed-income security, you need a spot rate for each cash flow (recall that the spot rate is the rate prevailing today for a zero-coupon bond with the same maturity as the cash flow being valued). Hence, to value your 7-year 9% bond, you will need unique spot rates for each of the 14 coupon payments and a spot rate for the return of principal. In order to obtain all the necessary spot rates, you will need to construct a **theoretical spot rate curve for Treasury securities**.

Bootstrapping spot rates from the yields on coupon Treasury securities was covered in the Level I curriculum. However, because bootstrapping is necessary for understanding the issues surrounding the construction of the spot rate curve, we will briefly review bootstrapping.

Bootstrapping is the process of sequentially calculating spot rates from securities with different maturities, using the yields on Treasury bonds from the yield curve, as shown in Figure 5.

Figure 5: Bootstrapping

For example, suppose that you know a 6-month U.S. Treasury bill has an annualized yield of 4% and a 1-year Treasury STRIP has an annualized yield of 4.5% (assume annual rates stated on a bond equivalent basis). Because these are both discount securities, the yields are spot rates. Given these spot rates, we can calculate the spot yield on a 1.5-year Treasury via bootstrapping. Assume that the 1.5-year Treasury is priced at \$95 and carries a 4% coupon (\$2 every six months). In this case, to calculate the 1.5-year spot rate, solve the following equation:

$$\text{price} = \frac{\$2}{\left(1+\frac{\text{6-month spot}}{2}\right)^1} + \frac{\$2}{\left(1+\frac{\text{12-month spot}}{2}\right)^2} + \frac{\$102}{\left(1+\frac{\text{18-month spot}}{2}\right)^3}$$

$$\$95 = \frac{\$2}{1.02^1} + \frac{\$2}{1.0225^2} + \frac{\$102}{\left(1+\frac{\text{18-month spot}}{2}\right)^3} \Rightarrow \text{18-month spot rate} = 7.66\%$$

Our abbreviated theoretical spot rate curve looks like this:

- 6-month spot rate = 4.00%.
- 12-month spot rate = 4.50%.
- 18-month spot rate = 7.66%.

Professor's Note: The U.S. Treasury currently issues Treasury bills with various maturities including 4 weeks, 13 weeks, 26 weeks, and 52 weeks; Treasury notes of 2 years, 5 years, and 10 years; and Treasury bonds with 30-year maturities.

LOS 43.c: Explain various universes of Treasury securities that are used to construct the theoretical spot rate curve, and evaluate their advantages and disadvantages.

CFA® Program Curriculum, Volume 5, page 289

There are four combinations of securities that can be used to construct a theoretical Treasury spot rate curve: (1) all on-the-run Treasury securities, (2) all on-the-run and some off-the-run Treasury securities, (3) all Treasury bonds, notes, and bills, and (4) Treasury strips. After the explanation of each combination of Treasury securities is a summary of their advantages and disadvantages.

All On-the-Run Treasury Securities

On-the-run Treasury issues refer to the newest Treasury issues of a given maturity as described:

- T-bills: Zero-coupon securities with 1-month, 3-month, 6-month, and 12-month maturities.
- T-notes: Coupon instruments with 2-year, 5-year, and 10-year maturities.
- T-bonds: Coupon instruments with 30-year maturities.

The on-the-run issues have the largest trading volume and are, therefore, the most accurately priced issues. However, due to the tax effects on premium priced and discounted on-the-run coupon instruments, it is not appropriate to use the observed yield for these issues unless they are trading at par. Instead, the yield that is necessary to make the issue trade at par must be computed. Using these adjusted yields and filling in the missing maturities using linear extrapolation, an on-the-run yield curve (called the **par coupon curve**) can be constructed. The bootstrapping methodology can then be used to generate a theoretical spot rate curve.

Advantage: Uses only the most accurately priced issues.
Disadvantage: Large maturity gaps after the 5-year note.

All On-the-Run and Some Off-the-Run Treasury Securities

Using just on-the-run issues creates problems because there aren't on-the-run issues at every maturity, which leaves large maturity gaps between the 5-year and longest maturities. To provide additional observed points on the par coupon curve, 20- and 25-year off-the-run issues are added to the on-the-run issues. Linear interpolation is used to estimate yields for missing on-the-run maturities, and bootstrapping is employed to generate the theoretical spot rate curve.

There are two problems with the "on-the-run plus selected issues" framework. First, information is lost regarding the yield on Treasury securities not included in the construction of the curve. Second, the true yield for on-the-run issues may be distorted if any of these issues is "cheap" in the repo market.

Advantage: Reduces maturity gaps.
Disadvantages: (1) Still doesn't use all the rate information contained in Treasury issues, and (2) rates may be distorted by the repo market.

All Treasury Coupon Securities and Bills

It has been argued that using only on-the-run issues, even with some off-the-run issues, ignores important information contained in other Treasury security prices. Therefore, some practitioners feel it is better to use *all* Treasury coupon securities and bills to construct the theoretical spot rate curve.

Bootstrapping is not useful in generating the theoretical spot rate curve when all Treasury securities and bills are used, because more than one yield may exist for each maturity. However, other statistical methodologies are available for fitting a curve to the data made available when all Treasury securities and bills are used.

A disadvantage of using all Treasury securities and bills to develop the theoretical spot rate curve is that current information is not available for all issues.

Advantage: Does not ignore information from issues excluded by other approaches.
Disadvantages: (1) Some maturities have more than one yield, and (2) current prices may not reflect accurate interest rates for all maturities.

Treasury Strips

Don't lose sight of the big picture: the goal of the different yield curve construction approaches is to determine the spot rates for all maturities. Treasury coupon strips are zero-coupon securities made by stripping the coupons from normal T-bonds (i.e., coupon strips are zero-coupon T-bonds, so their rates are expressed as spot rates—no bootstrapping necessary). Hence, a seemingly simple solution to the problems associated with the other approaches is to use Treasury coupon strips, because the rates on strips are spot rates.

Unfortunately, this intuitive solution does not work well for several reasons. First, the strips market is not as liquid as the Treasury coupon market, so observed strip rates include a liquidity premium. Second, Treasury strip yields reflect a tax disadvantage, because the accrued interest on strips is taxed even though no cash flows are realized. Finally, some non-U.S. tax laws allow investors to recognize the difference between the maturity value and the price of some types of principal strips as a favorably taxed capital gain.

Advantages: (1) Provides yields at most maturities and reduces maturity gaps; and (2) intuitive approach that does not require bootstrapping to derive spot rates.
Disadvantages: (1) Liquidity premium embedded in strip rates; and (2) tax treatment affects observed rates.

LOS 43.d: Explain the swap rate curve (LIBOR curve) and why market participants have used the swap rate curve rather than a government bond yield curve as a benchmark.

CFA® Program Curriculum, Volume 5, page 291

In the topic review of swaps in Study Session 17 we will explain how interest rate swaps are "priced," which means how the fixed interest rate is determined. For example, two parties might enter into a 2-year interest rate swap in which counterparty A agrees to pay a fixed rate of 8% quarterly on a notional principal amount of $25 million, and counterparty B agrees to pay a floating rate equal to 3-month LIBOR on $25 million. The 8% fixed rate is called the 2-year swap rate. As we explain in Study Session 17, it is derived from the series of LIBOR rates from three months to two years.

The **swap rate curve** (also known as the **LIBOR curve**) is the series of swap rates quoted by swap dealers over maturities extending from 2 to 30 years. For U.S. dollar LIBOR, the LIBOR curve specifically refers to swap rates in which one party pays the fixed swap rate in U.S. dollars. LIBOR-based swap spreads reflect only the credit risk of the counterparty, which is usually a bank, so the swap curve is a AA-rated curve, not a default-free curve. Other currencies will have their own unique swap rate curves.

There are a number of reasons that market participants tend to prefer the swap rate curve as a benchmark interest rate curve rather than a government bond yield curve.

- The swap market is not regulated by any government, which makes swap rates in different countries more comparable.

- The supply of swaps and the equilibrium pricing that results from the interaction of supply and demand depends only on the number of participants willing to enter into a swap. It is not affected by technical market factors that can affect government bonds.
- Swap curves across countries are also more comparable because they reflect similar levels of credit risk, while government bond yield curves also reflect sovereign risk unique to each country.
- The swap curve typically has yield quotes at 11 maturities between 2 and 30 years. The U.S. government bond yield curve, however, only has on-the-run issues trading at four maturities of at least two years (2-year, 5-year, 10-year, and 30-year).

LOS 43.e: Explain the pure expectations, liquidity, and preferred habitat theories of the term structure of interest rates and the implications of each for the shape of the yield curve.

CFA® Program Curriculum, Volume 5, page 295

We'll explain each of the theories referenced in the LOS, paying particular attention to the implications of each theory for the shape of the yield curve and the interpretation of forward rates.

Pure (Unbiased) Expectations Theory

The pure (unbiased) expectations theory suggests that forward rates are solely a function of expected future spot rates. In other words, *long-term interest rates equal the mean of future expected short-term rates*. This implies, for example, that an investor could earn the same return by investing in a 5-year bond or by investing in a 3-year bond and then a 2-year bond after the 3-year bond expires.

For example, suppose the 1-year spot rate is 5% and the 2-year spot rate is 7%. Under the pure expectations theory, the 1-year forward rate in one year must be 9%, because investing for two years at 7% yields approximately the same annual return as investing for the first year at 5% and the second year at 9%. In other words, the 2-year rate of 7% is the average of the expected future 1-year rates of 5% and 9%, and is shown in Figure 6.

Figure 6: Spot and Future Rates

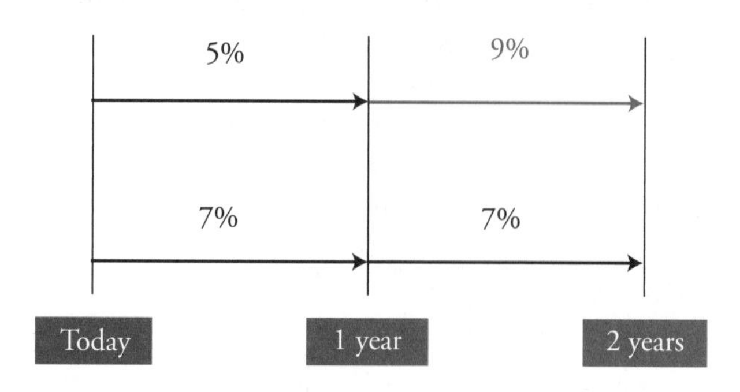

Notice that in this example, because short-term rates are expected to rise (from 5% to 9%), the yield curve is upward sloping, as depicted in Figure 7.

Figure 7: Upward Sloping Yield Curve

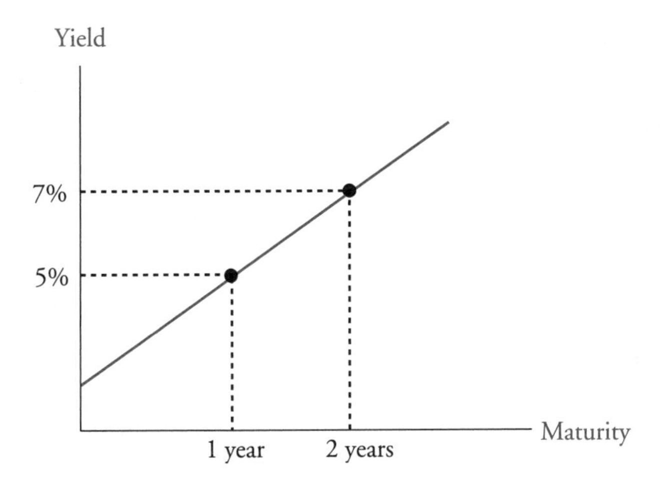

Therefore, the implications for the shape of the yield curve under the pure expectations theory are:

- If the yield curve is upward sloping, short-term rates are expected to rise.
- If the curve is downward-sloping, short-term rates are expected to fall.
- A flat yield curve implies that the market expects short-term rates to remain constant.

The 9% rate in the previous example is called the **implied forward rate**. We call it an implied rate because it's not a quoted rate; it's implied by the quoted spot interest rates for one and two years. There are three interpretations of this 9% forward rate:

1. **Breakeven rate** refers to the forward rate that leaves investors indifferent between investing for two years, or investing for one year and then reinvesting at the breakeven forward rate of 9% for the second year. An investor would be indifferent between investing for two years at 7%, or investing at 5% for the first year and reinvesting in one year at the 9% breakeven rate.

2. Forward rates can also be interpreted as the **locked-in rate** for some future period. Using this interpretation, the investor in the previous example could invest in the 2-year bond instead of the 1-year bond, and essentially lock in a 9% rate for the 1-year period starting in one year.

3. How do we interpret the 9% forward rate in relation to expected future spot rates in the context of the pure expectations theory? The pure expectations theory predicts that the **expected spot rate** in one year is equal to the implied 1-year forward rate of 9%. In other words, expectations are unbiased.

The pure expectations theory has a significant shortcoming because it fails to consider the riskiness of bond investing. Specifically, the pure expectations theory fails to recognize:

- Price risk—the uncertainty associated with the future price of a bond that may be sold prior to its maturity.
- Reinvestment risk—the uncertainty associated with the rate at which bond cash flows can be reinvested over an investment horizon.

Hence, the pure (or unbiased) expectations theory does not recognize the risk difference between investing in a 1-year bond and sequentially investing in two 6-month bonds. This leads to a discussion of the two biased term structure theories.

Liquidity Preference Theory

The liquidity preference theory of the term structure addresses the shortcomings of the pure expectations theory by proposing that forward rates reflect investors' expectations of future spot rates plus a **liquidity premium** to compensate them for exposure to interest rate risk. Furthermore, the theory suggests that this liquidity premium is positively related to maturity: a 25-year bond has a larger liquidity premium than a 5-year bond.

The liquidity theory says that forward rates are biased estimates of the market's expectation of future rates because they include a liquidity premium. Therefore, a positive-sloping yield curve may indicate that either: (1) the market expects future interest rates to rise; or (2) that rates are expected to remain constant (or even fall), but the addition of the liquidity premium results in a positive slope. A downward-sloping yield curve indicates falling short term rates according to the liquidity theory.

The size of the liquidity premiums need not be constant over time. They may be larger during periods of greater economic uncertainty, when risk aversion among investors is higher.

The liquidity preference theory says that the 2-year spot rate includes an extra return to compensate investors for the liquidity risk. Continuing our previous example, suppose the expected spot rate in the second year is only 8%, and the 2-year spot rate is still 7%. The 2-year spot rate must be equal to the average of the 1-year rates plus a liquidity premium or:

$$\text{2-year spot rate} = 7.0\% = \frac{5.0\% + 8.0\%}{2} + \text{2-year liquidity premium}$$

$$\text{2-year liquidity premium} = 7.0\% - 6.5\% = 0.5\%$$

Now the implied forward rate of 9% is not equal to the expected spot rate of 8%, so expectations are biased. Remember that this 0.5% extra return is a liquidity premium required by investors to induce them to hold the 2-year bond instead of two 1-year bonds. Furthermore, the liquidity theory predicts that this premium will be higher for longer-term investments, so if the 2-year premium is 0.5%, the 3-year premium might be 1%.

Preferred Habitat Theory

The preferred habitat theory also proposes that forward rates represent expected future spot rates plus a premium, but it *does not* support the view that this premium is directly related to maturity.

Instead, the preferred habitat theory suggests that the existence of an imbalance between the supply and demand for funds in a given maturity range will induce lenders and borrowers to shift from their **preferred habitats** (maturity range) to one that has the opposite imbalance. However, to get them to do so, they must be offered an incentive to compensate them for exposure to price and/or reinvestment rate risk in the "less-than-preferred" habitat. Borrowers require cost savings (i.e., lower yields) and lenders require a yield premium (i.e., higher yields) to move out of their preferred habitats.

Under this theory, premiums are related to supply and demand for funds at various maturities—not the term to maturity, as in the liquidity theory. This means that, for example, the 10-year bond might have a higher or lower risk premium than the 25-year bond. *It also means this theory can be used to explain almost any yield curve shape.*

The preferred habitat theory provides an interpretation of the implied forward rate that is similar to that of the liquidity theory. However, there are two subtle differences:

1. The premium is a *positive or negative risk* premium related to supply and demand for funds at various maturities, not necessarily a *liquidity* premium.
2. This risk premium is not necessarily related to maturity.

Warm-Up: Calculating Key Rate Duration

Recall that duration is an adequate measure of bond price risk only for small parallel shifts in the yield curve. The impact on nonparallel shifts can be measured using a concept known as **key rate duration**.

Rate duration is defined as the sensitivity of the value of a security or portfolio to changes in a single spot rate, holding all other spot rates constant. A security or portfolio will have a rate duration for every point (maturity) on the spot rate curve. Thus, a set of rate durations accompanies every security or portfolio.

To put this concept into practice, the analyst selects a certain number of maturities on the spot rate curve for which rate durations for bonds or bond portfolios are available. The set of rate durations associated with these maturities is referred to as the key rate durations. For example, the key rates might be 3 months, 1 year, 2 years, 3 years, 5 years, 7 years, 10 years, 15 years, and 20 years.

A key rate duration is defined as the approximate percentage change in the value of a bond or bond portfolio in response to a 100 basis point change in the corresponding key rate, holding all other rates constant. In other words, you can determine the key rate duration for the 5-year portion of the yield curve by changing the 5-year spot rate and observing the change in value of the portfolio. Keep in mind that every security or portfolio has a set of key rate durations, one for each key rate.

To keep it simple, we will use only four maturity points on the spot rate curve: the 2-year, 10-year, 20-year, and 25-year maturities, with key rate durations represented by D_1, D_2, D_3, and D_4, respectively. Also, assume that we have a portfolio of zero-coupon bonds with maturity and portfolio weights given in Figure 8.

Professor's Note: The use of a portfolio of zero-coupon bonds simplifies this example in two ways: (1) their duration is approximately equal to their maturity, and (2) because they have no intermediate cash flows, they are not sensitive to spot rate changes for other maturities. This does not change the analysis much, because we can always categorize the portfolio's cash flows this way by putting each cash flow into its appropriate maturity bucket.

Figure 8: Key Rate Duration Matrix

Bond	*Weight (%)*	D_1	D_2	D_3	D_4	*Total*
2-year	10	2	0	0	0	
10-year	20	0	10	0	0	
20-year	40	0	0	20	0	
25-year	30	0	0	0	25	
Portfolio Key Rate Duration	100	0.2	2	8	7.5	17.7

In this example, the bonds have exposure to only one key rate duration. This is so because these are zero-coupon bonds. If we used coupon bonds, there would be more than one rate duration for each of the issues. Portfolio key rate durations are computed as below:

$$
\begin{aligned}
D_1 &= (0.1 \times 2) + (0.2 \times 0) + (0.4 \times 0) + (0.3 \times 0) = 0.2 \\
D_2 &= (0.1 \times 0) + (0.2 \times 10) + (0.4 \times 0) + (0.3 \times 0) = 2.0 \\
D_3 &= (0.1 \times 0) + (0.2 \times 0) + (0.4 \times 20) + (0.3 \times 0) = 8.0 \\
D_4 &= (0.1 \times 0) + (0.2 \times 0) + (0.4 \times 0) + (0.3 \times 25) = \underline{7.5} \\
&\text{Effective portfolio duration} \quad 17.7
\end{aligned}
$$

The effective duration of a portfolio is the weighted average of the key rate durations of its individual security durations, where the weights are based on the market value of each bond relative to the market value of the portfolio. If the yield curve undergoes a parallel upward shift of 100 basis points, the value of the portfolio will decline by about 17.7 × 1.00% = 17.7%.

LOS 43.f: Calculate and interpret the yield curve risk of a security or a portfolio by using key rate duration.

CFA® Program Curriculum, Volume 5, page 302

Key rate duration is particularly useful for measuring the effect of a nonparallel shift in the yield curve on a bond portfolio. We can use the key rate duration for each key rate to compute the effect on the portfolio of the rate change at that maturity. The effect on the overall portfolio is the sum of these individual effects.

Example: Computing the effects of a nonparallel shift in the yield curve

Suppose that the yield curve shifts such that 2-year rates increase by 100 basis points, 10-year rates increase by 150 basis points, 20-year rates increase by 80 basis points, and 25-year rates decline by 100 basis points. Calculate the effect of this nonparallel shift in the yield curve on the portfolio with 2-year, 10-year, 20-year, and 25-year key rate durations of 0.2, 2.0, 8.0, and 7.5, respectively (same as Figure 8).

Answer:

The change in the portfolio's value can be determined by computing the change in value associated with each key rate change.

Change in Portfolio Value		
Change from 2-year key rate increase:	–(+1% × 0.2)	= –0.2% decrease
Change from 10-year key rate increase:	–(+1.5% × 2.0)	= –3.0% decrease
Change from 20-year key rate increase:	–(+0.80% × 8.0)	= –6.4% decrease
Change from 25-year key rate decrease:	–(–1% × 7.5)	= + 7.5% increase
Total		–2.1% decrease

Thus, the nonparallel shift in the spot rate curve caused a 2.1% decrease in the value of the portfolio. (The minus sign in front of each computation reminds us that prices and interest rates move in opposite directions.)

Now let's apply the concept of key rate duration to three common bond portfolio structures:

1. **Barbell portfolios** contain a relatively large percentage of long and short maturity bonds.
2. **Ladder portfolios** contain bonds that are evenly distributed throughout the maturity spectrum.
3. **Bullet portfolios** typically have a relatively high concentration of bonds at some intermediate maturity.

Consider the key rate durations provided in Figure 9 for each of these types of portfolios. The portfolio duration for each structure is 9.63, implying that for a parallel shift in the yield curve, the value of each of these portfolios will change by the same amount. Note that the sum of the portfolio's key rate durations equals the portfolio's effective duration. For example, if the yield curve experiences a parallel downward shift of 75 basis points, the value of each portfolio will increase by approximately 9.63 × 0.75% = 7.22%.

Figure 9: Complex Portfolio Structure Duration

Key Rate Maturity	*Bullet*	*Ladder*	*Barbell*
3-month	0.07	0.05	0.05
1-year	0.09	0.06	0.06
2-year	1.10	1.04	0.11
3-year	0.83	1.04	**2.25**
5-year	0.42	1.07	0.65
7-year	0.73	1.07	1.05
10-year	1.20	1.07	1.03
15-year	**4.22**	1.08	1.12
20-year	0.70	1.06	1.08
25-year	0.20	1.05	**2.15**
27-year	0.07	1.04	0.08
Effective portfolio duration	**9.63**	**9.63**	**9.63**

As you can see in Figure 9, the 15-year key rate duration dominates all other key rate maturities for the bullet structure. The ladder portfolio's key rate durations are fairly equal across all key rate maturities, and the barbell portfolio is characterized by relatively large key rate durations at the 3- and 25-year maturity levels.

To further illustrate key rate duration, now consider the impact of a 75 basis point increase in the 15-year spot rate while all other key rate maturity rates remain fairly stable. Because the bullet portfolio has the largest 15-year key rate duration, its value will decline more than the value of the ladder or barbell portfolios even though it has the same effective portfolio duration as the other two portfolios.

The concept of key rate duration allows us to assess the impact of nonparallel shifts in the yield curve on the value of our portfolio. The sensitivity of a portfolio to any type of yield curve change can be evaluated with the key rate concept.

LOS 43.g: Calculate and interpret yield volatility, distinguish between historical yield volatility and implied yield volatility, and explain how to forecast yield volatility.

CFA® Program Curriculum, Volume 5, page 306

Yield volatility measurement has applications when valuing callable bonds and interest rate derivatives, and when measuring interest rate risk. The standard deviation of yield changes is the common yield volatility measurement.

Using historical data, yield volatility is measured by the standard deviation of daily yield changes. Continuously compounded yield changes are computed as the natural log of the ratio of yield levels. The general formula for the variance of daily yield change (assuming continuous compounding) is:

$$\text{variance} = \sum_{t=1}^{T} \frac{(X_t - \overline{X})^2}{T-1}$$

$$\text{standard deviation} = \sqrt{\text{variance}}$$

where:

$$X_t = 100 \times \ln\left(\frac{y_t}{y_{t-1}}\right)$$

y_t = yield on day t

$\overline{X}$ = the average yield change over period t = 1 to t = T

Professor's Note: The natural logarithm function "ln" is labeled "LN" on your TI BAII Plus. On the HP, input [g] → LN.

Example: Calculating continuously-compounded yield changes

Assume that today's yield is 7.56% and yesterday's yield was 7.50%. Compute the percentage yield change from yesterday to today, assuming continuous compounding.

Answer:

$$X_t = 100 \times \ln\left(\frac{7.56}{7.50}\right) = 0.7968\%$$

Continuing this process over a specific period of analysis will generate a set of observations for which the variance and standard deviation can be calculated.

The choice of sample period can have a significant effect on the estimate of standard deviation. The appropriate number depends on the investment horizon of the user of the volatility measurement. For example, day traders may only be interested in volatility over the most recent week or two, whereas bond portfolio managers might be interested in the volatility of yields over the past month or longer.

Professor's Note: It is unlikely that you will be asked to calculate the standard deviation given a series of daily yields. Therefore, you should concentrate on the interpretation of yield volatility.

It is common practice to annualize the standard deviation of daily yield changes using the following formula:

$$\sigma_{annual} = \sigma_{daily} \times (\text{number of trading days in the year})^{1/2}$$

where:
σ_{annual} = annualized standard deviation
σ_{daily} = daily standard deviation

The number of days that constitute a year can be the number of calendar days (365), the number of weekdays (52 × 5 = 260), or the number of actual trading days (260 – 10 holidays = 250). On the exam, you will most likely be given the number of days to use. If not, use 250, the actual number of trading days.

Interpreting Historical Yield Volatility

What does an annualized standard deviation of 10% mean? If the yield on a portfolio is currently 8%, the standard deviation is 80 basis points (8% × 0.10). This standard deviation of yield changes in basis point form can be used to construct confidence intervals. If yield changes are normally distributed, then there is a 68.3% probability that the observed yield will be plus or minus one standard deviation from the expected (prevailing) yield. That is, if the prevailing yield is 8% and the annualized standard deviation is 80 basis points, there is a 68.3% chance that next year's yield will be between 7.2% and 8.8% (8.0% +/– 80bp). This is referred to as the 68.3% confidence interval.

Continuing with this process, there is a 99.7% probability that the yield next year will be plus or minus 3 standard deviations from the prevailing rate. In this example, the 99.7% confidence interval is 5.6% to 10.4% [8.0% +/– (3) × (80bp)].

Professor's Note: Confidence intervals are discussed in Study Session 3.

Implied Yield Volatility

In addition to using historical observations, yield volatility can be estimated using observed prices for interest rate derivatives and option pricing models. The method for doing this is to plug the observed price of an option into the option pricing model, along with the model's other observable variables, then solve the model for the unknown volatility (standard deviation). When yield volatility is derived from option prices in this manner, it is referred to as **implied volatility**.

The use of implied volatility is often criticized because:

- It is based on the assumption that the option pricing model is correct.
- Models make the simplifying assumption that volatility is constant.

FORECASTING YIELD VOLATILITY

Typically, the standard deviation of daily yield changes is calculated using the moving average of yield changes over some appropriate time interval. For forecasting purposes, it is more appropriate to use a zero value for the expected change in yields. Thus, the general formula for the variance changes is:

$$\text{variance} = \sum_{t=1}^{T} \frac{X_t^2}{T-1}$$

The easiest way to compute the variance is to assign equal weights to each observation. Investors, however, often feel it is necessary to weight recent observations more heavily than distant observations. The formula for forecasting variance can be modified to incorporate any desired weighting scheme as follows:

$$\text{variance} = \sum_{t=1}^{T} \frac{W_t X_t^2}{T-1}$$

where:
W_t = the weight assigned to each period's observation such that the sum of the weights equals 1

Yield volatility has been observed to follow patterns over time. These patterns can be used to forecast volatility using a statistical technique based on autoregressive conditional heteroskedasticity (ARCH) models.

Professor's Note: ARCH models are covered in Study Session 3.

Key Concepts

LOS 43.a
When the yield curve undergoes a parallel shift, the yield on all maturities change in the same direction and by the same amount. The slope of the yield curve remains unchanged following a parallel shift.

When the yield curve undergoes a nonparallel shift, the yields for the various maturities do not necessarily change in the same direction nor by the same amount. The slope of the yield curve after a nonparallel shift is not the same as it was prior to the shift.

- Twists refer to yield curve changes when the slope becomes either flatter or more steep. A flattening of the yield curve means that the spread between short- and long-term rates has narrowed.
- Butterfly shifts refer to changes in curvature of the yield curve. A positive butterfly means that the yield curve has become less curved. A negative butterfly means that there is more curvature to the yield curve.

LOS 43.b
Three factors that explain historical Treasury returns have been identified. In the order of relative importance, these are:

- Changes in the level of interest rates (by far the most important factor).
- Changes in the slope of the yield curve (distant second most influential factor).
- Changes in the curvature of the yield curve (slight impact).

LOS 43.c
All on-the-run Treasury issues:
Advantage: Uses only the most accurately priced issues.
Disadvantage: Large maturity gaps after the five-year note.

All on-the-run and selected off-the-run Treasury issues:
Advantage: Reduces maturity gaps.
Disadvantages: (1) Still doesn't use all issues, and (2) rates may be distorted by the repo market.

All Treasury coupon securities and bills:
Advantage: Uses information from issues excluded by other approaches.
Disadvantages: (1) Some maturities have more than one yield, and (2) current prices may not reflect accurate interest rates for all maturities.

Treasury coupon strips:
Advantages: (1) Provides yields at most maturities and reduces maturity gaps, and (2) intuitive approach that does not require bootstrapping to derive spot rates.
Disadvantages: (1) Liquidity premium embedded in strip rates, and (2) tax treatment affects observed rates.

LOS 43.d

The swap rate curve (also known as the LIBOR curve) is the series of swap rates quoted by swap dealers over maturities extending from 2 to 30 years. Reasons why market participants may prefer to use the swap rate curve as a benchmark:

- The swap market is not regulated by any government, which makes swap rates in different countries more comparable.
- The availability of swaps and the equilibrium pricing are only driven by the interaction of supply and demand. It is not affected by technical market factors that can affect government bonds.
- Swap curves across countries are also more comparable because they reflect similar levels of credit risk, while government bond yield curves also reflect sovereign risk unique to each country.
- The swap curve typically has yield quotes at 11 maturities between 2 and 30 years. The U.S. government bond yield curve only has on-the-run issues trading at four maturities between 2 and 30 years.

LOS 43.e

There are two versions of the expectations theory (pure expectations and biased expectations). Both are based on the premise that current rates are related to the market's expectations regarding future rates. The difference lies in whether or not other factors also affect forward rates and, if they do, how? The pure expectations theory argues that forward rates are solely a function of expected future spot rates. This implies that if the yield curve is upward (downward) sloping, short-term rates are expected to rise (fall), and if the yield curve is flat, the market expects short-term rates to be constant. The theory's drawback is that it fails to consider price risk and reinvestment risk.

The two forms of the biased expectations theory are the liquidity theory and the preferred habitat theory. They contend that other factors affect forward rates.

- The liquidity preference theory of the term structure proposes that forward rates reflect investors' expectations of future rates plus a liquidity premium to compensate them for exposure to interest rate risk.
- The preferred habitat theory proposes that forward rates represent expected future spot rates plus a premium, but it suggests that this premium is related to disequilibrium between the supply and demand for funds in a given maturity range. Investors will switch to another maturity range (habitat) only if they are offered a premium to compensate them for exposure to price and/or reinvestment rate risk in the "less-than-preferred" habitat.

LOS 43.f

Key rate duration is a methodology that can be used to measure the impact of nonparallel shifts in the yield curve.

- Rate duration is defined as the sensitivity of the value of a security or portfolio to changes in a single spot rate, holding all other spot rates constant.
- In practice, a certain number of maturities on the spot rate curve are selected for which bond durations are measured. The set of rate durations associated with these key maturities are the key rate durations.

LOS 43.g

Yield volatility is measured with variance (standard deviation) of changes in daily yields.

- Continuously compounded daily yield changes are used. The formula used is: $100[\ln(y_t / y_{t-1})]$, where y_t and y_{t-1} = the day *t* and day t – 1 yields, respectively.
- The number of daily observations of yield changes in the sample can have a significant effect on the computed standard deviation. The appropriate number depends on the investment horizon of the user of the volatility measurement.
- It is common practice to annualize the standard deviation using the formula: $\sigma_{annual} = \sigma_{daily} \times (\text{number of trading days in the year})^{1/2}$. Typically, the number of trading days is estimated as 250.
- The standard deviation of yield changes is used to construct confidence intervals and interpret yield volatility.

Implied volatility can be estimated using observed prices for interest rate derivatives and option pricing models. Implied volatility is criticized because it is based on the assumptions that the option pricing model is correct and that volatility is constant.

Yield volatility forecasts are based on the standard deviation of daily yield changes using the moving average of yield changes over some appropriate time interval.

- It is more appropriate to use zero as the value for the expected change in yields.
- The easiest way to compute the variance is to assign equal weights to each observation.
- Some investors weight recent observations more heavily than distant observations.

Yield volatility has been observed to follow patterns over time. This pattern can be modeled and used to forecast volatility using autoregressive statistical techniques.

Concept Checkers

1. Which of the following statements concerning yield curve shifts is *least accurate*?
   A. A twist results in a flatter or steeper yield curve.
   B. Butterfly shifts result in a change in curvature.
   C. A positive butterfly shift results in more curvature.

2. Of the three factors that have been observed to affect Treasury returns, which is the most important? Changes in the:
   A. slope of the yield curve.
   B. curvature of the yield curve.
   C. level of interest rates.

Use the following information for an equally weighted U.S. Treasury portfolio to answer Questions 3 and 4.

Maturity	Key rate duration
3-month	0.06
2-year	0.73
5-year	0.34
10-year	3.09
15-year	0.63
20-year	1.22
25-year	2.19
27-year	3.65

3. The effective duration of the portfolio for a parallel shift in the yield curve is *closest* to:
   A. 9.09.
   B. 10.29.
   C. 11.91.

4. What is the impact on the portfolio of a 25 basis point increase in the 5-year rate and a 50 basis point increase in the 20-year rate, holding other key rates constant? The portfolio will:
   A. decrease in value by 0.695%.
   B. decrease in value by 0.372%.
   C. decrease in value by 0.816%.

5. Which of the following statements describes an inverted yield curve?
   A. Short-term rates are higher than long-term rates.
   B. Medium-term rates are higher than both short-term rates and long-term rates.
   C. Long-term rates are higher than short-term rates.

6. Which of the following statements concerning theories of the term structure is *least accurate*?
   A. Under the pure expectations hypothesis, if the term structure is inverted, the market expects future short-term interest rates to be lower than current short-term interest rates.
   B. Under the pure expectations hypothesis, if the term structure is normal, the market expects future short-term interest rates to be higher than current short-term interest rates.
   C. Under the liquidity theory, if the term structure is normal, the market expects future short-term interest rates to be higher than current short-term interest rates.

7. Which of the following statements is the best definition of key rate duration?
   A. The duration-weighted sensitivity of a bond to a parallel shift in the term structure.
   B. The convexity-enhanced sensitivity of a bond to a non-parallel shift in the term structure.
   C. The approximate percentage change in the value of a bond or bond portfolio in response to a 100 basis point change in a key rate, holding all other rates constant.

8. Which of the following is a major criticism of the pure expectations theory of the term structure? It ignores:
   A. the duration of the bond.
   B. price risk and reinvestment risk of an investment.
   C. convexity of an investment.

9. Today's yield is 6.10% and yesterday's yield was 6.18%. The percentage yield change from yesterday to today, assuming continuous compounding, is *closest* to:
   A. –1.303%.
   B. –1.137%.
   C. –1.098%.

10. If there are 250 trading days in a year and the daily historical yield volatility is 0.34%, the annual standard deviation of the yield is *closest* to:
   A. 5.38%.
   B. 0.85%.
   C. 6.84%.

11. The current yield on a bond is 7.19% and the bond's standard deviation is 11.3%. The 99.7% confidence interval for the yield is *closest* to:
   A. [6.32%, 8.04%].
   B. [5.56%, 8.81%].
   C. [4.75%, 9.63%].

CHALLENGE PROBLEMS

12. Suppose you observe a 1-year (zero-coupon) Treasury security trading at a yield to maturity of 5% (price of 95.2381% of par). You also observe a 2-year T-note with a 6% coupon trading at a yield to maturity of 5.5% (price of 100.9232). And, finally, you observe a 3-year T-note with a 7% coupon trading at a yield to maturity of 6.0% (price of 102.6730). Assume annual coupon payments. Use the bootstrapping method to determine the 2-year and 3-year spot rates.

	2-year spot rate	3-year spot rate
A.	5.51%	5.92%
B.	5.46%	5.92%
C.	5.51%	6.05%

13. Former Treasury Secretary Robert Rubin decided to stop issuing 30-year Treasury bonds in 2001 and to replace them by borrowing more with shorter-maturity Treasury bills and notes (although the U.S. Treasury has since resumed issuing 30-year bonds). Which of the following statements concerning this decision is *most accurate*?
    A. If the pure expectations hypothesis of the term structure is correct, this decision will reduce the government's borrowing cost.
    B. If the liquidity theory of the term structure is correct, this decision will reduce the government's borrowing cost.
    C. If the liquidity theory of the term structure is correct, this decision will not change the government's borrowing cost.

14. Ynot Investments currently uses the yield on all on-the run Treasury securities to construct the theoretical spot curve the firm uses to price bonds. Frank Bristow, a fixed income analyst at Ynot, has proposed to his colleagues that the firm switch to using yields on U.S. Treasury strips. He defends his proposal by making two statements that he purports to be advantages of using Treasury strips vs. on-the-run Treasury securities:

    1. On-the-run Treasury yields reflect a liquidity premium that distorts the spot rate curve derived from those yields; that liquidity premium is not embedded in strip yields.

    2. Observable market yields on strips are available at a variety of maturities above 10 years; there are large gaps in on-the-run yields between 10 and 30 years.

    With regards to Bristow's statements justifying use of Treasury strip yields instead of on-the-run Treasury yields to derive the theoretical spot rate curve:
    A. both statements are correct.
    B. only one statement is correct.
    C. both statements are incorrect.

15. Do spreads on swap rates [based on the London Interbank Offered Rate (LIBOR) curve] over comparable Treasury yields reflect credit risk and/or sovereign risk?
    A. Yes on both counts.
    B. Yes on one count.
    C. No on both counts.

16. The use of implied volatility is often criticized for the assumption that:
    A. the option pricing model provides a poor estimate, at best.
    B. volatility is constant.
    C. historical observation has more predictive power than current interest rate derivatives prices.

17. Forecasting yield volatility is based on each assumption except:
    A. a statistical technique based on autoregressive conditional heteroskedasticity (ARCH) models can be used to forecast volatility.
    B. it is often desirable to weight recent observations more heavily than distant observations
    C. including weighting schemes when forecasting variance eliminates autoregressive conditional heteroskedasticity.

Answers – Concept Checkers

1. C A positive butterfly shift is a nonparallel shift in the yield curve that results in less curvature.

2. C The three factors that affect Treasury returns are: (1) changes in the level of yields, (2) changes in the slope of the yield curve, and (3) changes in the curvature of the yield curve. Changes in the level of yields are by far the most influential of these factors, explaining about 90% of the variation in Treasury security returns.

3. C Given the key rate durations for an equally weighted bond portfolio, effective duration for a parallel shift in the yield curve is the sum of the individual rate durations. In this case, the portfolio effective duration is 11.91.

4. A Change in Portfolio Value

Change from 5-year key rate increase:	–0.25% × 0.34	= 0.085% decrease
Change from 20-year key rate increase:	–0.50% × 1.22	= 0.610% decrease
Net change		0.695% decrease

Thus, the portfolio value will decrease by 0.695%.

5. A An inverted yield curve is one where short-term rates are higher than long-term rates.

6. C Under the liquidity theory, there is a premium in long-term borrowing rates. Therefore, the term structure may be upward-sloping (i.e., normal) even if future short-term interest rates are expected to be equal to current short-term rates. If the term structure is inverted, even with a positive liquidity premium, the expectation for future short-term rates must be lower. Under the pure expectations theory, an upward-sloping yield curve (i.e., a normal curve) means short-term spot rates are expected to increase. An inverted yield curve implies a decrease in short-term expected spot rates, according to the pure expectations theory.

7. C Key rate duration is the approximate percentage change in the value of a bond or bond portfolio in response to a 100 basis point change in a key rate, holding all other rates constant.

8. B The major criticism of the pure expectations theory is that it fails to recognize interest rate risk; specifically, price risk and reinvestment risk. Price risk is the uncertainty associated with future bond prices as a result of interest rate changes, and reinvestment risk reflects the uncertainty associated with the rate at which the bond's cash flows can be reinvested.

9. A percentage yield change = $100 \times \ln\left(\frac{6.10}{6.18}\right) = -1.303\%$

10. A annualized standard deviation = $0.0034 \times \sqrt{250} = 0.0538 = 5.38\%$

11. **C** The standard deviation is calculated as:

$$\sigma = 7.19\% \times 0.113 = 0.8125\% = 81.25 \text{ basis points}$$

The 99.7% confidence interval equals the current rate (7.19%) plus or minus three times the standard deviation:

$$7.19\% \pm (3 \times 0.8125\%) \Rightarrow [4.75\%, 9.63\%]$$

ANSWERS – CHALLENGE PROBLEMS

12. **C** Here are the cash flows associated with the three bonds:

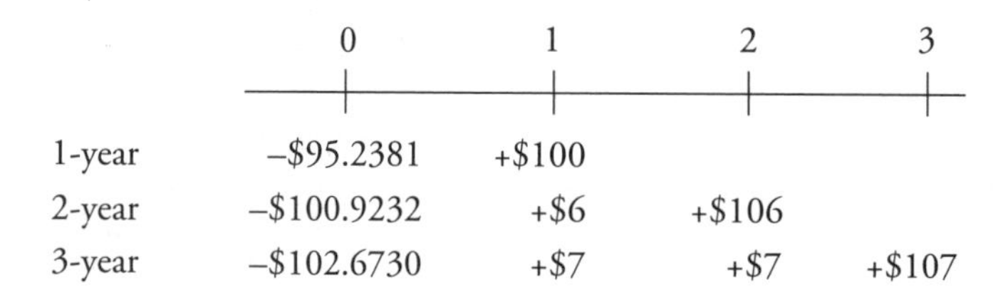

	0	1	2	3
1-year	–\$95.2381	+\$100		
2-year	–\$100.9232	+\$6	+\$106	
3-year	–\$102.6730	+\$7	+\$7	+\$107

To find Z_2, the 2-year spot rate:

$$\$100.9232 = \frac{\$6}{1.05^1} + \frac{\$106}{(1+Z_2)^2} \Rightarrow Z_2 = 5.51\%$$

To find Z_3, the 3-year spot rate:

$$\$102.6730 = \frac{\$7}{1.05^1} + \frac{\$7}{1.0551^2} + \frac{\$107}{(1+Z_3)^3} \Rightarrow Z_3 = 6.05\%$$

13. **B** If the pure expectations hypothesis of the term structure is correct, altering the maturity of the government's borrowing will not affect the government's borrowing cost (i.e., borrowing once for 30 years is the same as borrowing 30 times for one year at a time). If the liquidity theory is correct, the government's borrowing cost will go down, as it no longer has to compensate lenders with the liquidity premium for borrowing long term.

14. **B** An important disadvantage of using strip yields is that strip markets are less liquid, so strip yields contain a liquidity premium not embedded in on-the-run issues; therefore, Statement 1 is inaccurate and does not support Bristow's proposal. The primary advantage of using strip yields is that it reduces or eliminates the maturity gaps found in on-the-run Treasury yields; therefore, Statement 2 is accurate and supports Bristow's proposal.

15. **B** Swap curves are not default-free curves because the LIBOR-based swap spreads over U.S. Treasuries reflect counterparty credit risk. However, swap spreads over U.S. Treasuries do not reflect sovereign risk. The swap market is not regulated by any government, which makes swap spreads more comparable across borders than government bond yields, which do reflect sovereign risk.

16. **B** The use of implied volatility is often criticized for assuming that the option pricing model is correct, and that volatility is constant. The use of implied volatility does not assume that historical observation has more predictive power than current interest rate derivatives prices.

17. **C** Because yield volatility has been observed to follow patterns over time, a statistical technique based on (ARCH) models can be used to forecast volatility. Weighting schemes are common in forecasting, but are not used to eliminate autoregressive conditional heteroskedasticity.

The following is a review of the Fixed Income: Valuation Concepts principles designed to address the learning outcome statements set forth by CFA Institute. This topic is also covered in:

VALUING BONDS WITH EMBEDDED OPTIONS

Study Session 14

EXAM FOCUS

The binomial model is used to value bonds with embedded options (callable bonds and putable bonds), assess OAS, value the call feature, and calculate duration and convexity. The final section of this topic review addresses convertible bonds. Concentrate on valuation of option-free, callable, and putable bonds using interest rate trees, as well as the interpretation of a bond's OAS. You'll see these topics again in Study Session 15.

LOS 44.a: Evaluate, using relative value analysis, whether a security is undervalued, fairly valued, or overvalued.

CFA® Program Curriculum, Volume 5, page 334

Relative value analysis of bonds involves comparing the spread on the bond (over some benchmark) to the required spread and determining whether the bond is over or undervalued relative to the benchmark. The required spread is the spread available on comparable securities. In simple terms:

- Undervalued ("cheap") bonds have spreads larger than the required spread.
- Overvalued ("rich") bonds have spreads smaller than the required spread.
- Properly valued ("fairly priced") bonds have spreads equal to the required spread.

WARM-UP: BINOMIAL MODELS

A *binomial model* is a relatively simple single factor interest rate model that, given an assumed level of volatility, suggests that interest rates have an equal probability of taking on one of two possible values in the next period. The binomial interest rate model is used throughout this review to illustrate the issues that must be considered when valuing bonds with embedded options.

An interest rate model makes assumptions about interest rate volatility, along with a set of paths that interest rates may follow over time. This set of possible interest rate paths is referred to as an *interest rate tree.*

Binomial Interest Rate Trees

The set of possible interest rate paths that are used to value bonds with a binomial model is called a binomial interest rate tree. The diagram in Figure 1 depicts a binomial interest rate tree.

Figure 1: Two-Period Binomial Tree

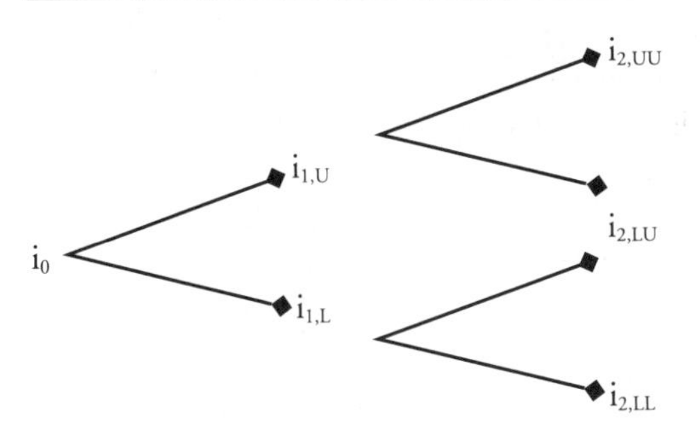

To understand this two-period binomial tree, consider the nodes indicated with the bold dots (♦). A node is a point in time when interest rates can take one of two possible paths, an upper path, *U*, or a lower path, *L*. Now, consider the node on the right side of the diagram where the interest rate $i_{2,LU}$ appears. This is the rate that will occur if the initial rate, i_0, follows the lower path from Node 0 to Node 1 to become $i_{1,L}$, then follows the upper of the two possible paths to Node 2, where it takes on the value $i_{2,LU}$. At the risk of stating the obvious, the upper path from a given node leads to a higher rate than the lower path. Notice also that an upward move followed by a downward move gets us to the same place on the tree as a down-then-up move, so $i_{2,LU} = i_{2,UL}$.

The interest rates at each node in this interest rate tree are 1-period forward rates corresponding to the nodal period. Beyond the root of the tree, there is more than one 1-period forward rate for each nodal period (e.g., at Year 1, we have two 1-year forward rates, $i_{1,U}$ and $i_{1,L}$). The relationship among the set of rates associated with each individual nodal period is a function of the interest rate volatility assumption of the model being employed to generate the tree.

Constructing an Arbitrage-Free Tree

The construction of an interest rate tree, binomial or otherwise, is a tedious process. In practice, the interest rate tree is usually generated using specialized computer software. There is one underlying rule governing the construction of an interest rate tree: the interest rate tree should generate **arbitrage-free values** for on-the-run issues of the benchmark security (benchmark interest rates are discussed in the next LOS). This means that the value of these on-the-run issues produced by the interest rate tree must equal their market prices, which excludes arbitrage opportunities. This requirement is very important because without it, the model will not properly price more complex callable and putable securities, which is the intended purpose of the model.

Valuing an Option-Free Bond With the Binomial Model

Remember that *the value of a bond at a given node in a binomial tree is the average of the present values of the two possible values from the next period*, because the probabilities of an up move and a down move are both 50%. The appropriate discount rate is the forward rate associated with the node under analysis.

Example: Valuing an option-free bond with the binomial model

A 7% annual coupon bond has two years to maturity. The interest rate tree is shown in the figure below. Fill in the tree and calculate the value of the bond today.

Valuing a 2-Year, 7.0% Coupon, Option-Free Bond

Today	1 year	2 years
		\$100.000 \$7.0
	\$???.?? \$7.0 7.1826%	
\$???.?? 4.5749%		\$100.000 \$7.0
	\$???.?? \$7.0 5.3210%	
		\$100.000 \$7.0

Answer:

Consider the value of the bond at the *upper* node for Period 1, $V_{1,U}$:

$$V_{1,U} = \frac{1}{2} \times \left[\frac{\$100 + \$7}{1.071826} + \frac{\$100 + \$7}{1.071826} \right] = \$99.830$$

Similarly, the value of the bond at the *lower* node for Period 1, $V_{1,L}$, is:

$$V_{1,L} = \frac{1}{2} \times \left[\frac{\$100 + \$7}{1.053210} + \frac{\$100 + \$7}{1.053210} \right] = \$101.594$$

Now calculate V_0, the current value of the bond at Node 0.

$$V_0 = \frac{1}{2} \times \left[\frac{\$99.830 + \$7}{1.045749} + \frac{\$101.594 + \$7}{1.045749} \right] = \$102.999$$

The completed binomial tree is shown below:

Valuing a 2-Year, 7.0% Coupon, Option-Free Bond

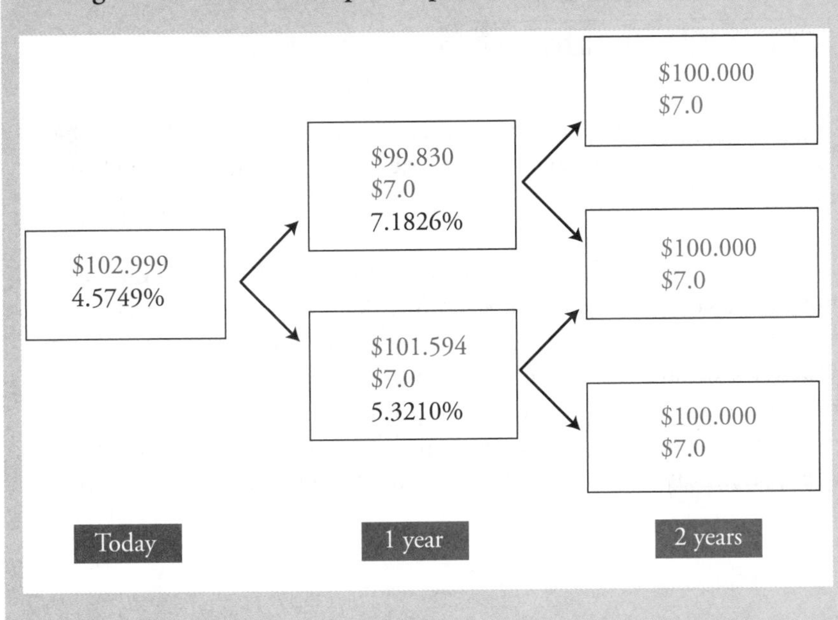

SPREAD MEASURES

There are three important spread measures that you must be able to interpret: nominal spread, zero-volatility spread (*Z*-spread), and option-adjusted spread (OAS). The first two were discussed in some detail at Level I; OAS was mentioned briefly, so we're going to spend more time on it at Level II. We'll provide a quick review of these three spread measures now before starting our discussion of benchmark interest rates and relative value analysis. LOS 44.g includes more detail on the OAS.

The *nominal spread* is the bond's yield to maturity minus the yield on a comparable-maturity treasury benchmark security. For example, if a 5-year AA bond has a yield to maturity of 8% and the 5-year U.S. Treasury note has a yield of 5%, the bond's nominal spread is 3%. The problem with the nominal spread is that it uses a single interest rate to discount each cash flow that makes up the bond; if the yield curve is not flat, each cash flow should instead be discounted at the appropriate spot rate for that maturity.

The *Z-spread* is the spread that when added to each spot rate on the yield curve, makes the present value of the bond's cash flows equal to the bond's market price. Therefore, it is a spread over the entire spot rate curve. The term *zero volatility* in the Z-spread refers to the fact that it assumes interest rate volatility is zero. If interest rates are volatile, the Z-spread is not appropriate to use to value bonds with embedded options because the Z-spread includes the cost of the embedded option. The nominal spread and the Z-spread are approximately equal to each other. The difference between the two is larger (1) if the yield curve is not flat, (2) for securities that repay principal over time such as mortgage-backed securities (MBS), and (3) for securities with longer maturities.

For example, suppose the 1-year spot rate is 4% and the 2-year spot rate is 5%. The market price of a 2-year bond with annual coupon payments of 8% is \$104.12. The Z-spread is the spread that solves the following equation:

$$\$104.12 = \frac{\$8}{(1+0.04+Z)^1} + \frac{\$108}{(1+0.05+Z)^2}$$

In this case, the Z-spread is 0.008, or 80 basis points. If you plug Z = 0.008 into the equation above, you'll find that the present value of the bond's cash flows (the right-hand side) will equal \$104.12.

The OAS is the spread on a bond with an embedded option after the embedded option cost has been removed. It's equal to the Z-spread minus the option cost. The OAS for a corporate bond must be calculated using a binomial interest rate model. Because the model is created using a spot rate curve, the OAS is also a spread over the spot rate curve. The relationship between the Z-spread, the OAS, and the option cost are shown in Figure 2. The line between the spot rate curve and the corporate yield curve is not usually identified separately, but technically it represents the spot rate curve plus the OAS.

Figure 2: *Z*-Spread, OAS, and Option Cost

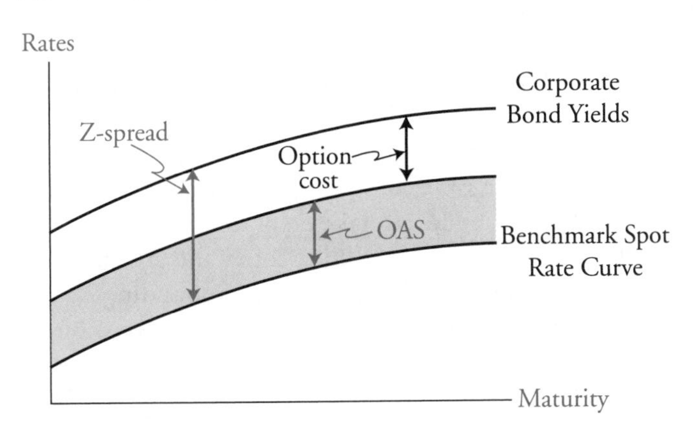

LOS 44.b: Evaluate the importance of benchmark interest rates in interpreting spread measures.

CFA® Program Curriculum, Volume 5, page 334

A nominal yield spread is the difference between the yield on a security and a benchmark yield, usually the comparable U.S. treasury yield of the same maturity. If we use a different benchmark (e.g., the AAA corporate yield), the spread and our interpretation of the spread will be different. The same concept applies to spreads measured from binomial interest rate trees. For example, later we'll see that the OAS that is derived from a binomial model, and our interpretation of the OAS, will depend on the benchmark rates used to create the tree.

In the previous example in which we valued the 7% coupon option-free bond, we used U.S. Treasury securities as benchmark rates to construct the interest rate tree. There are, in fact, three different benchmark interest rates that can be used to calculate spreads:

1. Treasury securities.
2. A specific sector of the bond market with a credit rating higher than the issue being valued.
3. A specific issuer.

Once again, our interpretation of a spread calculated for a specific security will depend on the benchmark rates we used.

LOS 44.c: Describe the backward induction valuation methodology within the binomial interest rate tree framework.

CFA® Program Curriculum, Volume 5, page 340

Backward induction refers to the process of valuing a bond using a binomial interest rate tree. The term "backward" is used because in order to determine the value of a bond at Node 0, you need to know the values that the bond can take on at Node 1. But to determine the values of the bond at the Year 1 nodes, you need to know the possible values of the bond at the Year 2 nodes. Thus, for a bond that has N compounding periods, the current value of the bond is determined by computing the bond's possible values at Period N and working backwards to Node 0.

LOS 44.d: Calculate the value of a callable bond from an interest rate tree.

CFA® Program Curriculum, Volume 5, page 347

The basic process for valuing a callable bond from an interest rate tree is similar to the process for a noncallable bond. When valuing a callable bond, however, the value used at any node corresponding to the call date and beyond must be either the price at which the issuer will call the bond at that date or the computed value if the bond is not called, *whichever is less*. The price at which the bond will be called is determined using a *call rule* (e.g., the issue will be called if the computed price exceeds 105% of the call price).

Example: Valuing a callable bond

Continuing with our example, assume that the 2-year bond can be called in one year at 100. The issuer will call the bond if the computed bond price exceeds 100 one year from today (this is the call rule). Calculate the value of the callable bond today.

Answer:

The call rule (call the bond if the price exceeds \$100) is reflected in the boxes in the completed binomial tree, where the second line of the boxes at the 1-year node is the lesser of the call price or the computed value. For example, the value of the bond in one year at the lower node is \$101.594. However, in this case, the bond will be called, and the investor will only receive \$100. Therefore, for valuation purposes, the value of the bond in one year at this node is \$100.

The calculation for the current value of the bond at Node 0 (today), assuming the simplified call rules of this example, is:

$$V_0 = \frac{1}{2} \times \left[\frac{\$99.830 + \$7}{1.045749} + \frac{\$100.00 + \$7}{1.045749} \right] = \$102.238$$

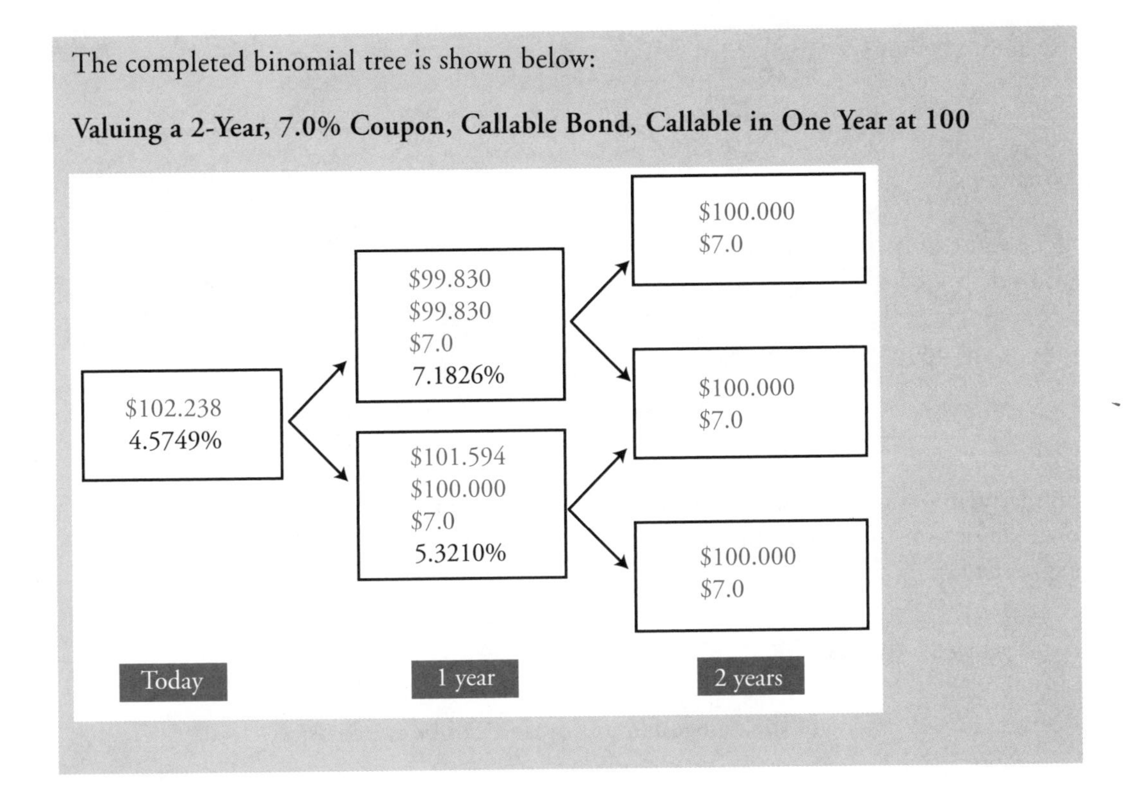

It should be noted that this example has been simplified for illustrative purposes. It is common for a callable bond to have a call schedule that specifies a different call price at different points in time. In this situation, the process described remains essentially the same, but the call prices at each node may not be equal.

In summary, the existence of an embedded option alters the cash flows that must be discounted when valuing a bond using the backward induction methodology with a binomial interest rate model.

LOS 44.e: Explain the relations among the values of a callable (putable) bond, the corresponding option-free bond, and the embedded option.

CFA® Program Curriculum, Volume 5, page 347

In essence, the holder of a callable bond owns a noncallable bond on which a call option has been written. The value of the embedded call option (V_{call}) is, therefore, simply the difference between the value of a noncallable ($V_{noncallable}$) bond and the value of the comparable callable bond ($V_{callable}$):

$$V_{call} = V_{noncallable} - V_{callable}$$

Example: Valuing an embedded call option

Calculate the value of the embedded call option from the previous example.

Answer:

The value of the call option is the difference between the noncallable bond and the callable bond:

$102.999 – $102.238 = $0.761

Similarly, investors are willing to pay a premium for a putable bond, since its holder owns an option-free bond plus a put option. The value of a putable bond can be expressed as:

$$V_{putable} = V_{nonputable} + V_{put}$$

Rearranging, the value of the embedded put option can be stated as:

$$V_{put} = V_{putable} - V_{nonputable}$$

LOS 44.f: Explain the effect of volatility on the arbitrage-free value of an option.

CFA® Program Curriculum, Volume 5, page 350

Like ordinary options, the value of an embedded call option, V_{call}, increases as interest rate volatility increases.

We can explain this relationship in the context of the callable bond by recalling that the upside price of a callable bond is capped at the call price. As volatility increases, the upside prices in the binomial tree will not rise above the call price, but the downside prices will fall. That means the callable bond value ($V_{callable}$) will fall as volatility rises. However, the arbitrage-free value of the noncallable bond ($V_{noncallable}$) will be unaffected by the increased volatility. Therefore, as volatility increases, the value of the call (V_{call}), which is the difference between the callable and noncallable bond values, will also increase. From the investor's perspective, increased volatility decreases the value of their callable bond. The issuer of the bond holds the call and benefits from the increased volatility.

WARM-UP: HOW OPTION-ADJUSTED SPREAD (OAS) IS CALCULATED

The interest rates used to value the callable bond in the previous example were derived to yield arbitrage-free values for on-the-run Treasury securities (i.e., the interest rates produced a theoretical value equal to the market price for Treasury securities). This does not mean that the interest rate tree will produce an arbitrage-free value for the callable bond. In order to produce an arbitrage-free value for a callable bond, interest rates must be adjusted for the option characteristics of the bond. The adjustment is called the **option-adjusted spread** (OAS).

The OAS is the interest rate spread that must be added to all of the 1-year rates in a binomial tree so that the theoretical value of a callable bond generated with the tree is equal to its market price (i.e., the OAS is the spread that forces the theoretical price to be arbitrage-free). Recognize that the underlying cash flows that are being discounted are adjusted to reflect the embedded option. By adjusting the cash flows, we assume that the option is exercised when it is in-the-money, as in the previous example (i.e., option is "removed" by the cash flow adjustment process). Thus, the option-adjusted spread is based on the same assumptions as those used to construct the binomial tree from which it is derived, particularly the interest rate volatility assumption. The only way to calculate the OAS from a binomial model is by trial and error, so you won't have to do it on the exam. However, the following example will give you a better understanding of what the OAS is and how to interpret it.

Example: Calculating the OAS

In the previous example, the value of the 2-year, 7% bond, callable in one year, was calculated as $102.238. If the market price of this bond is $101.531, the bond is selling at a discount relative to its theoretical value computed from the binomial model. Verify that if a spread of 50 basis points is added to each of the 1-year rates in the tree, the theoretical value of this bond will equal its market price of $101.531.

Answer:

Consider the value of the bond at the *upper* node for Period 1, $V_{1,U}$.

$$V_{1,U} = \frac{1}{2} \times \left[\frac{\$100 + \$7}{1.071826 + 0.005} + \frac{\$100 + \$7}{1.071826 + 0.005} \right] = \$99.366$$

Similarly, the value of the bond at the *lower* node for Period 1, $V_{1,L}$ is:

$$V_{1,L} = \frac{1}{2} \times \left[\frac{\$100 + \$7}{1.053210 + 0.005} + \frac{\$100 + \$7}{1.053210 + 0.005} \right] = \$101.114$$

Now calculate V_0, the current value of the bond at Node 0:

$$V_0 = \frac{1}{2} \times \left[\frac{\$99.366 + \$7}{1.045749 + 0.005} + \frac{\$100.000 + \$7}{1.045749 + 0.005} \right] = \$101.531$$

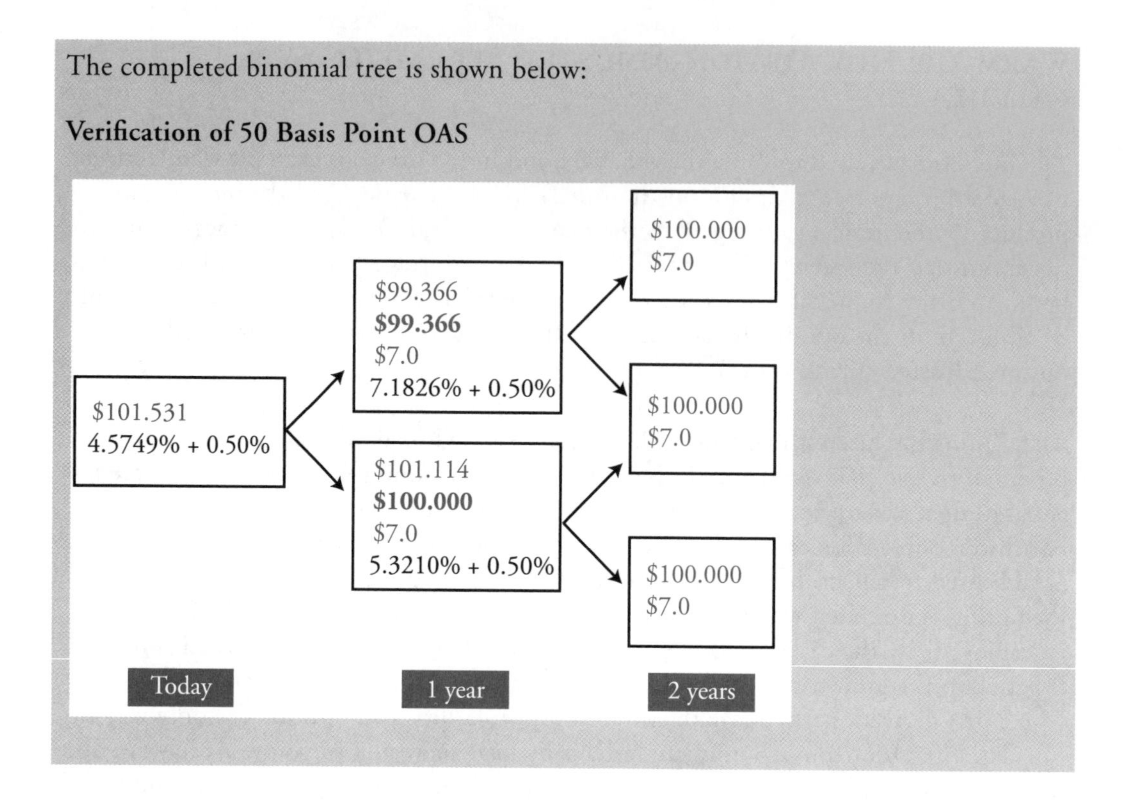

LOS 44.g: Interpret an option-adjusted spread with respect to a nominal spread and to benchmark interest rates.

CFA® Program Curriculum, Volume 5, page 350

Recall that:

- Undervalued ("cheap") bonds have spreads larger than the required spread.
- Overvalued ("rich") bonds have spreads smaller than the required spread.
- Properly valued ("fairly priced") bonds have spreads equal to the required spread.

In order to determine the appropriate required spread and interpret the bond's actual spread, however, we first have to determine what the spread is measuring, given the benchmark we used to calculate the spread. In general, a spread measures compensation for credit risk relative to the benchmark, liquidity risk relative to the benchmark, and option risk. Because the OAS removes the cost of the embedded option, the OAS measures only credit risk and liquidity risk relative to the benchmark.

Treasury Benchmark

If we use a Treasury benchmark, the nominal spread and *Z*-spread reflect:

- Credit risk relative to Treasuries.
- Liquidity risk relative to Treasuries.
- Option risk.

The OAS reflects:

- Credit risk relative to Treasuries.
- Liquidity risk relative to Treasuries.

Bond Sector Benchmark

If we use a higher-rated bond sector as the benchmark, the nominal spread and *Z*-spread reflect:

- Credit risk relative to the bond sector.
- Liquidity risk relative to the bond sector.
- Option risk.

The OAS reflects:

- Credit risk relative to the bond sector.
- Liquidity risk relative to the bond sector.

Issuer-Specific Benchmark

If we use the issuer's yield curve or spot curve as the benchmark, the nominal spread and *Z*-spread will not reflect any credit risk because the credit risk of the issue and the benchmark are assumed to be the same. Therefore, the nominal spread and *Z*-spread will reflect:

- Liquidity risk relative to the specific issuer's other securities (which is assumed to be very small).
- Option risk.

The OAS will reflect only:

- Liquidity risk relative to the specific issuer's other securities (which is assumed to be very small).

Relative OAS Valuation

In general, the interpretation of the OAS (i.e., whether the bond is over or undervalued) depends on the benchmark and, in some cases, the required OAS.

For example, if the benchmark is Treasuries or a bond sector (with a credit rating higher than the bond we're valuing), any corporate bond with an OAS less than or equal to zero is overvalued relative to the benchmark, because it must have more credit risk, and most likely more liquidity risk, than the benchmark. If the OAS is positive, the bond is undervalued relative to the benchmark only if the OAS is greater than the required OAS.

If we use an issuer-specific benchmark (assuming relative liquidity risk is zero), the bond is undervalued relative to the benchmark if the OAS is positive, fairly valued if the OAS is zero, and overvalued if the OAS is negative.

These concepts are summarized in Figure 3.

Figure 3: Relative OAS Valuation

	Treasury Benchmark	*Sector Benchmark*	*Issuer-Specific Benchmark*
OAS > 0	Overvalued ("rich") if actual OAS < required OAS; undervalued ("cheap") if actual OAS > required OAS	Overvalued ("rich") if actual OAS < required OAS; undervalued ("cheap") if actual OAS > required OAS	Undervalued ("cheap")
OAS = 0	Overvalued ("rich")	Overvalued ("rich")	Fairly priced
OAS < 0	Overvalued ("rich")	Overvalued ("rich")	Overvalued ("rich")

Example: Relative OAS valuation

An analyst makes the following spread estimates relative to U.S. Treasuries for a callable corporate bond:

- Nominal spread relative to the Treasury yield curve: 240 basis points.
- *Z*-spread relative to the Treasury spot curve: 225 basis points.
- OAS relative to the Treasury spot curve: 190 basis points.

The analyst also determines that the *Z*-spread over Treasuries on comparable option-free bonds (i.e., bonds with the same credit rating, maturity, and liquidity) in the market is 210 basis points. Determine whether the bond is overvalued, undervalued, or properly valued.

Answer:

The required OAS in this case is the *Z*-spread on comparable option-free bonds (because *Z*-spread is equal to OAS for option-free bonds), which is 210 basis points. This bond is overvalued, because its OAS of 190 basis points is less than the required OAS. It is not appropriate to compare the bond's *Z*-spread or nominal spread to the required spread because the embedded option cost is not reflected in those spread measures.

LOS 44.h: Explain how effective duration and effective convexity are calculated using the binomial model.

CFA® Program Curriculum, Volume 5, page 352

Recall from Level I that:

- Modified duration measures a bond's price sensitivity to interest rate changes, *assuming that the bond's cash flows do not change as interest rates change.*
- The standard measure of convexity can be used to improve price changes estimated from modified duration.

Modified duration and convexity are not useful for bonds with embedded options, however, because the cash flows from these bonds may change if the option is exercised. To overcome this problem, *effective* duration and convexity should be used because these measures take into account how changes in interest rates may alter cash flows.

The following expressions can be used to compute effective duration and convexity for *any* bond:

$$\text{effective duration} = \text{ED} = \frac{\text{BV}_{-\Delta y} - \text{BV}_{+\Delta y}}{2 \times \text{BV}_0 \times \Delta y}$$

$$\text{effective convexity} = \text{EC} = \frac{\text{BV}_{-\Delta y} + \text{BV}_{+\Delta y} - (2 \times \text{BV}_0)}{2 \times \text{BV}_0 \times \Delta y^2}$$

where:

Δy = change in required yield, in decimal form

$\text{BV}_{-\Delta y}$ = estimated price if yield decreases by Δy

$\text{BV}_{+\Delta y}$ = estimated price if yield increases by Δy

BV_0 = initial observed bond price

Calculating effective duration and effective convexity for bonds with embedded options is a complicated undertaking because you must calculate values of $\text{BV}_{+\Delta y}$ and $\text{BV}_{-\Delta y}$. Here's how it's done:

Step 1: Given assumptions about benchmark interest rates, interest rate volatility, and any call and/or put rules, calculate the OAS for the issue, using the binomial model.

Step 2: Impose a small parallel shift in the on-the-run yield curve by an amount equal to $+\Delta y$.

Step 3: Build a new binomial interest rate tree using the new yield curve.

Step 4: Add the OAS to each of the 1-year rates in the interest rate tree to get a "modified" tree. (We assume that the OAS does not change when interest rates change.)

Step 5: Compute $\text{BV}_{+\Delta y}$ using this modified interest rate tree.

Step 6: Repeat steps 2 through 5 using a parallel rate shift of $-\Delta y$ to obtain a value of $\text{BV}_{-\Delta y}$.

Note that the values for duration and convexity that result from this procedure are based on the computed values for $\text{BV}_{+\Delta y}$ and $\text{BV}_{-\Delta y}$, which are functions of: (1) the interest rate volatility assumption, (2) the call and/or put rule, and (3) the benchmark interest rates used to generate the binomial interest rate tree. Changes in any of these factors will likely alter the computed values for effective duration and convexity.

Professor's Note: Exam questions on effective duration and effective convexity are likely to deal with interpretation or calculation given values for $BV+_{\Delta y}$ and $BV-_{\Delta y}$. It is unlikely that you will be asked to calculate effective duration or effective convexity with the interest rate trees, although you may be asked to recognize the formula. Notice that the LOS says only to "explain how ... are calculated."

LOS 44.i: Calculate the value of a putable bond, using an interest rate tree.

CFA® Program Curriculum, Volume 5, page 354

A **putable bond** gives the holder the right to sell (put) the bond to the issuer at a predetermined price at some time prior to the bond's maturity. Putable bonds can be valued using the same procedure as for a callable bond, except that the relevant cash flows are dictated by the rules governing the exercise of the embedded put option.

Example: Valuing a putable bond

Consider a 2-year, 7% coupon, putable bond that is putable in one year at a price of 100. Further, assume that the put option will be exercised if the value of the bond is less than 100. Calculate the value of the putable bond.

Answer:

This situation is illustrated in the binomial tree shown in the following figure:

Valuing a 2-Year, 7.0% Coupon, Putable Bond, Putable in One Year at 100

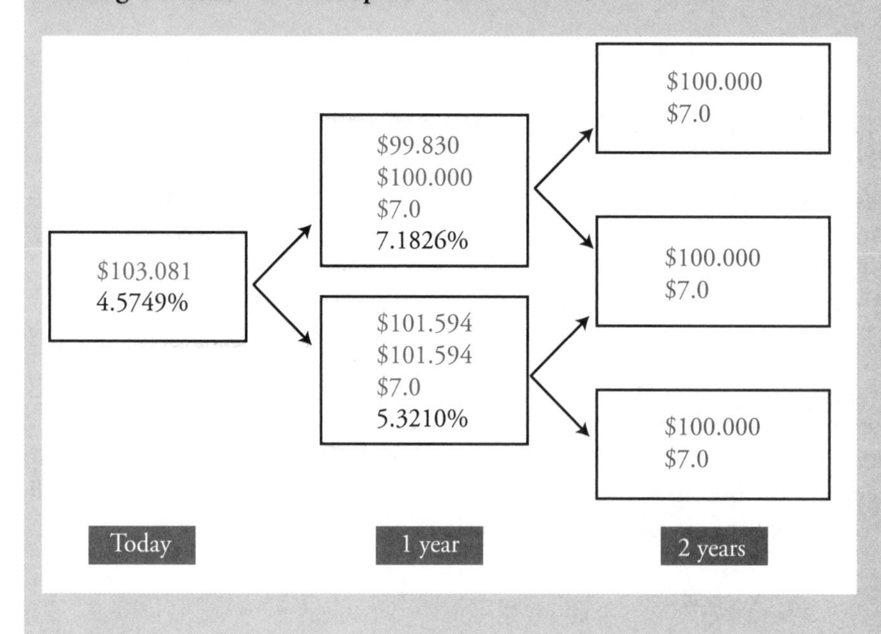

For the tree shown, the second line in the boxes at the 1-year node reflects the greater of the exercise price or the computed value. When valuing this putable bond, the value used at any node corresponding to the put date and beyond must be either the exercise price at that date or the computed value, *whichever is greater*.

Consider the value of the bond at the *upper* node for Period 1, $V_{1,U}$.

$$V_{1,U} = \frac{1}{2} \times \left[\frac{\$100 + \$7}{1.071826} + \frac{\$100 + \$7}{1.071826}\right] = \$99.830$$

Similarly, the value of the bond at the *lower* node for Period 1, $V_{1,L}$ is:

$$V_{1,L} = \frac{1}{2} \times \left[\frac{\$100 + \$7}{1.053210} + \frac{\$100 + \$7}{1.053210}\right] = \$101.594$$

Given our put rule, the current value of the bond at Node 0 (today) is:

$$V_0 = \frac{1}{2} \times \left[\frac{\$100.000 + \$7}{1.045749} + \frac{\$101.594 + \$7}{1.045749}\right] = \$103.081$$

Recall that the value of a putable bond is given by: $V_{putable} = V_{nonputable} + V_{put}$. Thus, the value of the embedded put option is: $V_{put} = V_{putable} - V_{nonputable}$.

Example: Valuing an embedded put option

The \$103.0810 value here is greater than the \$102.999 value that was computed earlier for the option-free bond. Compute the value of the embedded put option.

Answer:

The value of the embedded put option (to the bondholder) is:

\$103.081 – \$102.999 = \$0.082

As with all options, the value of the embedded put option increases as volatility increases. As such, it can be seen in the expression that the value of a putable bond will also increase as volatility increases. Intuitively, this makes sense; investors are willing to pay more for a bond that gives them the right to sell it at a price greater than the market value.

LOS 44.j: Describe and evaluate a convertible bond and its various component values.

CFA® Program Curriculum, Volume 5, page 361

The owner of a convertible bond has the right to convert the bond into a fixed number of common shares of the issuer. Hence, a convertible bond includes an embedded call option. The option is slightly different from the embedded option in a callable bond. First, the convertible bondholder owns the call option; the issuer owns the call option in a callable bond. Secondly, the holder has the right to buy shares with a bond that changes in value, not with cash at a fixed *exercise price* (the call price in a callable bond).

The **conversion ratio** is the number of common shares for which a convertible bond can be exchanged. For example, a convertible bond issued at par with a conversion ratio of 10 allows its holder to convert one $1,000 par bond into 10 shares of common stock. Equivalently, the **conversion price** of the bond is $1,000 / 10 shares = $100. For bonds not issued at par, the conversion price is the issue price divided by the conversion ratio.

Almost all convertible bonds are callable, which gives the issuer the ability to *force* conversion. If the bond is worth more than the call price and the issuer calls the bond, it's optimal for the holder to convert the bond into shares rather than sell back to the issuer at the lower call price.

Some convertible issues are putable. If the embedded put feature requires the issuer to redeem the bond with cash, the put is referred to as a hard put. If the issuer has a payment choice (cash, common stock, and/or subordinated notes), the embedded put is called a soft put.

Professor's Note: Exchangeable bonds are convertible at the option of the holder into shares of stock other than those of the issuer. The analysis of exchangeable bonds is the same as for convertible bonds.

The **conversion value** of a convertible bond is the value of the common stock into which the bond can be converted. The conversion ratio is the number of shares the holder receives from conversion for each bond. Conversion value is calculated as:

conversion value = market price of stock × conversion ratio

The **straight value**, or investment value, of a convertible bond is the value of the bond if it were not convertible—the present value of the bond's cash flows discounted at the required return on a comparable option-free issue.

The **minimum value of a convertible bond** must be the greater of its conversion value or its straight value. This must be the case, or arbitrage opportunities would be possible. For example, if a convertible bond were to sell for less than its conversion value, it could be purchased, immediately converted into common stock, and the stock could be sold for more than the cost of the bond.

Example: Calculating the minimum value of a convertible bond

Business Supply Company, Inc. operates retail office equipment stores in the United States and Canada. Consider a BSC convertible bond with a 7% coupon that is currently selling at $985 with a conversion ratio of 25 and a straight value of $950. Assume that the value of BSC's common stock is currently $35 per share, and that it pays $1 per share in dividends annually. Compute the bond's minimum value.

Answer:

The conversion value of this bond is 25 × $35 = $875. Since the straight value of $950 is greater than the conversion value of $875, the bond must be priced to sell for at least $950.

The **market conversion price**, or conversion parity price, is the price that the convertible bondholder would effectively pay for the stock if she bought the bond and immediately converted it. The market conversion price is given as:

$$\text{market conversion price} = \frac{\text{market price of convertible bond}}{\text{conversion ratio}}$$

Example: Calculating market conversion price

Compute and interpret the market conversion price of the BSC bond.

Answer:

The market conversion price is: $985 / 25 = $39.40. This can be viewed as the stock price at which an investor is indifferent between selling the bond or converting it.

The **market conversion premium per share** is the difference between the market conversion price and the stock's current market price:

market conversion premium per share = market conversion price – market price

Example: Calculating market conversion premium per share

Compute and interpret the market conversion premium per share of the BSC bond.

Answer:

Since BSC is selling for $35 per share, the market conversion premium per share for the BSC bond is: $39.40 – $35 = $4.40. This can be interpreted as the premium that investors are willing to pay for the chance that the market price of the stock will rise above the market conversion price. This is done with the assurance that even if the stock price declines, the value of the convertible bond will not fall below its straight value.

Market conversion premium per share is usually expressed as a ratio, appropriately called the **market conversion premium ratio**. Its formula is:

$$\text{market conversion premium ratio} = \frac{\text{market conversion premium per share}}{\text{market price of common stock}}$$

Example: Calculating market conversion premium ratio

Compute the market conversion premium ratio of the BSC bond.

Answer:

The BSC bond market conversion premium ratio is:

$$\frac{\$4.40}{\$35} = 12.57\%$$

Typically, the coupon income from a convertible bond exceeds the dividend income that would have been realized if the stock were owned directly. On a per-share basis, this tends to offset the market conversion premium. The time it takes to recoup the per-share premium is known as the **premium payback period** or the breakeven time and is expressed as:

$$\text{premium payback period} = \frac{\text{market conversion premium per share}}{\text{favorable income difference per share}}$$

where the favorable income difference per share is the annual per share difference in the cash flows from the convertible bond and the stock:

$$\begin{matrix}\text{favorable} \\ \text{income difference} \\ \text{per share}\end{matrix} = \frac{\text{coupon interest} - (\text{conversion ratio} \times \text{dividends per share})}{\text{conversion ratio}}$$

Example: Calculating premium payback period

Compute and interpret the premium payback period of the BSC bond.

Answer:

For the BSC bond:

$$\text{coupon interest} = 0.07 \times \$1{,}000.00 = \$70.00$$

$$\text{conversion ratio} \times \text{dividends per share} = 25 \times \$1.00 = \$25.00$$

$$\text{favorable income difference per share is } \frac{\$70.00 - \$25.00}{25} = \$1.80$$

$$\text{premium payback period is: } \frac{\$4.40}{\$1.80} = 2.44 \text{ years}$$

The convertible bond investor's downside risk is limited by the bond's underlying straight value because the price of a convertible bond will not fall below this value regardless of what happens to the price of the issuer's common stock.

This downside risk is measured by the **premium over straight value**, which is calculated as:

$$\text{premium over straight value} = \left(\frac{\text{market price of convertible bond}}{\text{straight value}}\right) - 1$$

Example: Calculating premium over straight value

Compute and interpret the premium over straight value of the BSC bond.

Answer:

The premium over straight value for the BSC bond is:

$$\left(\frac{\$985.00}{\$950.00}\right) - 1 = 3.68\%$$

Holding all other factors constant, the greater the premium over straight value, the less attractive the convertible bond.

Valuing Convertible Bonds Using an Option-Based Valuation Approach

Investing in a noncallable/nonputable convertible bond is equivalent to buying:

- An option-free bond.
- A call option on an amount of the common stock equal to the conversion ratio.

The value of a noncallable/nonputable convertible bond can be expressed as:

convertible, noncallable bond value = straight value + value of call option on stock

The Black-Scholes-Merton option pricing model can be used to establish the value of the call option. (See Study Session 17 for more information on the Black-Scholes-Merton option pricing model.) A key variable in this model is stock price volatility, which is positively related to the value of the call option. Therefore, as price volatility increases, so does the value of the convertible.

Most convertible bonds are callable, giving the issuer the right to call the issue prior to maturity. Incorporating this feature into the valuation of a convertible bond results in the following expression:

callable convertible bond value = straight value of bond
+ value of call option on stock
– value of call option on bond

Obviously, the valuation of a callable convertible bond involves the valuation of the call feature, which is a function of interest rate volatility and the economic conditions that can trigger the call feature. The Black-Scholes-Merton option pricing model *cannot* be used in this situation.

To further complicate the situation (just for fun), consider a convertible bond that is both callable and putable. The expression for value then becomes:

callable and putable convertible bond value = straight value of bond
+ value of call option on stock
– value of call option on bond
+ value of put option on bond

Here again, the Black-Scholes-Merton model is *not* appropriate to value options that are dependent on future interest rates.

From this discussion, it should be apparent that valuing convertible bonds can be challenging. The valuation of convertible bonds with embedded call and/or put options requires a model that links the movement of interest rates and stock prices. You will not be asked to deal with these complex models on the exam.

However, you should know the effects of changes in volatilities on the convertible bond value. For a callable convertible bond:

- An increase in stock price volatility will increase the value of the call on the stock and increase the value of the callable convertible bond.
- An increase in interest rate volatility will increase the value of the call on the bond and reduce the value of the callable convertible bond.

LOS 44.k: Compare the risk-return characteristics of a convertible bond with the risk-return characteristics of ownership of the underlying common stock.

CFA® Program Curriculum, Volume 5, page 367

Buying convertible bonds in lieu of stocks limits downside risk. The price floor set by the straight bond value provides this downside protection. The cost of the downside protection is reduced upside potential due to the conversion premium. Keep in mind though, that just like investing in nonconvertible bonds, convertible bond investors must be concerned with credit risk, call risk, interest rate risk, and liquidity risk.

Consider the following two examples based on our previous BSC example.

Example: Risk and return of a convertible bond, part 1

Calculate the return on the convertible bond and the common stock if the market price of BSC common stock increases to $45 per share.

Answer:

The return from investing in the convertible bond is:

$$\left(\frac{\$45.00}{\$39.40}\right)-1=14.21\%$$

The return from investing directly in the stock is:

$$\left(\frac{\$45.00}{\$35.00}\right)-1=0.2857=28.57\%$$

The lower return from the convertible bond investment is attributable to the fact that the investor effectively bought the stock at the market conversion price of $39.40 per share.

Example: Risk and return of a convertible bond, part 2

Calculate the return on the convertible bond and the common stock if the market price of BSC common stock falls to $30 per share.

Answer:

Recall that the bond will trade at the greater of its straight value or its conversion value. The conversion value in this scenario is 25 × $30.00 = $750.00. Assuming the straight value of the bond does not change, the bond will trade at $950.00. So, the return from investing in the convertible bond is:

$$\left(\frac{\$950}{\$985}\right)-1=-3.55\%$$

The return from investing directly in the stock is:

$$\left(\frac{\$30}{\$35}\right)-1=-14.29\%$$

The loss is less for the convertible bond investment because we assumed that the straight value of the bond did not change. Even if it had changed, the loss would probably still be less than the loss on the straight stock investment, thus emphasizing how the straight value serves as a floor to cushion a decline, even if it is a moving floor.

The following comparisons can be made between ownership of the underlying stock and the risk-return characteristics of the convertible bond:

- When the stock's price falls, the returns on convertible bonds exceed those of the stock, because the convertible bond's price has a floor equal to its straight bond value.
- When the stock's price rises, the bond will underperform because of the conversion premium. This is the main drawback of investing in convertible bonds versus investing directly in the stock.
- If the stock's price remains stable, the return on a convertible bond may exceed the stock return due to the coupon payments received from the bond, assuming no change in interest rates or the yield or credit risk of the issuer.

Sometimes the price of the common stock associated with a convertible issue is so low that it has little or no effect on the convertible's market price, and it trades as though it is a straight bond. When this happens, the convertible security is referred to as a *fixed-income equivalent* or *busted convertible*.

Other times, the price of the stock can be high enough that the price of the convertible behaves as though it were an equity security. When this happens, the convertible issue is referred to as a common stock equivalent. Most of the time, however, it is a *hybrid security* with the characteristics of equity and a fixed-income security.

KEY CONCEPTS

LOS 44.a

Relative value analysis of bonds involves comparing the spread on the bond (over some benchmark) to the required spread and determining whether the bond is over or undervalued relative to the benchmark. The required spread is the spread available on comparable securities. Undervalued bonds ("cheap") have spreads larger than the required spread; overvalued bonds ("rich") have spreads smaller than the required spread; and properly valued bonds ("fairly priced") have spreads equal to the required spread.

LOS 44.b

There are three different benchmark interest rates that can be used to calculate spreads: Treasury securities, a specific sector of the bond market with a certain credit rating higher than the issue being valued, or a specific issuer. Our interpretation of a spread calculated for a specific security will depend on the benchmark rates used to create the interest rate tree.

LOS 44.c

Backward induction methodology is a discounting process for valuing bonds with a binomial interest rate tree. "Backward" refers to the process of discounting distant values in a binomial tree, one node at a time, backwards through time to generate a current value.

LOS 44.d

Callable bonds can be valued by modifying the cash flows at each node in the interest rate tree to reflect the cash flow prescribed by the embedded call option according to the call rule.

LOS 44.e

The value of the embedded call option is the difference between the value of a noncallable bond and the value of a callable bond (i.e., $V_{call} = V_{noncallable} - V_{callable}$). Similarly, investors are willing to pay a premium for a putable bond since its holder owns an option-free bond plus a put option. The value of the embedded put option can be stated as $V_{put} = V_{putable} - V_{nonputable}$.

LOS 44.f

The value of an embedded option increases as volatility increases. This can be explained by recalling that the upside price of a callable bond is capped at the call price. As volatility increases, the upside prices in the binomial tree will not rise above the call price, but the downside prices will fall. This means that the callable bond value will fall as volatility rises. However, the arbitrage-free value of the noncallable bond will be unaffected by the increased volatility. Therefore, as volatility increases, the value of the call will increase.

LOS 44.g
Relative OAS Valuation

	Treasury Benchmark	*Sector Benchmark*	*Issuer-Specific Benchmark*
OAS > 0	Overvalued if actual OAS < required OAS; Undervalued if actual OAS > required OAS	Overvalued if actual OAS < required OAS; Undervalued if actual OAS > required OAS	Undervalued
OAS = 0	Overvalued	Overvalued	Fairly priced
OAS < 0	Overvalued	Overvalued	Overvalued

LOS 44.h
The binomial model can be used to compute the value of bonds with embedded options in the equations for effective duration and convexity. The general procedure for calculating $BV_{+\Delta y}$ (and $BV_{-\Delta y}$) is as follows:

Step 1: Given assumptions about benchmark interest rates, interest rate volatility, and a call and/or put rule, calculate the OAS for the issue using the binomial model.
Step 2: Impose a small parallel shift in the on-the-run yield curve by an amount equal to $+\Delta y$.
Step 3: Build a new binomial interest rate tree using the new yield curve.
Step 4: Add the OAS to each of the 1-year rates in the interest rate tree to get a *modified* tree. (We assume that the OAS does not change when interest rates change.)
Step 5: Compute $BV_{+\Delta y}$ using this modified interest rate tree.
Step 6: Repeat steps 2 through 5 using a parallel rate shift of $-\Delta y$ to obtain a value of $BV_{-\Delta y}$.

LOS 44.i
Putable bonds are valued using the same procedure as for a callable bond, except that the relevant cash flows are dictated by the rules governing the exercise of the embedded put option. The value of a putable bond is given by: $V_{putable} = V_{nonputable} + V_{put}$. The value of the embedded put option is: $V_{put} = V_{putable} - V_{nonputable}$.

LOS 44.j
The owner of a convertible bond can exchange the bond for the common shares of the issuer. A convertible bond includes an embedded call option giving the bondholder the right to buy the common stock of the issuer. Almost all convertible bonds are callable, and some convertible issues are putable.

The conversion ratio is the number of common shares for which a convertible bond can be exchanged.

The conversion price is the issue price divided by the conversion ratio. Conversion value is the value of the stock into which the bond can be converted. Conversion value = market price of stock × conversion ratio.

Straight value is the value of the bond if it were not convertible.

Market conversion price is the price that a convertible bondholder would effectively pay if the bond were purchased and immediately converted. Market conversion price = market price of convertible bond/conversion ratio.

Market conversion premium per share is the difference between the market conversion price and the current market price. It can also be expressed as the ratio of conversion price to market price, called the conversion premium ratio:

market conversion premium per share = market conversion price – market price

The coupon income from a convertible bond usually exceeds the dividend income that would have been realized if the stock were owned directly. The time it takes to recoup the per-share premium via this extra income is known as the premium payback period.

The minimum value at which a convertible bond trades is its straight value or its conversion value, whichever is greater.

Straight value is the usual measure of the downside risk for a convertible bond, because it sets a bond price floor that is independent of stock price.
- Downside risk is often measured using the premium over straight value.
- All other factors held constant, the greater the premium over straight value, the less attractive the convertible bond.

LOS 44.k
The major reason for investing in convertible bonds is the price appreciation resulting from an increase in the value of the common stock.
- The main drawback of investing in a convertible bond versus investing directly in the stock is that when the stock price rises, the bond will underperform because of the conversion premium of the bond.
- If the stock price remains stable, the return on the bond may exceed the stock returns due to the coupon payments received from the bond.
- If the stock price falls, the straight value of the bond limits downside risk. This is based on the assumption that bond yields remain stable.

CONCEPT CHECKERS

1. Which of the following statements concerning the calculation of value at a node in a binomial interest rate tree is *most accurate*? The value at each node is the:
   A. present value of the two possible values from the next period.
   B. average of the present values of the two possible values from the next period.
   C. sum of the present values of the two possible values from the next period.

2. An increase in interest rate volatility:
   A. increases the value of bonds with embedded call options.
   B. increases the value of bonds with embedded put options.
   C. increases the value of low-coupon bonds with embedded options, but decreases the value of high-coupon bonds with embedded options.

3. The option-adjusted spread (OAS) on a callable corporate bond is 73 basis points using on-the-run Treasuries as the benchmark rates in the construction of the binomial tree. The best interpretation of this OAS is the:
   A. cost of the embedded option is 73 basis points.
   B. cost of the option is 73 basis points over Treasury.
   C. spread that reflects the credit risk and liquidity risk is 73 basis points over Treasury.

4. An analyst has gathered the following information on a convertible bond and the common equity of the issuer.
   - Market price of bond: $925.00
   - Annual coupon: 7.5%
   - Conversion ratio: 30
   - Market price of stock: $28.50
   - Annual stock dividend: $2.15 per share

   The premium payback period for the convertible bond is *closest* to:
   A. 4.85 years.
   B. 5.29 years.
   C. 6.67 years.

5. Which of the following statements concerning the comparison between the risk and return of convertible bond investing and common stock investing is *least accurate,* assuming interest rates are stable?
   A. When stock prices fall, the returns on convertible bonds may exceed those of the stock because the convertible bond's price has a floor equal to the straight bond value.
   B. The main drawback of investing in convertible bonds versus direct stock purchases is that when stock prices rise, the convertible bond will likely underperform due to the conversion premium.
   C. Buying convertible bonds in lieu of direct stock investing limits upside potential to that of buying a straight bond at the cost of increased downside risk due to the conversion premium.

6. Which of the following statements concerning the option-adjusted spread (OAS) is *least accurate*?
   A. The OAS is the interest rate spread that must be added to all of the 1-year forward rates in the binomial tree so that the arbitrage-free value of a bond generated by the tree is equal to its market price.
   B. The OAS reflects credit and/or liquidity risk differences between the bond and the benchmark securities used to create the interest rate tree.
   C. The OAS is equal to the *Z*-spread plus the cost of the embedded option.

7. A convertible bond with a 9% annual coupon is currently selling for $1,073 with a conversion ratio of 30 and a straight value of $1,031. Assume that the common stock pays a $1.25 dividend and is currently selling for $32. The premium payback period is *closest* to:
   A. 2.64 years.
   B. 3.09 years.
   C. 2.15 years.

8. The difference between the value of a callable convertible bond and the value of an otherwise comparable option-free bond is *closest* to the value of the:
   A. call option on the stock minus value of the call option on the bond.
   B. put option on the stock plus value of the call option on the bond.
   C. call option on the stock plus value of call option on the bond.

9. With respect to the value of a callable convertible bond, what are the *most likely* effects of a decrease in interest rate volatility or a decrease in the underlying stock price volatility?
   A. Both will result in an increase in value.
   B. One will result in an increase in value, the other a decrease.
   C. Both will result in a decrease in value.

CHALLENGE PROBLEMS

10. Data on two convertible bonds are shown in the following table.

	Convertible Bond ABC	*Convertible Bond XYZ*
Conversion price	$40	$50
Current stock price	$123	$8

Which factors are *more likely* to influence the market prices of ABC and XYZ: factors that affect equity prices, or factors that affect option-free bond prices?
   A. Both will be more affected by equity factors.
   B. One will be more affected by equity factors, the other by bond factors.
   C. Both will be more affected by bond factors.

11. Ron Hyatt has been asked to do a presentation on how effective duration (ED) and effective convexity (EC) are calculated with a binomial model. His presentation includes the following formulas:

$$\text{effective duration} = \text{ED} = \frac{BV_{+\Delta y} - BV_{-\Delta y}}{2 \times BV_0 \times \Delta y}$$

$$\text{effective convexity} = \text{EC} = \frac{BV_{+\Delta y} + BV_{-\Delta y} - (2 \times BV_0)}{2 \times BV_0 \times \Delta y^2}$$

where:
Δy = change in required yield, in decimal form
$BV_{-\Delta y}$ = estimated price if yield decreases by Δy
$BV_{+\Delta y}$ = estimated price if yield increases by Δy
BV_0 = initial observed bond price

Are Hyatt's formulas for effective duration and effective convexity correctly presented?
A. The formulas are both correct.
B. One formula is correct, the other incorrect.
C. Both formulas are incorrect.

Use the following binomial interest rate tree to answer Questions 12 through 14.

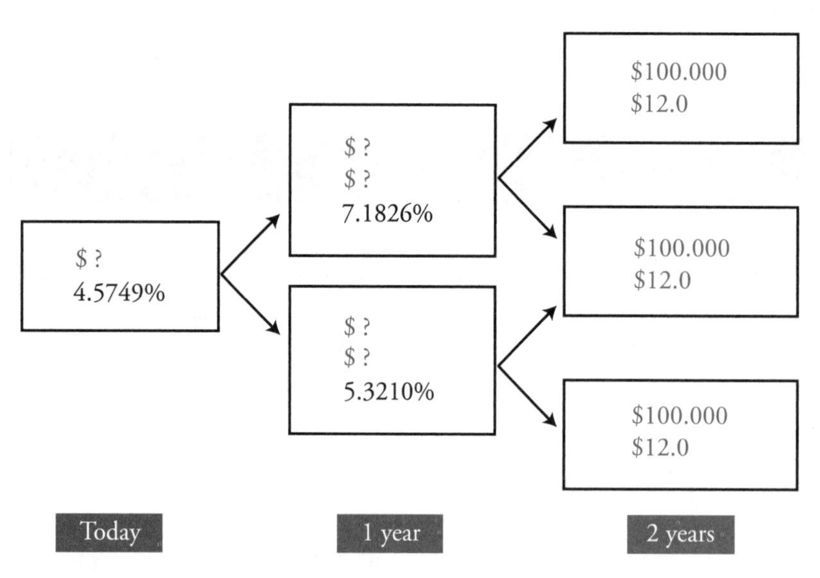

12. The value today of an option-free, 12% annual coupon bond with two years remaining until maturity is *closest* to:
A. 111.485.
B. 112.282.
C. 113.394.

13. The value of the bond and the value of the embedded call option, assuming the bond in Question 12 is callable at $105 at the end of Year 1, are *closest* to:

	Callable bond value	Embedded call option value
A.	110.573	1.709
B.	110.573	0.642
C.	111.640	0.642

14. The value of the bond and the value of the embedded put option, assuming the bond in Question 12 is putable at $105 at the end of Year 1, are *closest* to:

	Putable bond value	Embedded put option value
A.	112.523	0.241
B.	112.523	1.646
C.	113.928	1.646

15. Spamaloan, Inc., has issued a bond with an embedded call option that has been rated single A. Using the AA-rated bond sector as the benchmark, the bond's nominal spread is 60 basis points, the *Z*-spread is 45 points, and the option-adjusted spread (OAS) is 30 points. The nominal spread relative to the same benchmark on otherwise comparable option-free single A bonds with the same liquidity and maturity is 50 basis points. The OAS relative to the AA benchmark on other single A corporate bonds is 20 basis points. The Spamaloan bond is:
A. undervalued because its OAS is greater than the required OAS.
B. undervalued because its nominal spread is greater than the required nominal spread.
C. overvalued because its OAS is greater than the required OAS.

ANSWERS – CONCEPT CHECKERS

1. **B** The value at any given node in a binomial tree is the present value of the cash flows at the two possible states immediately to the right of the given node, discounted at the 1-period rate at the node under examination.

2. **B** Like ordinary options, the value of an embedded option increases as volatility increases. Furthermore, the arbitrage-free value of an option-free bond ($V_{option\text{-}free}$) is independent of the assumed volatility. This implies that the arbitrage-free value of a callable bond ($V_{callable}$) decreases as volatility increases the value of the embedded call option (V_{call}). This can be seen from the expression for the value of a callable bond:

   $$\downarrow V_{callable} = V_{option\text{-}free} - \uparrow V_{call}$$

   The value of the putable bond ($V_{putable}$) increases as the assumed volatility increases the value of the embedded put option (V_{put}).

   $$\uparrow V_{putable} = V_{option\text{-}free} + \uparrow V_{put}$$

3. **C** Let's construct a table of the risk differences between the issuer's callable bond and on-the-run Treasuries to help us answer this question.

Type of Risk	*Equal?*
Credit	No
Liquidity	No
Option	Removed by OAS

   Therefore, the OAS reflects the additional credit and liquidity risk of the corporate callable bond over Treasuries, since option risk has been removed.

4. **C** The premium payback period can be determined using the following formula:

   $$\text{premium payback period} = \frac{\text{market conversion premium per share}}{\text{favorable income difference per share}}$$

   The market conversion premium per share is the market conversion price per share minus the market price per share. The market conversion price per share is $\frac{925.00}{30} = \$30.833$, so the conversion premium per share is \$30.833 – \$28.50 = \$2.333.

   The per share coupon payment from the bond is the annual coupon divided by the conversion ratio, or $\frac{\$75.00}{30} = \$2.50$ per share. Since the stock dividend is \$2.15 per share, the favorable income difference per share is \$2.50 – \$2.15 = \$0.35.

   Thus, the premium payback period is $\frac{\$2.333}{\$0.35} = 6.67$ years.

5. C Buying convertible bonds in lieu of direct stock investing limits downside risk to that of straight bond investing at the cost of reduced upside potential, due to the conversion premium. Note that this analysis assumes that interest rates remain stable. Otherwise, the interest rate risk associated with the straight bond investing must be considered. When stock prices fall, the returns on convertible bonds may exceed those of the stock, because the convertible bond's price has a floor equal to the straight bond value. The main drawback of investing in convertible bonds versus direct stock purchases is that when stock prices rise, the convertible bond will likely underperform due to the conversion premium. If the stock price remains stable, the return on the bond may exceed the stock's return if the bond's coupon payment exceeds the dividend income of the stock.

6. C The OAS is equal to the *Z*-spread less the cost of the embedded option.

7. C First determine the market conversion price, as:

$$\frac{\$1{,}073}{30} = \$35.77$$

Next determine the market conversion premium per share, as:

$$\$35.77 - \$32.00 = \$3.77$$

Then determine the income difference per share, as $\frac{\$90 - (30 \times \$1.25)}{30} = \$1.75$.

The premium payback period is then $\frac{\$3.77}{\$1.75} = 2.15$ years.

8. A A bond that is both callable and convertible contains two embedded options: (1) a call option on the stock and (2) a call option on the bond. The investor has a short position in the call option on the bond (the issuer has the right to call the bond) and a long position in the call option on the stock (the investor has the right to convert the bond into shares of stock). Therefore, the difference in value between the callable convertible bond and the value of the comparable option-free bond to the investor is equal to the value of the call option on the stock minus the value of the call option on the bond.

9. B A decrease in interest rate volatility will decrease the value of the embedded short call on the bond (but have no effect on the value of the embedded call on the stock) and increase the value of the convertible bond.

A decrease in stock price volatility will decrease the value of the embedded call on the stock (but have no effect on the embedded call on the bond) and decrease the value of the convertible bond.

ANSWERS – CHALLENGE PROBLEMS

10. **B** ABC has a conversion price much less than the current stock price, so the conversion option is deep-in-the-money. Bond ABC effectively trades like equity and is more likely to be influenced by the same factors that affect equity prices, in general, rather than the factors that affect bond prices.

    A busted convertible like XYZ, with a stock price significantly less than the conversion price, trades like a bond (that's why a busted convertible is also called a fixed-income equivalent) and is therefore more likely to be influenced by the factors that affect bond prices.

11. **B** The numerator of the effective duration formula is presented incorrectly. The numerator should be the bond price if the yield decreases by Δy ($BV_{-\Delta y}$) minus the bond price if the yield increases by Δy ($BV_{+\Delta y}$). Bond price increases when yield falls for an option-free bond, and vice versa, so $BV_{-\Delta y}$ will be larger than $BV_{+\Delta y}$ and the numerator will be positive for an option-free bond. Hyatt has switched the order in his presentation of the effective duration formula, which will yield a negative effective duration measure for an option-free bond. The convexity formula is presented correctly, even though the typical order of the first two terms in the numerator is reversed; note that $BV_{+\Delta y} + BV_{-\Delta y}$ is equal to $BV_{-\Delta y} + BV_{+\Delta y}$. We were just trying to make sure you hadn't fallen asleep!

12. **B** The tree should look like this:

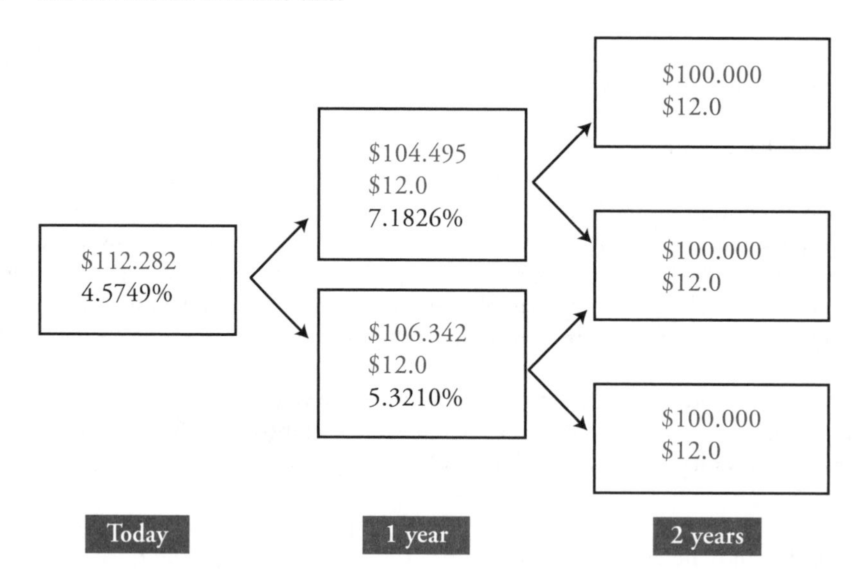

Consider the value of the bond at the upper node for Period 1, $V_{1,U}$:

$$V_{1,U} = \frac{1}{2} \times \left[\frac{\$100 + \$12}{1.071826} + \frac{\$100 + \$12}{1.071826} \right] = \$104.495$$

Similarly, the value of the bond at the lower node for Period 1, $V_{1,L}$ is:

$$V_{1,L} = \frac{1}{2} \times \left[\frac{\$100 + \$12}{1.053210} + \frac{\$100 + \$12}{1.053210} \right] = \$106.342$$

Now calculate V_0, the current value of the bond at Node 0:

$$V_0 = \frac{1}{2} \times \left[\frac{\$104.495 + \$12}{1.045749} + \frac{\$106.342 + \$12}{1.045749} \right] = \$112.282$$

13. C The tree should look like this:

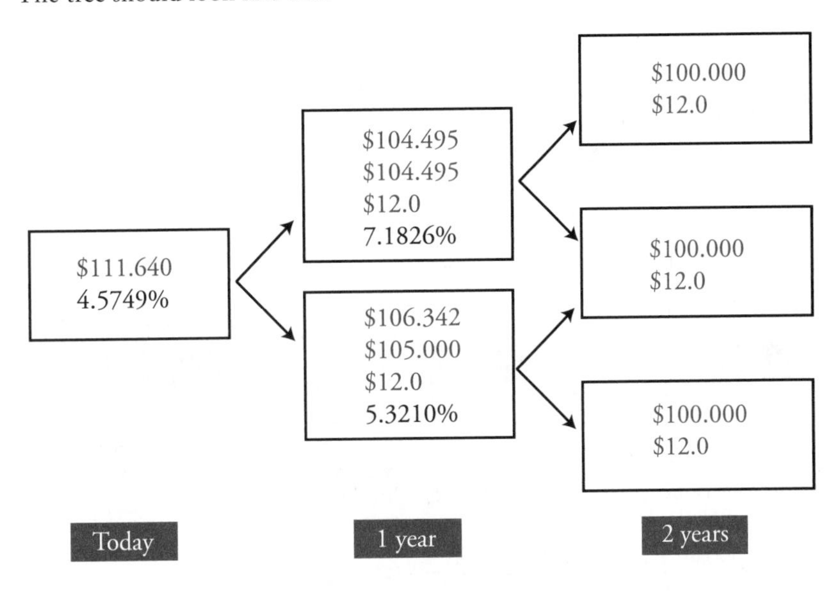

Consider the value of the bond at the upper node for Period 1, $V_{1,U}$:

$$V_{1,U} = \frac{1}{2} \times \left[\frac{\$100 + \$12}{1.071826} + \frac{\$100 + \$12}{1.071826} \right] = \$104.495$$

Similarly, the value of the bond at the lower node for Period 1, $V_{1,L}$ is:

$$V_{1,L} = \frac{1}{2} \times \left[\frac{\$100 + \$12}{1.053210} + \frac{\$100 + \$12}{1.053210} \right] = \$106.342$$

Now calculate V_0, the current value of the bond at Node 0:

$$V_0 = \frac{1}{2} \times \left[\frac{\$104.495 + \$12}{1.045749} + \frac{\$105.00 + \$12}{1.045749} \right] = \$111.640$$

The value of the embedded call option is $112.282 – $111.640 = $0.642.

14. **A** The tree should look like this:

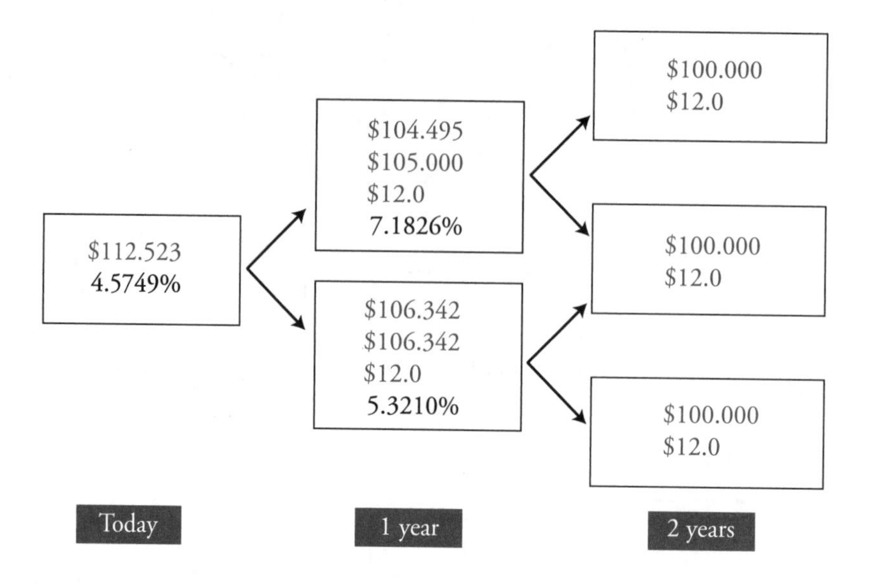

Consider the value of the bond at the *upper* node for Period 1, $V_{1,U}$:

$$V_{1,U} = \frac{1}{2} \times \left[\frac{\$100 + \$12}{1.071826} + \frac{\$100 + \$12}{1.071826} \right] = \$104.495$$

Similarly, the value of the bond at the lower node for Period 1, $V_{1,L}$, is:

$$V_{1,L} = \frac{1}{2} \times \left[\frac{\$100 + \$12}{1.053210} + \frac{\$100 + \$12}{1.053210} \right] = \$106.342$$

Now calculate V_0, the current value of the bond at Node 0:

$$V_0 = \frac{1}{2} \times \left[\frac{\$105.000 + \$12}{1.045749} + \frac{\$106.342 + \$12}{1.045749} \right] = \$112.523$$

The value of the embedded put option is \$112.523 – \$112.282 = \$0.241.

15. **A** The required OAS on the Spamaloan bond is the OAS relative to the AA benchmark on other single A corporate bonds, which is 20 basis points. The Spamaloan bond is undervalued because its OAS of 30 basis points is greater than the required OAS of 20 basis points.

The following is a review of the Fixed Income: Structured Securities principles designed to address the learning outcome statements set forth by CFA Institute. This topic is also covered in:

MORTGAGE-BACKED SECTOR OF THE BOND MARKET

Study Session 15

EXAM FOCUS

Mortgage-backed securities are securities backed by pools of residential or commercial mortgage loans. They include mortgage passthrough securities, collateralized mortgage obligations, and stripped mortgage-backed securities. Because the underlying mortgages can be prepaid, prepayment risk is a major concern for mortgage-backed security investors. Make sure you understand the relative prepayment risk exposure of the various collateralized mortgage obligation tranches (e.g., sequential, planned amortization class, and support tranches), as well as interest-only and principal-only strips. Also pay attention to the unique features and issues related to commercial mortgage-backed securities.

LOS 45.a: Describe a mortgage loan, and explain the cash flow characteristics of a fixed-rate, level payment, and fully amortized mortgage loan.

CFA® Program Curriculum, Volume 5, page 395

A mortgage is a loan that is collateralized with a specific piece of real property, either residential or commercial. The borrower must make a series of mortgage payments over the life of the loan, and the lender has the right to *foreclose* or lay claim against the real estate in the event of loan default. The interest rate on the loan is called the **mortgage rate** or **contract rate**.

A **conventional mortgage** is the most common residential mortgage. The loan is based on the creditworthiness of the borrower and is collateralized by the residential real estate that it is used to purchase. If a borrower's credit quality is questionable or the borrower is lacking a sufficient down payment, the mortgage lender may require mortgage insurance to guarantee the loan. Mortgage insurance is made available by both government agencies and private insurers. The cost of the insurance is borne by the borrower and effectively raises the interest rate on the mortgage loan.

There are a wide variety of mortgage designs that specify the rates, terms, amortization, and repayment methods. All of the concepts associated with risk analysis and valuation, however, can be understood through an examination of **fixed-rate, level payment, fully amortized mortgage loans**. This common type of mortgage loan requires equal payments (usually monthly) over the life of the mortgage. Each of these payments consists of an interest component and a principal component.

There are four important features of fixed-rate, level payment, fully amortized mortgage loans to remember when we move on to mortgage-backed securities (MBS):

1. The amount of the principal payment increases as time passes.
2. The amount of interest decreases as time passes.
3. The servicing fee also declines as time passes.
4. The ability of the borrower to prepay results in **prepayment risk.** Prepayments and curtailments reduce the amount of interest the lender receives over the life of the mortgage and cause the principal to be repaid sooner.

Example: Calculating a mortgage payment

Consider a 30-year, $500,000 level payment, fully amortized mortgage with a fixed rate of 12%. Calculate the monthly payment and prepare an amortization schedule for the first three months.

Answer:

The monthly payment is $5,143.06:

N = 360; I/Y = 1.0 (12/12); PV = –500,000; FV = 0; CPT → PMT = 5,143.06

With reference to the partial amortization schedule in the figure below, the portion of the first payment that represents interest is $5,000.00 (0.01 × $500,000). The remainder of the payment, $143.06 ($5,143.06 – $5,000.00), goes toward the reduction of principal. The portion of the second payment that represents interest is $4,998.57 (0.01 × $499,856.94). The remaining $144.49 ($5,143.06 – $4,998.57) goes toward the further reduction of principal.

Monthly Amortization Schedule for a 30-Year, $500,000 Mortgage Loan at 12%

Payment Number	*Initial Principal*	*Monthly Payment*	*Interest Component*	*Reduction of Principal*	*Outstanding Principal*
1	$500,000.00	$5,143.06	$5,000.00	$143.06	$499,856.94
2	499,856.94	5,143.06	4,998.57	144.49	499,712.45
3	499,712.45	5,143.06	4,997.12	145.94	499,566.51

Notice that the monthly interest charge is based on the beginning-of-period outstanding principal. As time passes, the proportion of the monthly payment that represents interest decreases, and, since the payment is level, the proportion that goes toward the repayment of principal increases. This process continues until the outstanding principal reaches zero and the loan is paid in full.

The incremental reduction of outstanding principal is referred to as scheduled amortization (or scheduled principal repayment). The figure above is a portion of what is commonly called an amortization schedule. Amortization schedules are easily constructed using an electronic spreadsheet. Also, your business calculator will compute the interest and principal components of any payment and the outstanding loan balance. The procedure is described in the calculator's guidebook.

The collection of payments and all of the other administrative activities associated with mortgage loans are paid for via a **servicing fee**, also known as the servicing spread, because it is usually built into the mortgage rate.

For example, if the mortgage rate is 10.5% and the servicing fee is 35 basis points, the provider of the mortgage funds will receive 10.15%. This amount is called the net interest or net coupon. The dollar amount of the servicing fee is based on the outstanding loan balance; thus, it declines as the mortgage is amortized.

Prepayment Risk

In the previous example, it was assumed that the borrower paid the exact amount of the monthly payment, and the interest and principal followed the amortization schedule. It is possible, however, for a borrower to pay an amount in excess of the required payment or even to pay off the loan entirely. Payments in excess of the required monthly amount are called **prepayments**, and prepayments for less than the outstanding principal balance are called **curtailments**.

Keep in mind that interest paid by the borrower (and received by the lender) is based on the outstanding principal at the beginning of each payment period. Thus, prepayments or curtailments will reduce the amount of interest the lender receives over the life of the loan. The likelihood of this situation actually occurring is very real and is known as **prepayment risk**. In order to reduce prepayment risk, some mortgages have prepayment penalties, which are intended to discourage prepayments when interest rates decline. However, residential mortgages in the United States typically do not contain prepayment penalties.

LOS 45.b: Explain investment characteristics, payment characteristics, and risks of mortgage passthrough securities.

CFA® Program Curriculum, Volume 5, page 398

A **mortgage passthrough security** represents a claim against a pool of mortgages. Any number of mortgages may be used to form the pool, and any mortgage included in the pool is referred to as a **securitized mortgage**. The mortgages in the pool have different maturities and different mortgage rates. The **weighted average maturity** (WAM) of the pool is equal to the weighted average of all the mortgages in the pool, each weighted by the relative outstanding mortgage balance to the value of the entire pool. The **weighted average coupon** (WAC) of the pool is the weighted average of the mortgage rates in the pool. The investment characteristics of a mortgage passthrough are a function of its cash flow features and the strength of its government guarantee.

As illustrated in Figure 1, passthrough security investors receive the monthly cash flows generated by the underlying pool of mortgages, less any servicing and guarantee/insurance fees. The fees account for the fact that **passthrough rates** (i.e., the coupon rate on the passthrough) are less than the average coupon rate of the underlying mortgages in the pool.

Figure 1: Mortgage Passthrough Cash Flow

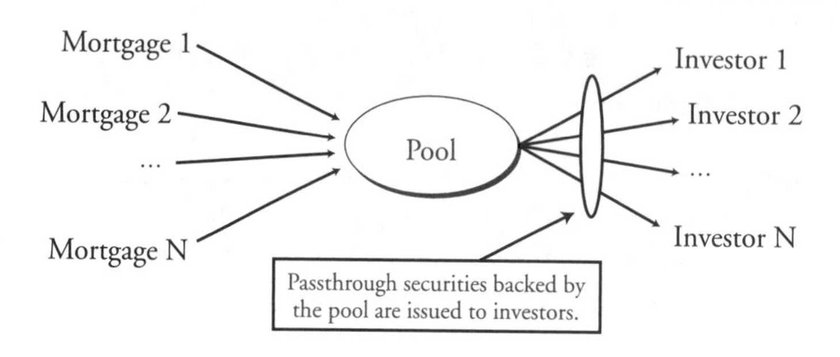

Since passthrough securities may be traded in the secondary market, they effectively convert illiquid mortgages into liquid securities (this process is called **securitization**). As we will see later, more than one class of passthrough securities may be issued against a single mortgage pool.

The timing of the cash flows to passthrough security holders does not exactly coincide with the cash flows generated by the pool. This is due to the delay between the time the mortgage service provider receives the mortgage payments and the time the cash flows are *passed through* to the security holders.

The three major types of agency passthrough securities issued in the United States are:

1. *Ginnie Mae*. Issued by the Government National Mortgage Association (GNMA), an agency of the U.S. government under the Department of Housing and Urban Development. Thus, its guarantee is backed by the full faith and credit of the U.S. government, and there is no credit risk.

2. *Freddie Mac*. Issued by the Federal Home Loan Mortgage Corporation (FHLMC).

3. *Fannie Mae*. Issued by the Federal National Mortgage Association (FNMA).

The securities issued by all three of these entities are referred to as agency passthrough securities. However, FHLMC and FNMA are not truly government agencies, but government-sponsored enterprises originally created by the U.S. government. Thus, a guarantee from Freddie or Fannie is not backed by the full faith and credit of the U.S. government, but they are considered to be of very high credit quality.

The most important characteristic of passthrough securities is their prepayment risk; because the mortgages used as collateral for the passthrough can be prepaid, the passthroughs themselves have significant prepayment risk. Most of this topic review deals specifically with the prepayment risk in passthroughs: how to measure prepayment speeds, the factors that affect prepayment speeds, and how to create securities collateralized by passthroughs that have different levels of prepayment risk and are therefore more attractive to investors.

LOS 45.d: Compare the conditional prepayment rate (CPR) with the Public Securities Association (PSA) prepayment benchmark.

CFA® Program Curriculum, Volume 5, page 402

Prepayments cause the timing and amount of cash flows from mortgage loans and MBS to be uncertain; they speed up principal repayments and reduce the amount of interest paid over the life of the mortgage. Thus, it is necessary to make specific assumptions about the rate at which prepayment of the pooled mortgages occurs when valuing passthrough securities. Two industry conventions have been adopted as benchmarks for prepayment rates: the **conditional prepayment rate** (CPR) and the **Public Securities Association** (PSA) prepayment benchmark.

The *CPR* is the annual rate at which a mortgage pool balance is assumed to be prepaid during the life of the pool. A mortgage pool's CPR is a function of past prepayment rates and expected future economic conditions.

We can convert the CPR into a monthly prepayment rate called the **single monthly mortality rate** (SMM) using the following formula:

$$\text{SMM} = 1 - (1 - \text{CPR})^{1/12}$$

An SMM of 10% implies that 10% of a pool's beginning-of-month outstanding balance, less scheduled payments, will be prepaid during the month.

The *PSA prepayment benchmark* assumes that the monthly prepayment rate for a mortgage pool increases as it ages, or becomes seasoned. The PSA benchmark is expressed as a monthly series of CPRs.

The PSA standard benchmark is referred to as 100% PSA (or just 100 PSA). 100 PSA (see Figure 2) assumes the following graduated CPRs for 30-year mortgages:

- CPR = 0.2% for the first month after origination, increasing by 0.2% per month up to 30 months. For example, the CPR in month 14 is 14 (0.2%) = 2.8%.
- CPR = 6% for months 30 to 360.

Figure 2: 100 PSA

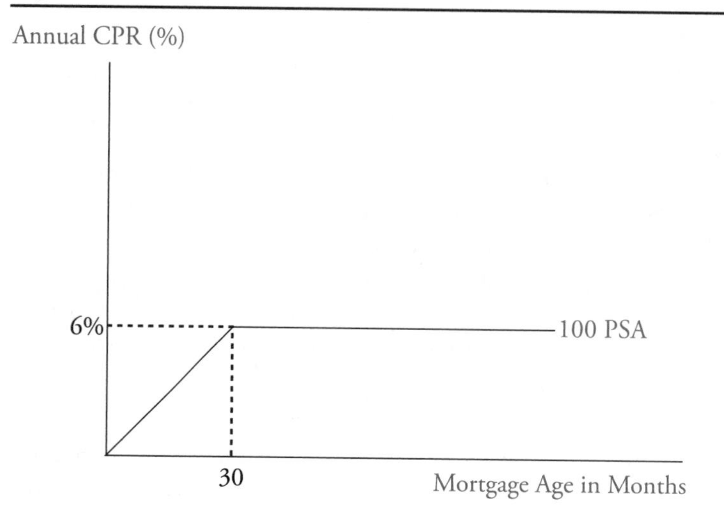

Remember that the CPRs are expressed as annual rates.

A particular pool of mortgages may exhibit prepayment rates faster or slower than 100% PSA, depending on the current level of interest rates and the coupon rate of the issue. A 50% PSA refers to one-half of the CPR prescribed by 100% PSA, and 200% PSA refers to two times the CPR called for by 100% PSA.

The SMM is computed from the CPR. Let's look at an example.

Example: Computing the SMM

Compute the CPR and SMM for the 5th and 25th months, assuming 100 PSA and 150 PSA.

Answer:

Assuming 100 PSA:

$$\text{CPR}(\text{month } 5) = 5 \times 0.2\% = 1\%$$
$$100 \text{ PSA} = 1 \times 0.01 = 0.01$$
$$\text{SMM} = 1 - (1 - 0.01)^{1/12} = 0.000837$$

$$\text{CPR}(\text{month } 25) = 25 \times 0.2\% = 5\%$$
$$100 \text{ PSA} = 1 \times 0.05 = 0.05$$
$$\text{SMM} = 1 - (1 - 0.05)^{1/12} = 0.004265$$

Assuming 150 PSA:

$$\text{CPR}(\text{month } 5) = 5 \times 0.2\% = 1\%$$
$$150 \text{ PSA} = 1.5 \times 0.01 = 0.015$$
$$\text{SMM} = 1 - (1 - 0.015)^{1/12} = 0.001259$$

$$\text{CPR}(\text{month } 25) = 25 \times 0.2\% = 5\%$$
$$150 \text{ PSA} = 1.5 \times 0.05 = 0.075$$
$$\text{SMM} = 1 - (1 - 0.075)^{1/12} = 0.006476$$

Prepayment Speeds for 5th and 25th Months at 100 and 150 PSA

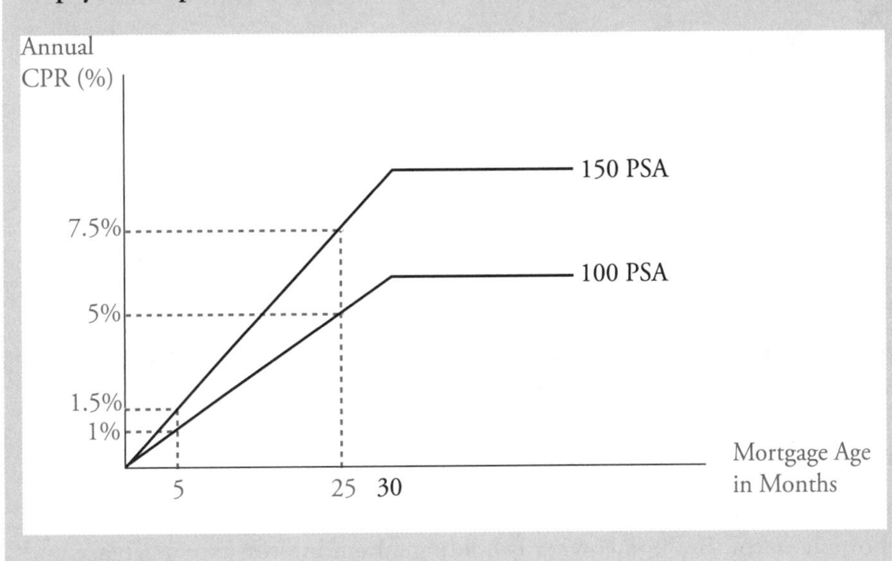

It is important for you to recognize that the nonlinear relationship between CPR and SMM implies that the SMM for 150% PSA does *not* equal 1.5 times the SMM for 100% PSA. Also, keep in mind that the PSA standard benchmark is nothing more than a market convention. It is not a model for predicting prepayment rates for MBS. In fact, empirical studies have shown that actual CPRs differ substantially from those assumed by the PSA benchmark.

LOS 45.c: Calculate the prepayment amount on a mortgage passthrough security for a month, given the single monthly mortality rate.

CFA® Program Curriculum, Volume 5, page 401

The estimated prepayment for any month *m* can be expressed as:

$$\text{Prepayment}_m = \text{SMM}_m \times (\text{mortgage balance at beginning of month m} - \text{scheduled principal payment for month m})$$

Example: Calculating prepayment amount

Assume that you have invested in a mortgage pool with a $100,000 principal balance outstanding at the beginning of the 25th month. The scheduled monthly principal payment for month 25 is $28.61. Borrowing from the previous example, the CPR and SMM, assuming 100 PSA, are 5% and 0.4265%, respectively. Compute the prepayment for the 25th month.

Answer:

This means that 0.4265% of the pool balance, less scheduled payments, will be prepaid this month. So the estimated prepayment amount is:

$$\text{Prepayment}_{25} = (0.004265)(\$100{,}000 - \$28.61) = \$426.38$$

LOS 45.f: Explain factors that affect prepayments and the types of prepayment risks.

CFA® Program Curriculum, Volume 5, page 412

There are *three* main factors that have been shown to affect prepayments: prevailing mortgage rates, housing turnover, and characteristics of the underlying mortgages.

Prevailing mortgage rates affect prepayments by influencing the:

- *Spread between the current mortgage rate and the original mortgage rate.* This is the most important factor. If a homeowner is holding a high interest rate mortgage and current mortgage rates fall, the incentive to refinance is large.
- *Path of mortgage rates.* The path that mortgage rates follow on their way to the current level will affect prepayments today. Consider a mortgage pool that was formed when rates were 12%, then interest rates dropped to 9%, rose to 12%, and then dropped again to 9%. Many homeowners will have refinanced when interest rates dipped the first time. On the second occurrence of 9% interest rates, most homeowners in the pool who were able to refinance would have already taken advantage of the opportunity. This tendency is called **refinancing burnout**.

Housing turnover increases as rates fall and housing becomes more affordable. This increases refinancings and prepayments. Housing turnover is also higher when economic growth is higher. As the level of general economic activity rises, personal income increases, and workers move to pursue career opportunities. The result is an increase in housing turnover and mortgage prepayments.

Two particular *characteristics of the underlying mortgages* also affect the level of prepayments: seasoning (i.e., the age of the loan) and property location. Prepayments are low for new mortgages but increase as the loan seasons (the PSA benchmark reflects this idea). Local economics also influence prepayments, which tend to be faster in some parts of the country and slower in others.

Types of Prepayment Risk

Contraction risk refers to the shortening of the expected life of the mortgage pool due to falling interest rates and higher prepayment rates. There are two undesirable consequences for passthrough investors when interest rates decline:

1. First, MBS exhibit **negative convexity** as rates decline due to the embedded call option granting the mortgage borrower the right to prepay. Hence, the upside price potential of passthrough securities is restricted, because investors receive principal sooner than expected (like a callable bond).

2. The second undesirable outcome is **reinvestment rate risk**. Declining interest rates stimulate prepayments resulting in the earlier-than-expected receipt of principal. This means that investors are faced with having to reinvest at relatively lower rates.

Extension risk is associated with interest rate increases and falling prepayment rates. Bond prices typically fall when interest rates rise. With passthroughs, the accompanying decrease in prepayments compounds this price decline, because the timing of the passthrough cash flows is extended further than originally expected (i.e., the duration of the bond is extended). This is undesirable for mortgage investors, particularly short-term investors, because they would prefer to recapture their principal as soon as possible and reinvest at the current higher rates. Essentially, investors' capital must remain invested at the lower rate.

LOS 45.e: Explain why the average life of a mortgage-backed security is more relevant than the security's maturity.

CFA® Program Curriculum, Volume 5, page 408

Because of contraction and extension risk, the stated maturity of a mortgage passthrough security is unlikely to equal its true life. Instead, investors calculate **average life** (weighted average life), which is the weighted average time until both scheduled principal payments and expected prepayments are received. It's similar to Macaulay duration, except time is weighted by the projected principal to be received at time t, rather than the *present value* of the projected principal.

Remember that contraction and extension risk are functions of the security's average life:

- Contraction risk occurs as mortgage rates fall, prepayment rates increase, and the average life of the passthrough security decreases.
- Extension risk occurs as mortgage rates rise, prepayment rates slow, and the average life of the passthrough security increases.

LOS 45.g: Explain how a collateralized mortgage obligation (CMO) is created and how it provides a better matching of assets and liabilities for institutional investors.

CFA® Program Curriculum, Volume 5, page 412

Institutional investors have varying degrees of concern about exposure to prepayment risk. Some are primarily concerned with extension risk, while others want to minimize exposure to contraction risk. Fortunately, all of the passthrough securities issued on a pool of mortgages do not have to be the same. The ability to partition and distribute the cash flows generated by a mortgage pool into different risk packages has led to the creation of **collateralized mortgage obligations** (CMOs).

CMOs are securities issued against passthrough securities (i.e., they are securities secured by other securities) for which the cash flows have been reallocated to different bond classes called **tranches**, each having a different claim against the cash flows of the mortgage passthroughs or pool from which they were derived. Each CMO tranche represents a different mixture of contraction and extension risk. Hence, CMO securities can be more closely matched to the unique asset/liability needs of institutional investors and investment managers.

It is important to note that the redistribution of the original passthrough securities' cash flows does not eliminate contraction and extension risk. It merely repackages these risks and apportions them to different classes of bondholders. However, the distribution of these risks to investors most able to deal with a specific type of risk enhances the investment value of the mortgage pool.

LOS 45.h: Distinguish among the sequential pay tranche, the accrual tranche, the planned amortization class tranche, and the support tranche in a CMO.

CFA® Program Curriculum, Volume 5, page 413

Sequential Pay CMO

A popular arrangement for separating the cash flows from a mortgage pool is a **sequential pay CMO**, in which each class of bonds is retired sequentially. To illustrate, consider a simple CMO structure with two tranches in which both tranches receive interest payments at a specified coupon rate, but all principal payments are directed to tranche one until it is completely amortized (the *short tranche*). Principal payments would then accrue to Tranche 2 until it was fully amortized and the underlying pool was exhausted.

Contraction and extension risk still exist with this structure, but they have been redistributed to some extent between the two tranches. The short tranche, which matures first, offers investors relatively more protection against extension risk. The other tranche provides relatively more protection against contraction risk. Let's expand this example with some specific numbers to illustrate how sequential pay structures work.

Consider the simplified CMO structure presented in Figure 3. Payments to the two sequential-pay tranches are made first to Tranche A and then to Tranche B.

Figure 3: Sequential Pay CMO Structure

	CMO Structure	
Tranche	*Outstanding Par Value*	*Coupon Rate*
A	$200,000,000	8.50%
B	50,000,000	8.50%

Payments from the underlying collateral (which has a passthrough coupon rate of 8.5%) for the first five months, as well as months 183 through 187, are shown in Figure 4. These payments include scheduled payments plus projected prepayments based on an assumed prepayment speed. *Note: Some totals might not add due to rounding.*

Figure 4: CMO Projected Cash Flows

Month	*Beginning Principal Balance*	*Principal Payment*	*Interest*	*Total Cash Flow = Principal Plus Interest*
1	$250,000,000	$391,128	$1,770,833	$2,161,961
2	249,608,872	454,790	1,768,063	2,222,853
3	249,154,082	518,304	1,764,841	2,283,145
4	248,635,778	581,620	1,761,170	2,342,790
5	248,054,157	644,690	1,757,050	2,401,741
183	$51,491,678	$545,153	$364,733	$909,886
184	50,946,525	540,831	360,871	901,702
185	50,405,694	536,542	357,040	893,582
186	49,869,152	532,287	353,240	885,526
187	49,336,866	528,065	349,469	877,534

Professor's Note: This example is provided as an illustration of how a basic CMO is created. The LOS does not require you to do the calculations that underlie the numbers in Figure 4. Concentrate on how the cash flows are allocated to each tranche.

Example: Calculating principal payments on a sequential pay tranche

Calculate the principal payments, ending principal balance, and interest payments to each tranche in the first month using the data in Figure 4.

Answer:

Tranche A gets the entire principal payment as well as its share of the interest. Tranche B only receives interest.

Tranche A principal payment = \$391,128
Tranche A ending principal balance = \$200,000,000 – \$391,128 = \$199,608,872

$$\text{Tranche A interest} = \$200{,}000{,}000 \times \frac{0.085}{12} = \$1{,}416{,}667$$

Tranche B principal payment = \$0
Tranche B ending principal balance = \$50,000,000 – \$0 = \$50,000,000

$$\text{Tranche B interest} = \$50{,}000{,}000 \times \frac{0.085}{12} = \$354{,}167$$

Cash Flow to Sequential Pay Tranches: Month 1

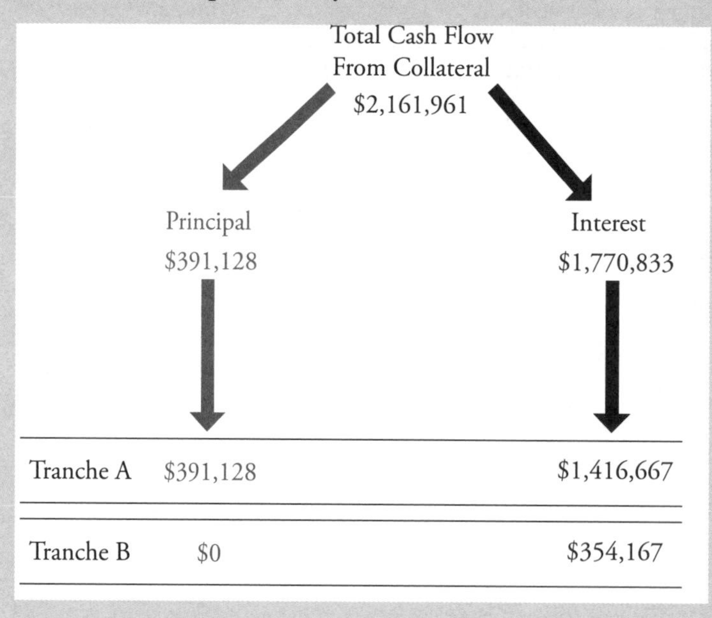

Example: Calculating principal payments – Part 2

Calculate the principal payments, ending principal balance, and interest payments to each tranche in the 185th month, assuming the principal balance of Tranche A is now $405,694.

Answer:

From Figure 4 you can see that the total principal payment is $536,542 and the total interest payment is $357,040. Tranche A receives enough principal to pay off its balance, as well as its share of the interest. Tranche B receives the remaining principal as well as its interest.

$$\text{Tranche A principal payment} = \$405{,}694$$
$$\text{Tranche A ending principal balance} = \$405{,}694 - \$405{,}694 = \$0$$
$$\text{Tranche A interest} = \$405{,}694 \times \frac{0.085}{12} = \$2{,}874$$

$$\text{Tranche B principal payment} = \$536{,}542 - \$405{,}694 = \$130{,}848$$
$$\text{Tranche B ending principal balance} = \$50{,}000{,}000 - \$130{,}848 = \$49{,}869{,}152$$
$$\text{Tranche B interest} = \$50{,}000{,}000 \times \frac{0.085}{12} = \$354{,}167$$

Cash Flow to Sequential Pay Tranche: Month 185

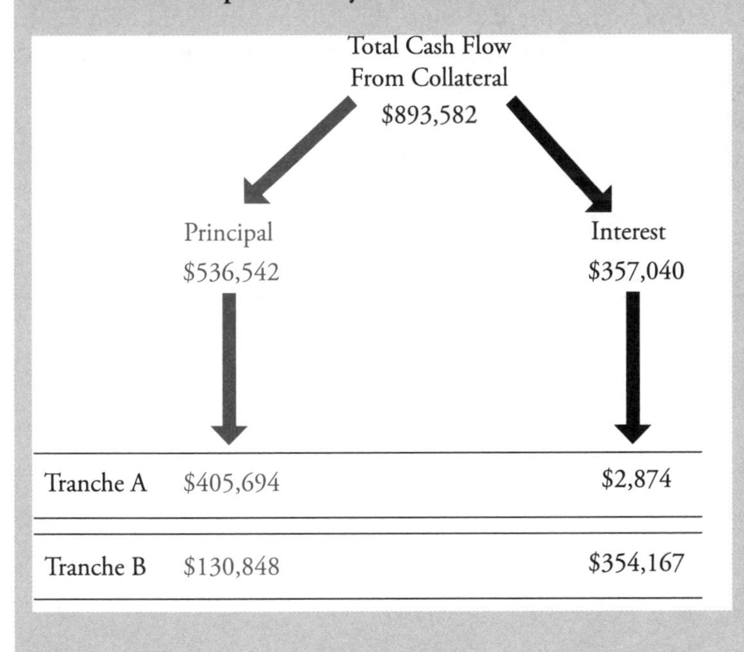

The time period between the first and last principal payments on a CMO tranche is called the **principal pay down window**. The principal pay down window of Tranche A in the previous example is 185 months because the principal balance of Tranche A falls to zero in month 185.

For many sequential-pay CMO structures, the last tranche to receive principal also does not receive current interest until the other tranches have been paid off. This tranche is called the *Z*-**tranche** or **accrual tranche**, and the securities that represent a claim against its cash flows are called *Z*-bonds or accrual bonds. The interest that would ordinarily be paid to the accrual tranche is applied against the outstanding principal of the other tranches, in sequence. The diverted interest from the accrual tranche accrues. That is, it is added to the outstanding principal balance of the *Z*-tranche.

Planned Amortization Class (PAC) CMO

The most common type of CMO today is the **planned amortization class** (PAC). A PAC is a tranche that is amortized based on a sinking fund schedule that is established within a range of prepayment speeds called the **initial PAC collar**.

There are two principal repayment schedules associated with a PAC bond, one for the lower prepayment rate and one for the upper rate of the initial PAC collar. PAC bondholders are guaranteed a principal payment that is equal to the lesser amount prescribed by these two repayment schedules. This *planned amortization* schedule gives the PAC tranche a highly predictable life.

Figure 5 illustrates the planned amortization schedule for a PAC I tranche with an initial collar of 90 PSA to 300 PSA. Notice that the principal payments (which include scheduled payments and prepayments) increase up to month 30 at both prepayment speeds and then slow down. The principal payments at 300 PSA are much higher through the 30 months because of higher prepayments, then decline much more quickly than the 90 PSA after 30 months. After approximately 90 months, principal payments on the 90 PSA begin to exceed the 300 PSA because the higher earlier prepayments under the 300 PSA significantly reduced the outstanding balance. *The planned amortization schedule promised to the PAC I tranche is the minimum of the two prepayment speeds.*

Figure 5: Planned Amortization Schedule for PAC Tranche

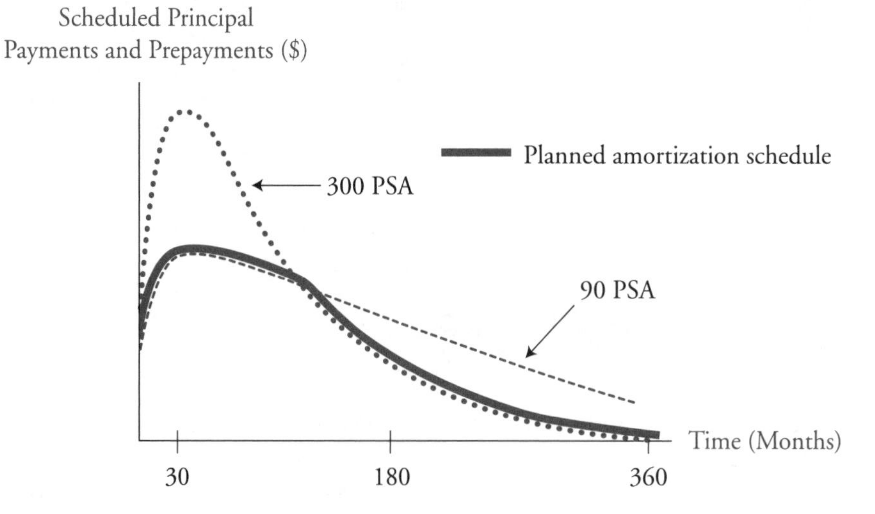

The time period over which principal is expected to be paid on a PAC tranche is called a **PAC window**. The narrower the window, the more the PAC tranche resembles a corporate bond with a bullet payment.

Support Tranche

What makes a PAC bond work is that it is packaged with a **support**, or **companion, tranche** created from the original mortgage pool. Support tranches are included in a structure with PAC tranches specifically to provide prepayment protection for the PAC tranches (each tranche is, of course, priced according to the timing risk of the cash flows). If the prepayment speed of the collateral stays at one level between the lower prepayment rate (90 PSA in Figure 5) and the upper prepayment rate (300 PSA in Figure 5), the principal will be received as scheduled because the support tranche will absorb excess principal or provide principal as needed. If prepayment speeds are outside the initial collar (above 300 or below 90), or even if prepayment speeds vary but stay within the collar, the PAC tranche principal amortization schedule will not necessarily be met. It should be pointed out that the extent of prepayment risk protection provided by a support tranche increases as its par value increases relative to its associated PAC tranche.

There is an inverse relationship between the prepayment risk of PAC tranches and the prepayment risk associated with the support tranches. In other words, *the certainty of PAC bond cash flow comes at the expense of increased risk to the support tranches.*

To understand the relatively high prepayment risk for support tranches, consider the situation where prepayments are slower than planned. Since the PAC tranches have priority claim against the cash flows, principal payments to the support tranches must be deferred until the PAC repayment schedule is satisfied. Thus, the average life of the support tranche is extended. Similarly, when actual prepayments come faster than expected, the support tranches must absorb the amount in excess of that required to maintain the repayment schedule for the PAC. In this case, the average life of the support tranche is contracted. If these excesses continue to occur, the support tranches will eventually be paid off, and the principal will then go to the PAC holders. When this happens, the PAC is referred to as a *broken* or *busted* PAC, and any further prepayments go directly to the PAC tranche. Essentially, the PAC tranche becomes an ordinary sequential-pay structure.

Notice that the prepayment risk protection provided by the support tranches causes their average life to extend and contract. This relationship is such that as the prepayment risk protection for a PAC tranche increases, its average life variability decreases, and the average life variability of the support tranche increases.

For example, Figure 6 shows the average life for a hypothetical structure that includes a PAC I tranche and a support tranche at various PSA speeds, assuming the PSA speed stays at that level for the entire life of the PAC tranche.

Figure 6: Average Life Variability of PAC I Tranche vs. Support Tranche

PSA Speed	*PAC I Tranche*		*Support Tranche*
0	13.2		24.0
50	8.8		21.2
100	6.5	↑	17.1
150	6.5		13.3
200	6.5	Effective Collar	10.4
250	6.5		5.2
300	6.5	↓	2.9
350	5.9		2.4
400	5.4		1.8
450	4.6		1.5
500	4.2		1.2

Figure 6 illustrates the fact that the PAC I tranche has less prepayment risk than the support tranche because the variability of its average life is significantly lower:

- When prepayment speeds fall and prepayments decrease, the support tranche average life is significantly higher than the average life of the PAC I tranche. Thus the support tranche has significantly more extension risk.
- When prepayment speeds rise and prepayments increase, the support tranche average life is much shorter than that of the PAC I tranche. Thus the support tranche also has significantly more contraction risk.
- Over a relatively wide range of prepayment speeds (100 PSA to 300 PSA), the average life of the PAC I tranche is constant at 6.5 years. This range is called the *effective collar.*

Support tranches are usually subdivided into other tranches. Support tranches can also be split to create support tranches that have a schedule for principal payments just like a PAC tranche. Thus, there are CMO PAC tranches with support tranches that have a PAC schedule. The following definitions may help clarify this type of structure.

- **PAC I tranche** (or level I PAC tranche): A PAC structure having a support tranche with a PAC principal repayment schedule.
- **PAC II tranche** (level II PAC tranche or scheduled tranche): The support tranche for a PAC I tranche that has a PAC schedule of principal repayments. PAC II tranches have higher prepayment risk (and average life variability) than PAC I tranches but more prepayment protection (and less average life variability) than support tranches without schedules for principal repayment.

LOS 45.i: Evaluate the risk characteristics and relative performance of each type of CMO tranche, given changes in the interest rate environment.

CFA® Program Curriculum, Volume 5, page 435

Let's repeat something we said earlier:

- Prepayment risk encompasses contraction risk and extension risk.
- Contraction risk occurs as mortgage rates fall, prepayment rates increase, and the average life of the passthrough security decreases.
- Extension risk occurs as mortgage rates rise, prepayment rates slow, and the average life of the passthrough security increases.

CMO structures are designed to redistribute contraction and extension risk among the tranches. The risk characteristics and relative price performance of each CMO tranche is a function of how well protected it is against these risks.

First, let's analyze the contraction and extension risk of a simple sequential pay CMO with four sequential pay tranches (A, B, C, and D) and a one accrual tranche (*Z*-bond).

Figure 7: Contraction and Extension Risk

Tranche	*Contraction Risk*	*Extension Risk*
A (sequential pay)	HIGH	LOW
B (sequential pay)		
C (sequential pay)	↑	↓
D (sequential pay)		
Z (accrual)	LOW	HIGH

The *early* tranches are protected against extension risk, while the later tranches are protected against contraction risk. The *Z*-bond has low contraction risk, because reinvestment risk is eliminated until the other tranches have paid off.

Now let's consider a more realistic CMO structure with four PAC I tranches (A through D), two PAC II tranches (E and F), and an unscheduled support tranche. The PAC I tranches receive principal in order (A first, then B, and so on), as do the PAC II tranches. The support tranche provides support to the PAC tranches. We can characterize the relative prepayment risk of each tranche based on our previous discussions.

Figure 8: Prepayment Risk of PAC Tranches

Tranche	*Prepayment Risk*
A (PAC I)	LOW
B (PAC I)	↓
C (PAC I)	↓
D (PAC I)	↓
E (PAC II)	↓
F (PAC II)	↓
Support	HIGH

Notice the PAC I tranches (which have a specified prepayment collar that limits both contraction and extension risk) have lower prepayment risk than the PAC II tranches, which have lower prepayment risk than the support tranche. Within the PAC I and II tranches, the *early* tranches have lower prepayment risk than the *later* tranches. The unscheduled support tranche absorbs most of the prepayment risk.

LOS 45.j: Explain investment characteristics of stripped mortgage-backed securities.

CFA® Program Curriculum, Volume 5, page 435

A distinguishing characteristic of a traditional passthrough security is that the interest and principal payments generated by the underlying mortgage pool are allocated to the bondholders on a pro rata basis. This means that each passthrough certificate holder receives the same amount of interest and the same amount of principal. **Stripped mortgage-backed securities** differ in that principal and interest are not allocated on a pro rata basis. The unequal allocation of principal and interest results in a price/yield relationship for the stripped securities that is significantly different from that of the underlying passthrough. The two most common types of stripped MBS are **principal-only (PO) strips** and **interest-only (IO) strips**.

POs are a class of securities that receive only the principal payment portion of each mortgage payment. They are sold at a considerable discount to par. The PO cash flow stream starts out small and increases with the passage of time as the principal component of the mortgage payments grows. The entire par value of a PO is ultimately paid to the PO investor. The only question is whether realized prepayment rates will cause it to be paid sooner or later than expected.

IOs are a class that receives only the interest component of each payment. IO strip cash flow starts out big and gets smaller over time. Thus, IOs have shorter effective lives than POs. The major risk associated with IO strips is that the value of the cash flow investors receive over the life of the mortgage pool may be less than initially expected and possibly less than the amount originally invested. Why? The amount of interest produced by the pool depends on its beginning-of-month balance. If market rates fall, the mortgage pool will be paid off sooner than expected, leaving IO investors with no interest cash flows. Therefore, IO investors benefit when prepayments are low.

The price/yield relationships for IO and PO securities are shown in Figure 9. Notice the following *investment characteristics of IOs and POs*:

- The investment performance of a PO is extremely sensitive to prepayment rates. Higher prepayment rates result in a faster-than-expected return of principal and, thus, a higher return. Since prepayment rates increase as mortgage rates decline, PO prices increase when interest rates fall. They also exhibit some negative convexity at low rates.
- The IO price is positively related to mortgage rates at low current rates. When market rates decline below the average mortgage rate in the pool, prepayment rates increase and the principal amount falls. Interest payments to the IO decrease because they are based on the outstanding principal on the underlying pool. The diminished cash flow usually causes the IO price to decline despite the fact that the cash flows are now being discounted at a lower rate. On the other hand, as interest rates rise above the contract rate, the expected cash flows improve. Even though the higher rate must be used to discount these improved cash flows, there is usually a range above the contract rate for which the price increases.
- Both IOs and POs exhibit greater *price volatility* than the passthrough from which they were derived. This occurs because IO and PO returns are negatively correlated (their prices respond in opposite directions to changes in interest rates), but the combined price volatility of the two strips equals the price volatility of the passthrough.

Figure 9: Investment Characteristics of IOs and POs

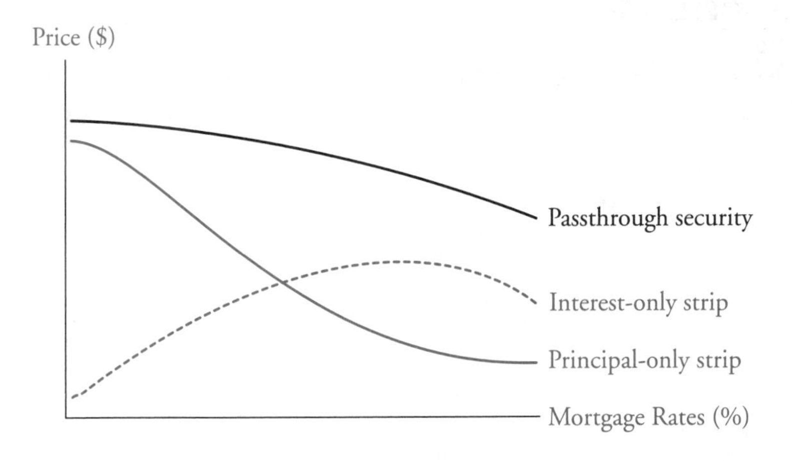

LOS 45.k: Compare agency and nonagency mortgage-backed securities.

CFA® Program Curriculum, Volume 5, page 438

Up to this point, the MBS that we have discussed have been backed by residential mortgage loans issued by agencies of the federal government. There also are MBS that are issued by private entities. These are referred to as **nonagency mortgage-backed securities** or, simply, nonagency securities.

The nonagency securities discussed in this section are backed by a pool of one to four single-family residential first-lien mortgages issued by private entities. However, nonagency securities are sometimes backed by second mortgage loans, manufactured housing loans, and a variety of commercial real estate loans.

The loans that form the mortgage pool for agency securities must conform to the underwriting standards of the issuing or guaranteeing agency. The loans that are used to back nonagency securities are usually those that fail to meet the agency's underwriting standards. These loans are referred to as **nonconforming mortgage loans**. The underwriting standards are primarily concerned with the *maximum* loan-to-value ratio, payment-to-income ratio, and loan amount.

In the agency market, CMOs are formed by splitting up a pool of passthrough securities. However, since it is rare for nonconforming mortgage loans to be securitized, nonagency CMOs are usually created directly from the nonconforming mortgages. Nonagency CMOs are often referred to as **whole-loan CMOs**, because unsecuritized loans are called whole loans. In other words, the collateral behind nonagency CMOs is a pool of loans rather than passthrough securities.

The key difference between agency issued MBS and nonagency issues is that the agency issues are backed by a pseudo-governmental guarantee and, as such, may have a relatively more certain cash flow stream. Consequently, the risk and expected return of agency issues is lower than nonagency issues. Since the cash flows from nonagency securities are affected by mortgage default rates, they require credit enhancement (i.e., additional support against default).

WARM-UP: COMMERCIAL MBS

Commercial mortgage-backed securities (CMBS) are backed by income-producing real estate, typically in the form of:

- Apartments (multi-family).
- Warehouses (industrial use property).
- Shopping centers.
- Office buildings.
- Health care facilities.
- Senior housing.
- Hotel/resort properties.

These loans are typically originated by conduit organizations (commercial mortgage companies). They negotiate and close commercial real estate loans which are then incorporated into a CMBS. Conduit-originated transactions are the most popular way to generate mortgages to securitize. Other, less popular, CMBS structures include liquidating trusts and multi-property single-borrower programs.

LOS 45.l: Compare credit risk analysis of commercial and residential nonagency mortgage-backed securities.

CFA® Program Curriculum, Volume 5, page 440

The biggest difference between residential and commercial MBS loans is the obligation of the underlying borrower. Residential MBS loans are repaid by homeowners; commercial MBS loans are repaid by real estate investors who, in turn, rely on tenants and customers to provide the cash flow to repay the mortgage loan. CMBS mortgages are structured as **nonrecourse loans**, meaning that the lender can *only* look to the collateral as a means to repay a delinquent loan if the cash flows from the property are insufficient. In contrast, the residential mortgage lender can go back to the borrower personally in an attempt to collect a delinquent mortgage loan.

For these reasons, the analysis of CMBS securities focuses on the credit risk of the property and not the credit risk of the borrower. The analysis of CMBS structures focuses on two key ratios to assess credit risk.

1. **Debt-to-service coverage ratio** is a basic cash flow coverage ratio of the amount of cash flow from a commercial property available to make debt service payments.

   $$\text{debt-to-service coverage ratio} = \frac{\text{net operating income}}{\text{debt service}}$$

   Net operating income (NOI) is calculated after the deduction for real estate taxes but before any relevant income taxes. This ratio, which is typically between one and two, provides increased comfort to the lender as it increases. Debt service coverage ratios below one indicate that the borrower is not capable of making the debt payments and is likely to default. Remember: the *higher the better* for this ratio from the perspective of the lender and the MBS investor.

2. **Loan-to-value ratio** compares the loan amount on the property to its current fair market or appraisal value.

   $$\text{loan-to-value ratio} = \frac{\text{current mortgage amount}}{\text{current appraised value}}$$

   The lower this ratio, the more comfortable the mortgage lender is in making the loan. Loan-to-value ratios determine the amount of collateral available, above the loan amount, to provide a cushion to the lender should the property need to be foreclosed on and sold. Remember: *the lower the better* for this ratio from the perspective of the lender and the MBS investor.

LOS 45.m: Describe the basic structure of a commercial mortgage-backed security (CMBS), and explain the ways in which a CMBS investor may realize call protection at the loan level and by means of the CMBS structure.

CFA® Program Curriculum, Volume 5, page 440

The basic **CMBS structure** is created to meet the risk and return needs of the CMBS investor. As with residential MBS securities, rating organizations such as S&P and Moody's assess the credit risk of each CMBS issue and determine the appropriate credit rating. Each CMBS is segregated into tranches that are repaid in a specific sequence with the highest credit quality tranche being repaid first.

As with any fixed income security, call protection for the investor is important. CMBS provide call protection in two ways: loan-level call protection provided by the structure of the individual mortgage, and call protection provided by the CMBS structure.

There are several means of creating **loan-level call protection**:

- *Prepayment lock out.* For a specific period of time (typically two to five years), the borrower is prohibited from prepaying the mortgage loan.
- *Defeasance.* Should the borrower insist on making payments on the mortgage loan, the mortgage loan can be defeased, which means the loan proceeds are received by the loan servicer and invested in U.S. Treasury securities, essentially creating cash collateral against the loan. Upon completion of the defeasance period, these U.S. Treasuries are liquidated and the proceeds are used to repay the mortgage. Treasuries provide higher-quality collateral than the underlying real estate, so defeased loans increase the credit quality of a CMBS loan pool.
- *Prepayment penalty points.* A penalty fee may be charged if the borrower prepays the mortgage loan. This penalty fee is typically much higher in the early years of the loan (e.g., 5% of the loan amount in the first year) and then steps down over time until it finally disappears after several years. In many cases, this penalty fee is quoted as a 5-4-3-2-1, which means the penalty fee is 5% of the principal amount of the loan in the first year, and 1% of the principal amount if repaid in the fifth year of the mortgage. Beginning in the sixth year of the mortgage, there is no prepayment penalty to the borrower.
- *Yield maintenance charges.* The borrower is charged the amount of interest lost by the lender should the loan be prepaid. This *make whole* charge makes the lenders indifferent to prepayment, as they are in the same economic position whether the loan is prepaid or not.

With all loan call protection programs, any prepayment penalties received are distributed to the CMBS investors in a manner determined by the structure of the CMBS issue.

To create **CMBS-level call protection**, CMBS loan pools are segregated into tranches with a specific sequence of repayment. Those tranches with a higher priority for prepayment or collateral position will have a higher credit rating than lower priority tranches because loan defaults will first affect the lower tranches. A wide variety of features can be used to provide call protection to the more senior tranches of the CMBS.

KEY CONCEPTS

LOS 45.a

A mortgage is a loan that is collateralized with a specific piece of real estate, either residential or commercial. The interest rate on the loan is called the mortgage rate, or contract rate.

A fixed-rate, level payment, fully amortized mortgage loan requires equal monthly payments, each consisting of an interest component and a principal component.

- The monthly interest component is based on the amount of outstanding principal at the beginning of the month.
- The incremental reduction of outstanding principal is referred to as scheduled amortization (or scheduled principal repayment).
- A servicing fee is built into the mortgage rate to cover the cost of payment collection and other administrative activities.

Payments in excess of the required monthly amount are called prepayments, and prepayments for less than the outstanding principal balance are called curtailments.

- Prepayments or curtailments will reduce the amount of interest the lender receives over the life of the loan.
- Prepayment risk refers to the likelihood that prepayments or curtailments will actually occur.

LOS 45.b

A mortgage passthrough security represents a claim against a pool of mortgages. Any number of mortgages may be used to form the pool. A mortgage that is included in the pool is called a *securitized mortgage*.

- Passthrough investors receive the monthly cash flows generated by the underlying pool.
- More than one class of passthrough security may be issued against a single mortgage pool, each representing a unique claim on the pool's cash flows.
- The most important characteristic of passthrough securities is their *prepayment risk*; because the mortgages used as collateral for the passthrough can be prepaid, the passthroughs themselves have significant prepayment risk.

LOS 45.c

The single monthly mortality rate (SMM) is derived from the conditional prepayment rate (CPR) and is used to estimate monthly prepayments for a mortgage pool.

- $\text{SMM} = 1 - (1 - \text{CPR})^{1/12}$

The estimated prepayment for any month *m* can be expressed as:

- $\text{Prepayment}_m = \text{SMM} \times$ (mortgage balance at beginning of month *m* – scheduled principal payment for month *m*)

LOS 45.d

CPR and the PSA prepayment benchmark are industry benchmarks for assumed prepayment rates. CPR is the annual rate at which a mortgage pool balance is assumed to be prepaid during the life of the pool. A mortgage pool's CPR is a function of past prepayment rates and economic conditions.

The PSA prepayment benchmark assumes that the monthly prepayment rate for a mortgage pool increases as the mortgage pool ages (becomes seasoned).

- PSA is expressed as a monthly series of CPRs.
- For 30-year mortgages, the 100% PSA standard benchmark is:
  - CPR = 0.2% for the first month, increasing by 0.2% per month up to 30 months.
  - CPR = a flat 6% for months 30–360.

LOS 45.e

Investors calculate average life or weighted average life for passthrough securities since prepayment risk usually results in the stated maturity of a passthrough being different than its actual life.

- As mortgage rates fall, prepayment rates increase, and the average life of a passthrough security decreases.
- As mortgage rates rise, prepayment rates slow, and the average life of a passthrough security increases.

LOS 45.f

Three factors affect prepayments:

- Prevailing mortgage rate.
  - The spread between the current mortgage rate and the original mortgage rate is the most important factor. Historically, if mortgage interest rates fall more than 2%, refinancing activity increases dramatically.
  - The path that mortgage rates follow on their way to the current level will affect prepayments today. When mortgage rates drop, rebound, and drop again, most homeowners have already refinanced. This tendency is called refinancing burnout.
- Housing turnover increases as mortgage rates fall and housing becomes more affordable, and as the general level of economic activity increases. The result is higher prepayments.
- Prepayments are also affected by seasoning and property location.

Contraction risk for an MBS refers to undesirable consequences of declining interest rates: (1) MBS exhibit negative convexity, and (2) cash flows must be reinvested at a lower rate.

Extension risk refers to the drop in bond prices and the slowing of prepayments as interest rates increase. Investors would prefer to recapture their principal without a capital loss and reinvest at the current higher rates.

LOS 45.g

CMOs are securities issued against a pool of mortgages for which the cash flows have been allocated to different classes called tranches. Each tranche has a different claim against the assets of the pool and a different mixture of contraction and extension risk. CMOs can be matched to the unique asset/liability needs of investors.

LOS 45.h
Sequential-pay tranches are a common arrangement for separating mortgage cash flows into classes to create CMOs where each class of bond is retired sequentially.

PAC tranches, the most common type of CMO, have a payment schedule that is established within a range of prepayment speeds called the initial PAC collar. The time period over which principal is expected to be paid on a PAC tranche is called a PAC window.

Each PAC has a companion or support tranche that has a second priority claim to the cash flows. If prepayments are too high, the support tranche is paid off faster. If too slow, the support tranche provides the funds needed to keep the PAC on schedule.

LOS 45.i
The following table shows the contraction and extension risk of a simple sequential pay CMO containing four sequential pay tranches and one accrual tranche.

Tranche	*Contraction Risk*	*Extension Risk*
A (sequential pay)	HIGH	LOW
B (sequential pay)		
C (sequential pay)	↑	↓
D (sequential pay)		
Z (accrual)	LOW	HIGH

The *early* tranches are protected against extension risk, while the later tranches are protected against contraction risk. The Z bond has low contraction risk because reinvestment risk is eliminated until the other tranches have been paid off.

LOS 45.j
Stripped MBS differ from traditional passthroughs in that the principal and interest are not allocated on a pro rata basis.

- PO strips are a class of securities that receive only the principal payment portion of each mortgage payment. The PO exhibits some negative convexity at low rates.
- IO strips are classes that receive only the interest component of each payment. The IO price is positively related to mortgage rates at low current rates.
- PO and IO prices are more volatile than the underlying passthroughs.

LOS 45.k
Nonagency MBS (nonagency securities) are issued by private entities and are usually backed with nonconforming mortgage loans (loans that fail to meet the agency's underwriting standards). Nonagency security cash flows are affected by mortgage default rates and thus require credit enhancement (i.e., additional support against default).

LOS 45.l
CMBS are structured as nonrecourse loans, meaning that the lender can only look to the collateral as a means to repay the loan. In contrast, the residential mortgage lender can go back to the borrower, personally, in an attempt to repay a delinquent mortgage loan. The analysis of CMBS structures focuses on two key ratios to assess the credit risk of the property: debt-to-service coverage ratio and loan-to-value ratio.

LOS 45.m
Methods of call protection for the CMBS at the loan level include:

- Prepayment lock outs prevent the borrower from repaying the loan for a set period of time.
- Defeasance increases the quality of a CMBS loan pool by reinvesting any prepayments in Treasury securities.
- Penalty fees may be assessed against a borrower for prepayment.
- Yield maintenance charges require the borrower to *make whole* the amount of interest that would be paid to the lender upon prepayment.

At the CMBS pool level, cash prepayments are assigned to tranches, which mitigates the amount of prepayment risk of the more senior tranches.

CONCEPT CHECKERS

1. Which of the following statements concerning interest-only (IO) and principal-only (PO) passthrough securities is *least accurate*?
   A. IO passthroughs generally increase in value when interest rates rise.
   B. PO passthroughs generally increase in value when interest rates fall.
   C. If interest rates have fallen, risen, and then fallen again, the values of IOs and POs will be more affected by the second rate decrease.

2. Which of the following statements concerning the role of a support tranche in a planned amortization class collateralized mortgage obligation (PAC CMO) is *least accurate*?
   A. The purpose of a support tranche is to provide prepayment protection for one or more PAC tranches.
   B. The support tranches are exposed to extremely high levels of credit risk.
   C. If prepayments are too low to maintain the PAC schedule, the shortfall is provided by the support tranche.

Use the following information to answer Questions 3 through 5.

Assume that an investor has invested in a mortgage pool with a $100,000 principal balance outstanding. The scheduled monthly principal payment is $28.61.

3. The mortgage pool has a conditional prepayment rate (CPR) of 6% and the pool is seasoned. The single monthly mortality rate is *closest* to:
   A. 0.005098.
   B. 0.005113.
   C. 0.005143.

4. Using the information from Question 3, the estimated prepayment for the month is *closest* to:
   A. $509.92.
   B. $514.15.
   C. $529.25.

5. Using the Public Securities Association (PSA) standard prepayment benchmark, the single monthly mortality rate (SMM) in month 10, assuming 175% PSA, is *closest* to:
   A. 0.002363.
   B. 0.002793.
   C. 0.002965.

6. Consider a collateralized mortgage obligation (CMO) structure with one planned amortization class (PAC) class and one support tranche outstanding. Also, assume that the prepayment speed is higher than the upper collar on the PAC. Which of the following statements is *most accurate*? The:
   A. PAC tranche has no risk of prepayments.
   B. average life of the support tranche will contract.
   C. average life of the PAC tranche will extend.

7. Which of the following is *least likely* an important factor affecting the prepayment rate of a pool of mortgages?
   A. The location of the underlying real estate.
   B. Seasonal factors (i.e., the time of year when the mortgages were initiated).
   C. General economic conditions.

8. Which of the following scenarios is *most likely* to lead to the highest risk of prepayments on a mortgage pool?
   A. The mortgage pool has an average mortgage rate of 6.25% and an average life remaining of 84 payments. The current mortgage rate is 6.0%.
   B. A strong economy has caused gross domestic product to rise and unemployment to decline.
   C. Mortgage rates are currently at 7.5% and are now declining after varying between 7 and 10% for the last three years.

9. Which of the following statements regarding a planned amortization class (PAC) is *least accurate*?
   A. The average life of a PAC bond can remain stable even if prepayment rates go outside of the initial PAC collar for short time periods.
   B. A broken PAC is one where the support tranches have been fully repaid.
   C. PAC II tranches give investors in all PAC II tranches equal prepayment risk.

10. The average life of a mortgage-backed security (MBS) is more relevant than the security's final maturity because it represents the average time to the receipt of:
    A. scheduled principal payments.
    B. expected prepayments.
    C. both expected prepayments and scheduled principal payments.

11. Commercial mortgage-backed securities (CMBS) loans typically have greater call protection than residential MBS loans because:
    A. CMBS typically receive higher credit ratings from credit agencies than residential MBS.
    B. commercial mortgages may have yield maintenance charges.
    C. smaller dollar-sized mortgages typically are not refinanced if interest rates fall.

12. Commercial mortgage-backed securities (CMBS) mortgages are structured as nonrecourse loans, which means the:
    A. borrower cannot be forced into bankruptcy.
    B. lender cannot litigate the loan.
    C. lender can only look to the collateral as a means to repay a delinquent loan.

Challenge Problems

13. What is *most likely* to happen to the prepayment rate and the average life of a typical passthrough security if mortgage rates rise?
    A. Both will increase.
    B. One will increase, one will decrease.
    C. Both will decrease.

14. Tiffany Childers is reviewing various mortgage-backed securities (MBS) and is interested in the calculation of single monthly mortality (SMM) rates. Childers is using the Public Securities Association (PSA) standard prepayment benchmark. She calculates the SMM for month 22, assuming a 140 PSA, to be 0.37%. She calculates the SMM for month 200, assuming a 90 PSA, to be 0.46%. Childers is:
    A. correct for both months.
    B. correct for one month, but incorrect for the other month.
    C. incorrect for both months.

15. Two different structures of collateralized mortgage obligations (CMO) are being considered for issuance:
    - Structure 1: $400 million of passthroughs will be used as collateral for two sequential pay tranches: $325 million worth of bonds of Tranche X and $75 million of bonds of Tranche Y. The principal for Tranche X must be completely paid off before any payments are made to Tranche Y.
    - Structure 2: $400 million of passthroughs will be used as collateral for $325 million of E bonds in a planned amortization class (PAC) tranche and $75 million of F bonds in a support tranche.

    Which of the following statements is *least accurate*? The:
    A. X bonds have less contraction risk than the Y bonds.
    B. X bonds have less extension risk than the Y bonds.
    C. E bonds have less contraction risk than the F bonds.

16. Nonagency issues have all of the following characteristics *except*:
    A. they are usually created using nonconforming mortgages.
    B. they include 1 to 4 family residential homes but exclude second mortgage loans and manufactured housing loans.
    C. the collateral is a pool of loans rather than passthrough securities.

Answers – Concept Checkers

1. **C** The values of IOs and POs will be less affected by the second rate decrease. This occurs because of refinancing burnout, wherein many borrowers will have refinanced at the first rate decrease.

2. **B** The support tranches are exposed to extremely high levels of prepayment risk, not credit risk.

3. **C** *Seasoned* means that the pool is older than 30 months.

$$SMM = 1-(1-0.06)^{1/12} = 0.005143$$

4. **B** 0.005143 × ($100,000 – $28.61) = $514.15

5. **C** $CPR = 6\% \times \frac{10}{30} = 2\%$

$$175PSA = 1.75 \times 2\% = 3.50\%$$
$$SMM = 1-(1-0.035)^{1/12} = 0.002965$$

6. **B** If the prepayment speed is faster than the PAC collar, the support tranche receives a higher level of prepayments (so that the PAC tranche remains at the upper collar of the PAC). The average life of the support tranche will contract (shorten). The PAC tranche *could* receive higher prepayments if eventually the support tranche is fully repaid its principal (i.e., a busted PAC). However, the question says that the support tranche is still outstanding, which means that hasn't happened yet.

7. **B** The four main factors that have been shown to affect prepayments are (1) prevailing mortgage rates; (2) the characteristics of the underlying mortgage pool (such as the location of the real estate); (3) seasonal factors (i.e., the time of year in which the prepayment rate is measured, *not* the time of year when the mortgages were initiated); and (4) general economic activity.

8. **B** As the economy grows, personal income rises and workers transfer to new or better paying jobs. This leads to an increase in housing turnover, which results in mortgage payoffs and prepayments. The other scenarios do not carry a large risk of prepayments. The incentive to refinance is not great for only a 0.25% spread in mortgage rates and a relatively short time left on the mortgage; a mortgage rate that follows a down, up, and back down path can lead to refinancing burnout; and home-buying and prepayments are typically strongest in the spring.

9. **C** A PAC II tranche does not require equal distribution of prepayment risk. The PAC II tranche can be divided into classes of investors with different prepayment risk through a PAC schedule. The other statements are accurate. The average life of a PAC bond *can* remain stable in certain circumstances even if the prepayment speed *temporarily* goes outside the initial collar. Figure 6 in the topic review illustrates the case in which the prepayment speed jumps immediately to a speed outside the initial collar and stays at that speed for the life of the tranche.

10. **C** The average life is more relevant for mortgage backed securities because it represents the average time to receipt of both principal payments and expected prepayments.

11. **B** Any type of call protection structured into the loan itself (in this case, yield maintenance charges) increases the overall call protection of the CMBS. Residential mortgages can be prepaid without penalty at any time and do not provide any call protection at the individual loan level.

12. **C** Nonrecourse loans mean that the lender can only look to the collateral as a means to repay a delinquent loan, not the borrower's personal assets.

ANSWERS – CHALLENGE PROBLEMS

13. **B** Prepayment rates will most likely decrease if mortgage rates rise. This will be associated with an increase in the average life.

14. **B** Under PSA, the conditional prepayment rate rises 0.2% per month for months 1–30 and levels off at a rate of 6%. Under the first scenario,

$$CPR = 6\% \times \frac{22}{30} = 4.4\%$$

$$140PSA = 1.40 \times 4.4\% = 6.16\%$$
$$SMM = 1-(1-0.0616)^{1/12} = 0.0053 = 0.53\%$$

Under the second scenario, the CPR is after month 30, so CPR = 6%.

$$CPR = 6\%$$
$$90PSA = 0.9 \times 6\% = 5.4\%$$
$$SMM = 1-(1-0.054)^{1/12} = 0.0046 = 0.46\%$$

Childers is incorrect in her estimate of the month 22 SMM, but correct in her estimate of the month 200 SMM.

15. **A** In Structure 1, we have two sequential pay tranches. If prepayments slow, it will take longer for cash flows to get to the Y bonds, so the X bonds have less extension risk. The X bonds have more contraction risk than the Y bonds because they will get cash flows more quickly if prepayments accelerate. The X bonds protect the Y bonds against contraction risk. In the case of Structure 2 where there are two PAC tranches, the F support tranche will absorb the impact of both accelerated and slower than expected prepayments, resulting in the E bonds having both less contraction risk and less extension risk than the F bonds.

16. **B** The nonagency securities are backed by a pool of one to four single-family residential first-lien mortgages issued by private entities. However, nonagency securities are sometimes backed by second mortgage loans, manufactured housing loans, and a variety of commercial real estate loans.

The following is a review of the Fixed Income: Structured Securities principles designed to address the learning outcome statements set forth by CFA Institute. This topic is also covered in:

Asset-Backed Sector of the Bond Market

Study Session 15

Exam Focus

Asset-backed securities (ABS) are securities created from the pooling of non-mortgage assets (e.g., auto loans, credit card receivables, and corporate bonds). You should have a solid understanding of the basic structure of each of these different types of ABS. Also focus on the similarities and differences between mortgage-backed securities (MBS) and ABS; both are exposed to varying degrees of prepayment risk, but credit risk is a more important consideration for ABS investors. Remember that you're being tested on your skills as an analyst, not as an investment banker; concentrate on the risks faced by investors who hold ABS, not on the details of how various ABS are created.

LOS 46.a: Describe the basic structural features of and parties to a securitization transaction.

CFA® Program Curriculum, Volume 5, page 468

Let's illustrate the basic structure of a securitization transaction with a simplified, fictitious example of Fred Motor Company.

Fred Motor Company manufactures and sells automobiles in a wide range of styles and prices. Most of the company's sales are done on retail sales installment contracts (i.e., auto loans). The customer buys the automobile, and Fred loans the customer the proceeds for the purchase (i.e., Fred originates the loan) using the auto as collateral and receives principal and interest payments on the loan until it matures. The loans have maturities of 48 to 60 months at varying interest rates. Fred is also the **servicer** of the loan: the company collects principal and interest payments, sends out delinquent notices, and repossesses and disposes of the auto if the customer doesn't make timely payments.

Fred has 50,000 auto loans totaling $1 billion that it would like to remove from its balance sheet. It accomplishes this by selling the loans to a special purpose vehicle (SPV) called Auto Owner Trust for $1 billion (which is why Fred is called the **seller**). The SPV, which is set up for the specific purpose of buying these auto loans, is referred to as the **trust** or the **issuer**. The SPV then issues asset-backed securities (ABS) to investors using the portfolio of auto loans as collateral.

Let's review the parties to this transaction and their functions:

- The **seller** (Fred Motor Company) originates the auto loans and sells the portfolio of loans to Auto Owner Trust, the SPV.
- The **issuer/trust** (Auto Owner Trust) is the SPV that buys the loans from the seller and issues ABS to investors.
- The **servicer** (Fred Motor Company) services the loans.

- In this case, the seller and the servicer are the same entity (Fred Motor Company), but that is not always the case in asset securitizations.

The structure of this securitization transaction is shown in Figure 1.

Figure 1: Structure of Fred Motor Company Asset Securitization

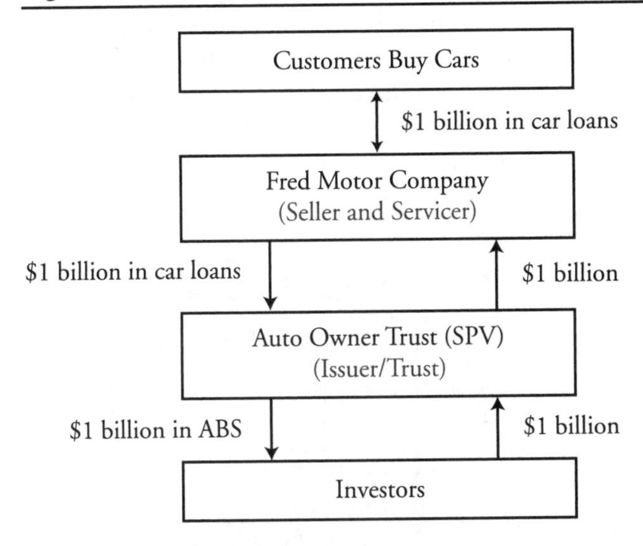

Subsequent to the initial transaction, the principal and interest payments on the original loans are paid by the customers to the servicer. This cash flow is then allocated to pay servicing fees to the servicer and principal and interest payments to the investors in the various tranches of the ABS according to the priority rules set out in the prospectus. This flow of funds structure is called the **waterfall**.

ABS are most commonly backed by automobile loans, credit card receivables, home equity loans, manufactured housing loans, student loans, Small Business Administration (SBA) loans, corporate loans, corporate bonds, emerging market bonds, and structured financial products.

LOS 46.b: Explain and contrast prepayment tranching and credit tranching.

CFA® Program Curriculum, Volume 5, page 473

Recall from the previous topic review that agency mortgage-backed securities (MBS) structures are divided into different tranches to distribute the prepayment risk to various investors using, for example, sequential-pay or planned amortization class (PAC) structures. ABS are also structured to distribute the prepayment risk; this is called **prepayment tranching**, or **time tranching**.

ABS can have credit risk in addition to prepayment risk. The credit risk of ABS is reduced by various forms of credit enhancement. The most common form of credit enhancement is a senior-subordinated structure in which the subordinated bonds absorb all losses first up to their par value, after which any additional losses are absorbed by the senior bonds, so that credit risk is shifted from the senior bonds to the subordinated bonds. This type of structure is called **credit tranching**.

Often ABS are structured with both prepayment and credit tranching, as illustrated in Figure 2.

The structure represented in Figure 2 has senior bonds, which are divided so that some have relatively short and some have relatively long target maturities. Other senior (in terms of credit risk) bonds serve as the support tranches for the short and long target maturities of the senior bonds in the first tier. The bonds in the lowest tier are the junior or subordinated bonds, which absorb defaults up to their par values, increasing the credit rating of both the senior target maturity and senior support tranches. These bonds may also be structured to provide support for the target maturity of the senior bonds as well, and therefore may have the highest levels of both prepayment and credit risk.

Figure 2: Prepayment and Credit Tranching of an ABS

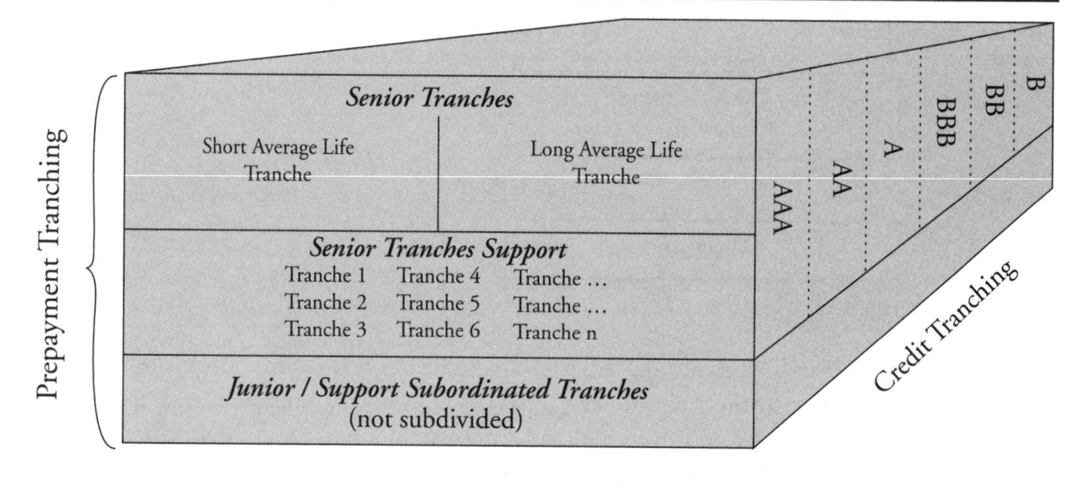

LOS 46.c: Distinguish between the payment structure and collateral structure of a securitization backed by amortizing assets and non-amortizing assets.

CFA® Program Curriculum, Volume 5, page 473

Amortizing assets are loans for which the borrower makes periodic scheduled payments that include both principal and interest. The interest amount is subtracted from the total payment, and the balance is applied toward the principal, reducing the outstanding loan. Amounts in excess of the scheduled periodic payment are applied to a further reduction of principal. Such additional payments are called **prepayments**. A residential mortgage is an example of an amortizing loan.

Non-amortizing assets are loans that do not have a scheduled payment amount. Instead, a minimum payment, which is applied against accrued interest, is required. If the minimum payment exceeds the accrued interest, the excess is applied toward reducing the outstanding principal. If the payment falls short of the accrued interest, the outstanding loan balance is increased by the amount of the shortfall. A revolving credit card loan is an example of a non-amortizing asset.

The structure of the ABS transaction is affected by whether the assets backing the bonds are amortizing or non-amortizing. For amortizing assets like auto loans, once the assets are securitized, the composition of the loans in the pool doesn't change. Loans disappear from the pool as they are paid off or default, but no new loans are added to the pool to replace them. Principal payments and prepayments on the remaining loans are distributed to the bondholders according to the distribution rules of the structure.

For non-amortizing assets like credit card receivables, however, the composition of the loans in the pool can and does change. During the *lockout period* (e.g., the first 18 months), principal payments and prepayments are not distributed to the bondholders as is the case with amortizing assets. Instead, the cash flow from these principal payments is used to invest in new loans to replace the amounts paid off. This type of structure is called a *revolving structure*.

The bonds issued in a revolving structure can be retired early under certain conditions by requiring cash flows to be directed to the reduction of principal rather than the purchase of new loans. The call provision can be triggered by several different types of events, the most common being poor performance of the collateral.

In the case of non-amortizing collateral, due to the call provision on the ABS, while the underlying collateral (loans) has no prepayment risk, the securities backed by such collateral may have a prepayment (call) risk.

In some cases, revolving structures are possible for amortizing assets as well. In such cases, the principal and prepayments during the lockout period are used to acquire additional collateral.

LOS 46.d: Distinguish among various types of external and internal credit enhancements.

CFA® Program Curriculum, Volume 5, page 475

Credit enhancements accompany all ABS. The level of credit enhancement is directly proportional to the level of rating desired by the issuer. Rating agencies determine the exact amount of credit enhancement necessary for an issue to hold a specific rating. There are two types of credit enhancements: internal and external.

External Credit Enhancements

External credit enhancements are financial guarantees from third parties that support the performance of the bond. They are used to supplement other forms of credit enhancements. Third-party guarantees impose a limit on the guarantor's liability for losses at a specified level. They protect against losses before internal credit enhancements are used. External credit enhancements include the following:

- **Corporate guarantees**. The sponsor (effectively the seller of the securities) agrees to guarantee a portion of the offer.
- **Letter of credit**. A bank letter of credit provides a guarantee against loss up to a certain level.
- **Bond insurance**. Bond insurance provides for protection against losses through the purchase of insurance against nonperformance.

The problem with third-party guarantees is the "weak link" philosophy adopted by rating agencies: the credit quality of an issue cannot be higher than the credit rating of the third-party guarantor. If the guarantor is downgraded, the issue itself may also be downgraded, even if there has not been a decline in the credit quality of the underlying collateral.

Internal Credit Enhancements

Internal credit enhancements include reserve funds, overcollateralization, and structures that contain senior and subordinated debt. Internal credit enhancements do not rely on a third-party guarantee.

There are two types of **reserve funds**—cash reserve funds and excess servicing spread funds.

1. **Cash reserve funds** are cash deposits that come from issuance proceeds. This excess cash provides for the establishment of a reserve account to pay for future losses.
2. **Excess servicing spread funds** consist of reserve funds in the form of excess spread or cash after paying for servicing and other expenses. The excess servicing spread funds can be used to fund credit losses on the collateral. However, if defaults exceed those initially projected, the effectiveness of the excess servicing spread diminishes. Thus, default-related assumptions should be examined when assessing the extent of the default protection provided by an excess servicing spread account.

Overcollateralization occurs when the ABS is issued with a face value less than the value of the underlying collateral. For example, if the liability structure is $100 million and the collateral's value is $105 million, the issue is overcollateralized by $5 million. The overcollateralization can be used to absorb losses.

A **senior/subordinated structure** contains at least two tranches—a *senior* tranche and a junior, or *subordinated*, tranche. The subordinated tranches absorb the first losses up to their limits. The level of protection for the senior tranches increases with the percentage of subordinated bonds in the structure.

Let's look at an example to illustrate how overcollateralization and a senior/subordinated structure enhance the creditworthiness of an ABS. Consider the following ABS structure:

Senior tranche	$300,000,000
Subordinated tranche A	$80,000,000
Subordinated tranche B	$30,000,000
Total	$410,000,000

The collateral value for the structure is $450,000,000, and Tranche B is first to absorb losses (the first loss tranche). The amount of overcollateralization for this structure is the difference between the value of the collateral and the combined value of all the tranches. That is:

overcollateralization = $450,000,000 – $410,000,000 = $40,000,000

This means that losses up to $40 million will be absorbed by the overcollateralization, and none of the tranches will experience a loss. Losses between $40 million and $70 million will be absorbed by Tranche B. Losses between $70 million and $150 million will be absorbed by Tranche A. Losses greater than $150 million will be absorbed by the senior tranche.

The **shifting interest mechanism** is a mechanism for addressing the change in the level of credit protection provided by junior tranches as prepayments occur in a senior/subordinated structure. The key point to remember is that the shifting interest mechanism reduces the credit risk of the senior tranches, but the trade-off is greater prepayment risk.

Junior tranches are designed to provide loss protection for senior tranches by absorbing credit losses first. The percentage share of the junior or subordinate tranches to the total outstanding balance is called as the subordinate interest. As the principal on junior tranches is reduced by prepayments, subordinate interest declines, and the level of protection for senior tranches is reduced. In other words, the subordinate interest shifts, hence, the term "shifting interest." To maintain subordinate interest at a desirable level, prepayments are allocated among the senior tranches at a relatively higher proportion in the early years.

The bond prospectus contains the schedule for the shifting interest percentage required to calculate the *senior prepayment percentage* (i.e., the proportion of prepayments that are applied to the senior tranche). A commonly used shifting interest schedule is shown in Figure 3.

Figure 3: Example of Senior Prepayment Percentage Schedule

Years After Issuance	*Senior Prepayment Percentage*
1-5	100
6	70
7	60
8	40
9	20
after 9	0

Suppose, for example, that if prepayments of $80,000 occur in the 46th month (the fourth year), all of the prepayments will be allocated to the senior tranches. If there are prepayments of $80,000 in the seventh year, 60%, or $48,000, will be allocated to the senior tranches, and only 40%, or $32,000, will go to the subordinated tranches. If there are prepayments of $80,000 in the tenth year, all of the prepayments will be allocated to the subordinated tranches.

Keep in mind that the shifting interest schedule that is stated in the prospectus is not fixed. The issue's trustees may change the initial schedule if credit losses cause the credit risk of the senior tranches to increase. The decision to change the shifting interest schedule is based on performance tests that are specified in the prospectus.

It is important to realize that while the shifting interest mechanism can be effectively used to maintain the desired level of credit risk protection, it comes at the expense of increased contraction risk for the senior tranches. This is a result of the increase in the proportion of the prepayments allocated to the senior tranches. Shifting interest mechanism is commonly used for real-estate-related ABS and non-agency MBS.

LOS 46.e: Describe cash flow and prepayment characteristics for securities backed by home equity loans, manufactured housing loans, automobile loans, student loans, SBA loans, and credit card receivables.

CFA® Program Curriculum, Volume 5, page 479

Home Equity Loans

As the name implies, a home equity loan (HEL) is a loan backed by residential property. HEL used to be a second lien on a property with an existing first lien. Lately, a HEL is frequently a first lien on property owned by a borrower that has a marginal credit history or a loan that does not meet agency requirements for a qualified loan. HELs are also commonly used to consolidate consumer debt.

There are two basic types of HELs: closed-end and open-end. We will focus on *closed-end HELs*, which are structured just like a standard fixed-rate, fully amortizing mortgage. As such, a closed-end HEL is a one-time lump sum loan with a fixed maturity and a payment structure such that the loan is fully amortized at maturity. An ABS issued on a pool of closed-end HELs is very similar to a standard mortgage-backed security (MBS). In the absence of tranching, each HEL-backed certificate holder receives a proportional share of the principal and interest paid on the underlying HELs. Thus, a prepayment model, such as the conditional prepayment rate model used for an MBS, must be employed to estimate cash flows to the HEL pool.

Prepayments

The pattern of prepayments from HELs differs from MBS prepayment patterns, primarily because of differences in the credit traits of the borrowers. Generally, higher prepayments at lower rates are more likely for higher credit quality borrowers.

In the prospectus for an HEL-backed issue, an assumption is made regarding the initial speed of prepayments and time until the issue is expected to become seasoned (i.e., the point where prepayments stabilize). This is known as the *base case prepayment assumption*. The benchmark speed stated in the prospectus for HEL-backed securities is called the *prospectus prepayment curve* (PPC). PPCs are used in a manner similar to the Public Securities Association (PSA) curves. If the speed of seasoning for an issue is faster or slower than that stated in the prospectus, an analyst would employ a multiplication factor to adjust the PPC to reflect the actual seasoning behavior. As with the PSA benchmark, the speed of prepayment measured using a PPC benchmark is measured as the *conditional prepayment rate* (CPR). Unlike the PSA benchmark, however, the PPC is not generic; it is an issuer-specific benchmark for prepayment rates associated with HELs.

Payment Structure

HEL-backed securities that are collateralized with variable rate HELs are known as *HEL floaters*. While the individual variable rate HELs commonly use the 6-month London Interbank Offered Rate (LIBOR) as their reference rate, 1-month LIBOR is used as the reference rate for HEL floaters. This practice is a response to investor preferences. The mismatch between the reference rates for HEL floaters and the variable rate HELs used to collateralize them may result in cash shortfalls over time. As a consequence of this potential shortfall and the periodic and lifetime caps on the underlying variable rate loans, HEL floaters must have coupon rate caps. Unlike most floating-rate securities, which have fixed caps over the term of the security, the effective periodic and lifetime caps for HEL floaters are variable. This effective cap is called the *available funds cap*. Its level is determined on the basis of net coupon-generated funds, less all applicable fees. You can think of the available funds cap as a variable cap on interest rate adjustments in the HEL floaters.

HEL structures frequently include non-accelerating senior tranches and planned amortization class (PAC) tranches. The characteristics of these tranches include:

- *Non-accelerating senior tranches* (NAS). An NAS tranche receives principal payments on the basis of a predetermined schedule. This is a schedule of principal payments that shows the proportion of principal that is to be distributed to the NAS tranche for a given month. Typically, the schedule is such that an NAS tranche receives no prepayments in the early years—its share is paid to the other senior tranches. This structure reduces contraction risk for the NAS tranche(s). In the latter years, an NAS tranche receives a relatively high percentage of prepayments, thus reducing extension risk.
- *PAC tranche*. The prepayments to PACs are stable if prepayments fall within the specified PAC collar. The concept of a PAC as it applies to HEL-backed securities is similar to that of standard MBSs.

Manufactured Housing-Backed Securities

As the name implies, manufactured housing-backed securities are backed by loans for manufactured homes (e.g., mobile homes). These loans are similar to standard mortgage loans in that they fully amortize over the life of the loan. Ginnie Mae, as well as private organizations, issues manufactured housing-backed securities.

Cash Flow and Prepayments

The *cash flows* for manufactured housing-backed securities include interest, scheduled principal payments, and prepayments, much like residential mortgage loans and HELs. Prepayments are also typically measured in terms of a conditional prepayment rate. In contrast to MBSs and HEL-backed assets, however, prepayments for manufactured housing-backed securities are less significant, because the underlying loans are not as sensitive to refinancing, because:

- Loan balances are usually small, reducing the extent of savings resulting from refinancing.
- The depreciation of mobile homes during the earlier years may be greater than the reduction of the loan principal, resulting in the value of the asset being less than the outstanding loan amount.
- Borrowers are likely to have relatively low credit ratings, which makes it difficult for them to refinance.

Payment Structure

The payment structure for manufactured housing-backed loans is like that of nonagency MBS and HEL-backed securities. Each issue is divided into different classes, each with a different claim against the cash flow components of the underlying collateral pool.

Auto Loan ABS

Auto loan-backed securities are backed by loans for automobiles. Auto loans have maturities from 36 to 72 months. Issuers include the financial subsidiaries of auto manufacturers, commercial banks, credit unions, S&Ls, finance companies, and other small financial institutions.

The cash flow components of auto loan-backed securities include scheduled monthly interest and principal payments and prepayments. Auto loans prepay if the cars are sold, traded in, or repossessed. Prepayments also occur if the car is stolen or wrecked and the loan is paid off from insurance proceeds. Finally, the borrower may simply use excess cash to reduce or pay off the loan balance.

Refinancing, however, is not a major factor contributing to auto loan prepayments because:

- Loan balances are usually small, reducing the extent of savings resulting from refinancing, especially because used-car refinancing rates are significantly higher than new car rates. (How many people do you know who refinance their cars when rates drop?)
- The automobile's value may depreciate faster than the loan balance in the early years, resulting in the value of the asset being less than the outstanding loan amount, particularly if the loans were originally done at below-market rates because of sales promotions.

That means prepayments from a pool of auto-loans are much more predictable and much less dependent on interest rate changes than prepayments on mortgage loans. This significantly reduces the prepayment risk of auto-loan ABS.

Absolute prepayment speed (ABS) is the measure of prepayments associated with securities backed by auto loans. It is calculated as the monthly prepayment expressed as a percentage of the value of the initial collateral.

Professor's Note: The absolute prepayment speed is denoted as "ABS," which is confusing since "ABS" is also used for "asset-backed security." You will have to examine the context of the question to determine which "ABS" is being discussed if you see it on the exam.

The absolute prepayment speed is conceptually similar to the CPR discussed in the previous topic review. The relationship between the absolute prepayment speed and the single monthly mortality rate (SMM) is shown in the following equation.

$$SMM = \frac{ABS}{1-[ABS \times (m-1)]}$$

where:
ABS = absolute prepayment speed
m = number of months since loan origination

Example: SMM calculation

If the absolute prepayment speed ten months after origination is 1.8% (0.018), compute the SMM.

Answer:

$$SMM = \frac{0.018}{1-[0.018 \times (10-1)]} = 0.0215 = 2.15\%$$

Student Loan-Backed Securities

Student loan asset-backed securities (SLABS) have structural features similar to the other asset-backed securities we have discussed. The student loans that are most often securitized are those made by lending institutions under the U.S. Government's Federal Family Education Loan Program (FFELP). Under FFELP, the U.S. government guarantees loans made by private lenders to students. If an FFELP loan goes into default, the U.S. government guarantees up to 98% of the loan principal and accrued interest on the condition that the loan has been serviced properly. Student loans that are not part of the FFELP program (known as *alternative loans*) have been securitized but are not guaranteed by the U.S. Government.

The cash flows associated with SLABSs occur during three periods:

1. The deferment period, when the borrower makes no payments and the loan accrues no interest.
2. The grace period, when the borrower makes no payments, but interest does accrue.
3. The loan repayment period, when the borrower makes principal and interest payments based on a reference rate plus a margin.

Prepayments may occur because of defaults (inflows from the Government guarantee process) or loan consolidation.

Small Business Administration Loan-Backed Securities

The Small Business Administration (SBA) is a U.S. government agency that guarantees loans made by private lenders to borrowers who meet specified guidelines. The private lenders must be approved by the SBA for their loans to be eligible for the guarantee. Because the SBA is a U.S. government agency, its guarantees are backed by the full faith and credit of the U.S. government.

Pooled SBA loans must have similar terms and features. Most SBA loans are variable-rate loans, based on the prime rate, and are reset either monthly or quarterly. The monthly payment for individual variable-rate SBA loans includes an interest component and a repayment-of-principal component. Level amortizing loan payments are calculated based on a reference rate at the beginning of each reset period.

An SBA-backed security investor receives the following *cash flows*:

- *Interest* based on the coupon rate set at the beginning of the reset period.
- The *principal repayment* that is based on the amortization schedule developed at the time of loan origination.
- *Prepayments* received by the lender that are applied to the outstanding loan.

Credit Card Receivable-Backed Securities

Credit card receivable-backed securities are ABS backed by the pools of receivables owed to banks, retailers, travel and entertainment companies, and other credit card issuers.

Credit card receivable-backed securities use a structure that enables the issuer to sell more than one series from the same pool of receivables. This means more receivables are added each time a new series is issued. Thus, the balance may never be reduced to zero.

The cash flow to a pool of credit card receivables includes finance charges, annual fees, and principal repayments. Credit cards have periodic payment schedules, but because their balances are revolving, the principal is not amortized. Because of this characteristic, interest on credit card ABS is paid periodically, but no principal is paid to the ABS holders during the *lockout period*, which may last from 18 months to 10 years.

If the underlying credit card holders make principal payments during the lockout period, these payments are used to purchase additional underlying assets or receivables, keeping the overall value of the receivables pool relatively constant. Once the lockout period ends, principal payments are passed on to the security holders. This post-lockout period is known as the **principal amortization period**.

The distribution of payments usually follows one of three **amortization payment structures:**

- **Passthrough structure.** Principal payments received from credit card holders are distributed pro rata to investors.

- **Controlled-amortization structure.** This structure relies on the mechanism of a "principal window" similar to a PAC bond. To protect against the impact of cash shortfalls due to inadequate principal repayments or slow payments by cardholders, the ABS is designed with a relatively low principal payment in the schedule. If there is cash flow shortfall, the ABS investor receives the lower of the scheduled principal payment or a pro rata portion of the principal repayment.
- **Bullet-payment structure.** As "bullet" implies, investors receive the total principal amount in a single payment. The uncertain nature of principal payments by credit card holders, however, allows for no guarantee that the total principal amount will be available when the bullet payment is due. To overcome this problem, a soft bullet structure is often used. Under this structure, the ABS trustees place the monthly principal payments in an interest-bearing account that is expected to generate enough interest over time to fund the payment of the bullet. The period over which interest is earned, called the "accumulation period," usually begins a few months prior to the scheduled bullet payment. Despite the lack of a guaranteed maturity, the scheduled bullet payment is seldom missed in practice.

Several metrics are typically used to assess the performance of the credit card receivable portfolio and the issuer's ability to make the interest and principal payments required by the various tranches in a credit card ABS, as shown in Figure 4.

Figure 4: Assessing the Performance of the Receivables Portfolio

Performance Measure	*Definition*	*Warning Signal*
Net portfolio yield	Gross portfolio yield minus charge offs.	If the weighted average coupon promised to the ABS tranches is greater than the net portfolio yield, there is risk that tranches will not get paid off as promised.
Delinquencies	Percentage of past due receivables.	High delinquencies signal potential future charge offs and lower net portfolio yield.
Monthly repayment rate (MPR)	Monthly payments (interest, fees, principal) as percent of outstanding receivables at previous month end.	Low MPR signals: • increased extension risk of the ABS tranches and, • insufficient cash flow to pay off tranches.

Gross portfolio yield equals finance charges and fees collected as percent of outstanding receivables. Charge offs equal percent of uncollectible accounts that are charged off.

Early amortization of the principal in credit card receivable-backed securities can be triggered by certain events. This **early amortization trigger** protects the investor against declines in the credit quality of the underlying receivables. The most common trigger is when the 3-month average excess spread earned on the receivables declines to zero. Hence, even though there is no principal repayment schedule for credit card borrowers, an early amortization trigger provision creates the potential for contraction risk in a receivables-backed structure.

LOS 46.f: Describe collateralized debt obligations (CDOs), including cash and synthetic CDOs.

CFA® Program Curriculum, Volume 5, page 492

COLLATERALIZED DEBT OBLIGATIONS

A **collateralized debt obligation** (CDO) is an ABS that is collateralized by a pool of debt obligations. Examples include:

- Corporate bonds with ratings below investment grade.
- MBS and ABS (called structured financial products).
- Bond issues in emerging markets.
- Corporate loans advanced by commercial banks.
- Special situation loans and distressed debt.

A CDO has the following structure:

- One or more senior tranches.
- Several levels of mezzanine tranches.
- A subordinate tranche, also known as the **equity tranche**, to provide prepayment and credit protection to the other tranches.

The senior tranche, which typically comprises about 70% to 80% of the entire deal, is assigned a floating-rate payment to attract investors who are looking for a floating-rate investment. The mezzanine tranches are assigned a fixed-coupon payment. As with other ABS, payments received from the collateral are paid to the security holders associated with the different tranches.

A CDO's collateral pool typically contains a mix of floating-rate and fixed-rate debt instruments. However, payments made to a majority of the tranche holders (the senior tranche holders) are based on a floating rate. This creates a potential cash flow mismatch. In order to control for the interest rate risk imposed by this mismatch, asset managers often use interest rate swaps. Interest rate swaps are derivative instruments that can be used to convert fixed-rate interest receipts into floating-rate payments. The inclusion of swaps in a CDO deal is almost always mandated by the rating agencies.

Cash Flow CDO

The objective of a cash flow CDO is for the portfolio manager to generate sufficient cash flow (from interest and principal payments) to repay the senior and mezzanine tranches. A cash flow CDO has three phases:

1. *Ramp up phase.* In this phase, which usually lasts one to two months, the portfolio manager puts together a portfolio financed with the help of the sale of different tranches to investors.

2. *Reinvestment phase*. After the portfolio has been assembled, the asset manager monitors its performance and reinvests prepayments and cash flows from calls and loan default recoveries.

3. *Pay down phase*. During this phase, which may last from three to five years, principal payments are made to junior and senior tranche holders. As the name implies, this is a winding-down period of the CDO.

Income from the portfolio is used first to pay administration and management fees, then to pay interest on the senior tranches. If certain coverage tests are met, interest is paid to the mezzanine tranches, and any remaining cash flow is paid to the equity tranche. If the coverage tests are not met, the cash flow is used to retire senior tranche principal until the coverage tests are met. Coverage tests include par value tests and interest coverage tests.

During the reinvestment period, principal proceeds from the portfolio are reinvested in new securities (assuming the coverage tests are met). After the reinvestment period, principal proceeds are used first to pay down the senior tranches, then the mezzanine tranches, and finally the equity tranche.

The portfolio manager actively manages the portfolio, but does not try to generate trading profits to meet the cash flow obligations of the tranches. Instead, the manager structures the portfolio so that the interest and principal repayments are sufficient to meet the cash flow obligations, and rebalances as necessary.

Market Value CDO

In a market value CDO the manager actively manages the portfolio and sells assets to generate cash flows to meet the CDO tranches' obligations. Because of this, the manager of a market value CDO has more flexibility than the manager of a cash flow CDO.

Synthetic CDO

In a synthetic CDO, the bondholders take on the economic risks of the underlying assets but do not take legal ownership of them. This is accomplished by linking certain contingent payments to a reference asset (e.g., a bond index, or a portfolio of loans held by a bank).

The CDO is divided into a senior "section" and a junior "section"; debt obligations are only issued to fund the junior section, in the same manner as a cash CDO, but no securities are issued to fund the senior section. The junior section absorbs losses up to a certain level before the senior section is forced to absorb any losses. The proceeds from the junior section are invested by the portfolio manager in high-quality debt securities.

For example, a synthetic arbitrage CDO might have a notional amount of credit exposure to the reference asset of $100 million. The $100 million is referred to as notional exposure because it is not fully funded. The senior section has $90 million in exposure and the junior section has $10 million.

The note holders also sell a $90 million *credit default swap*. In a credit default swap the seller receives a premium in return for the obligation to pay the buyer a specific amount if a credit event occurs on the reference asset (e.g., the issuer of one of the bonds in the bond index declares bankruptcy or fails to pay interest). In the case of a credit event the seller is required to pay the difference between the par value and the fair market value of the bond. The senior note holders receive a small premium in return for the obligation to fund any losses in excess of $10 million. Because the deal is structured so that the chance of losses exceeding $10 million is very small, the senior notes usually carry a AAA rating.

Professor's Note: Credit default swaps are discussed in the Study Session on derivative investments.

The bottom line is that the junior bondholders receive income from the high-quality debt securities in the portfolio, as well as the insurance premium on the credit default swap. However, they are also exposed to credit losses in the reference asset. Therefore, they are in a similar position to junior bondholders in a cash CDO.

The question you're probably asking yourself is, "Why construct the complicated synthetic CDO when you can just do the simple cash CDO?" There are several advantages to using a synthetic structure instead of a cash structure for an *arbitrage* CDO:

- The senior section doesn't require funding.
- The ramp-up period is shorter.
- It is cheaper to acquire an exposure to the reference asset through the credit default swap instead of buying the asset directly.

LOS 46.g: Distinguish among the primary motivations for creating a collateralized debt obligation (arbitrage and balance sheet transactions).

CFA® Program Curriculum, Volume 5, page 494

The motivations for creating CDOs fall into two basic categories:

- CDOs can be **arbitrage-driven**, in which the motivation is to generate an arbitrage return on the spread between return on the collateral and the funding costs.
- CDOs can be **balance sheet-driven**, in which the motivation is to remove assets (and the associated funding) from the balance sheet. For example, a bank can use a synthetic *balance sheet* CDO to remove the credit risk of a loan portfolio from its balance sheet and reduce its regulatory capital requirements. The advantage to the bank of using the synthetic structure versus a cash CDO is they don't need to obtain the consent of the borrowers to move the credit risk off the balance sheet.

Arbitrage-driven cash CDOs make up the majority of cash CDO deals, so an example of a typical transaction is presented next.

Arbitrage-Driven Cash CDO

Although this LOS asks you to "describe," but not "construct," this is an excellent tie-in to the swap material coming up in Study Session 17. Therefore, let's examine how an equity tranche gets paid in an arbitrage-driven CDO deal.

Example: CDO cash flows

Assume the following:

- The CDO is a \$200 million structure—the collateral will have an initial value of \$200 million.
- The collateral consists entirely of bonds with 15 years remaining until maturity and a coupon rate equal to the 15-year Treasury rate plus 350 basis points.
- The senior tranche represents \$150 million (75% of the structure) and carries a floating-coupon rate equal to LIBOR plus 150 basis points. There is one \$20 million mezzanine tranche, and it carries a fixed coupon equal to the Treasury rate at origination plus 175 basis points.
- The manager of the trust has entered into an interest rate swap under which the trust will pay an annual fixed rate equal to the Treasury rate plus 125 basis points and receive LIBOR. The notional amount for this swap is \$150 million.
- The 15-year Treasury rate is 7.5% at the time of origination for this CDO.

Calculate the interest received by the CDO from the collateral and the swap counterparty; the total interest paid by the CDO to the senior and mezzanine tranches and the swap counterparty; and the net cash flow to the equity tranche.

Answer:

Because the senior tranche and mezzanine tranche are initially valued at \$150 million and \$20 million, respectively, the equity tranche has an initial par amount of \$30 million.

Let's look at the various cash flows.

- Assuming no defaults, the collateral will pay annual interest equal to the Treasury rate plus 350 basis points. Because the Treasury rate is 7.5%, the collateral will pay:

  $$\text{interest from collateral} = (0.075 + 0.035) \times \$200{,}000{,}000 = \$22{,}000{,}000$$

- The senior tranche will receive LIBOR plus 150 basis points. This amounts to:

  $$\text{interest to senior tranche} = \$150{,}000{,}000 \times (\text{LIBOR} + 0.015)$$

- The mezzanine tranche will receive the Treasury rate plus 175 basis points, fixed over the term of the issue. This amounts to:

  $$\text{interest to mezzanine tranche} = \$20{,}000{,}000 \times (0.075 + 0.0175) = \$1{,}850{,}000$$

- Now let's look at the swap. The amount that must be paid to the counterparty in the swap agreement is the Treasury rate (assumed here to be 7.5%) plus 125 basis points, or 8.75%. The dollar amount of this payment is based on the notional amount of the swap. In this case, the notional amount of the swap equals the par value of the senior tranche, or $150 million. So, the trust must pay the following:

  interest to swap counterparty: 0.0875 × $150,000,000 = $13,125,000

Similarly, the floating rate that the trust will receive under the swap agreement is:

interest from swap counterparty = $150,000,000 × LIBOR

Putting it all together we have:

Interest received by the CDO:

Interest from collateral	$22,000,000
Interest from swap counterparty	150,000,000 × LIBOR

Total incoming interest $22,000,000 + ($150,000,000 × LIBOR)

Interest paid to senior and mezzanine tranches:

Interest to senior tranche	$150,000,000 × (LIBOR + 0.015)
Interest to mezzanine tranche	1,850,000
Interest to swap counterparty	$13,125,000
Total interest paid	$14,975,000 + $150,000,000 × (LIBOR + 0.015)

Netting payment inflows and outflows we have:

Total interest received	$22,000,000 + ($150,000,000 × LIBOR)
– Total interest paid	$14,975,000 + $150,000,000 × (LIBOR + 0.015)
Net interest	$7,025,000 – $150,000,000 × 0.015
	= $7,025,000 – $2,250,000
	= $4,775,000

So, the cash flow each year available to pay the equity tranche is $4,775,000, less management and other fees (and assuming no defaults). The cash flow risk from the interest rate mismatch has been eliminated, and the structure has created an equity tranche with a guaranteed return of $4,775,000/$30,000,000 = 15.9%, which is an arbitrage profit.

KEY CONCEPTS

LOS 46.a

The key parties to a securitization transaction are the:

- Seller, who originates the loans and sells them to the issuer/trust.
- Issuer/trust, who buys the loans from the seller and issues the ABS.
- Servicer, who services the original loans.

The flow of funds structure in a securitization transaction is known as the waterfall.

LOS 46.b

ABS structures are divided into different tranches to distribute the prepayment risk to various investors using, for example, sequential-pay or PAC structures; this is called prepayment tranching or time tranching. In a senior-subordinated structure, the subordinated bonds absorb losses first up to their par value, after which losses are absorbed by the senior bonds. The result is to transfer some of the credit risk from the senior bonds to the subordinated bonds. This type of structure is called credit tranching.

LOS 46.c

The structure of the ABS transaction is affected by whether the assets backing the bonds are amortizing or non-amortizing. For amortizing assets like auto loans, once the assets are securitized, the composition of the loans in the pool doesn't change. Loans disappear from the pool as they are paid off or default, but no new loans are added to the pool to replace them. For non-amortizing assets like credit card receivables, the composition of the loans in the pool can and does change. During the lockout period, cash flow from principal payments is used to invest in new loans to replace the amounts paid off.

LOS 46.d

External credit enhancements are financial guarantees from a third party that are used to supplement other forms of credit enhancements. The third-party guarantee effectively links the ABS to the credit risk of the third-party guarantor. Third-party guarantees include: corporate guarantee, letter of credit, and bond insurance.

Internal credit enhancements are "internal" to the issue—they do not rely on a third-party guarantee. Internal credit enhancements include reserve funds, overcollateralization, and senior/subordinated structure.

LOS 46.e

Closed-end HELs are secondary mortgages that are structured just like a standard fixed-rate, fully amortizing mortgage. The pattern of prepayments from HELs differs from MBS prepayment patterns, primarily because of differences in the credit traits of the borrowers. Therefore, analysts must consider the credit of the borrowers when analyzing HEL-backed securities. HEL floaters have a variable coupon rate cap called the available funds cap. HEL structures frequently include non-accelerating senior tranches and planned amortization class (PAC) tranches.

Manufactured housing ABS are backed by loans for manufactured homes. Prepayments for manufactured housing ABS are relatively stable because the underlying loans are not as sensitive to refinancing for the following reasons:

- Small loan balances reduce the extent of savings resulting from refinancing.
- Initial depreciation of mobile homes may be such that the loan principal exceeds the asset value.
- Borrowers often have relatively low credit ratings, making it difficult to refinance.

Auto loan-backed securities are backed by loans for automobiles. Auto loans have 36- to 72-month maturities and are issued by the financial subsidiaries of auto manufacturers, commercial banks, credit unions, etc. Prepayments for auto loan-backed securities are caused by sales and trade-ins, the repossession/resale process, insurance payoffs due to thefts and accidents, borrower payoffs, and refinancing. Refinancing is of minor importance, because many auto loans are frequently below market rates due to sales promotions.

Student loan ABS are most often securitized by loans made under the U.S. government's FFELP. Qualifying FFELP loans carry a U.S. government guarantee. Prepayments may occur because of defaults (inflows from the Government guarantee process) or loan consolidation.

SBA loan-backed securities are backed by pools of SBA loans with similar terms and features. Most SBA loans are variable-rate loans, reset quarterly or monthly, and based on the prime rate.

Credit-card receivables ABS are backed by pools of receivables owed by banks, retailers, travel and entertainment companies, and other credit card issuers. The cash flow to a pool of credit card receivables includes finance charges, annual fees, and principal repayments. Credit cards have periodic payment schedules, but because their balances are revolving, the principal is not amortized. Because of this characteristic, interest on credit card ABS is paid periodically, but no principal is paid to the ABS holders during the lockout period, which may last from 18 months to 10 years.

LOS 46.f

A CDO is an ABS that is collateralized by a pool of debt obligations. A CDO has the following structure: one or more senior tranches, several levels of mezzanine tranches, and a subordinate (equity) tranche to provide prepayment and credit protection.

A CDO's collateral pool typically contains a mix of floating-rate and fixed-rate debt instruments. However, the majority of payments made are based on a floating rate. Managers often address this potential cash flow mismatch by using interest rate swaps to convert fixed-rate interest receipts into floating-rate payments.

In a cash flow CDO, the portfolio manager seeks to generate sufficient cash flow (from interest and principal payments) to repay the senior and mezzanine tranches.

In a synthetic CDO, the bondholders take on the economic risks (but not legal ownership) of the underlying assets. There are three advantages to a synthetic CDO versus a cash CDO:

- The senior section doesn't require funding.
- The ramp-up period is shorter.
- It's cheaper to acquire an exposure to the reference asset through a credit default swap instead of buying the asset directly.

LOS 46.g

The motivations for creating CDOs fall into two basic categories:

- CDOs can be arbitrage-driven, in which the motivation is to generate an arbitrage return on the spread between return on the collateral and the funding costs.
- CDOs can be balance sheet-driven, in which the motivation is to remove assets (and the associated funding) from the balance sheet. For example, a bank can use a synthetic balance sheet CDO to remove the credit risk of a loan portfolio from its balance sheet and reduce its regulatory capital requirements. The advantage to the bank of using the synthetic structure versus a cash CDO is that they don't need to obtain the consent of the borrowers to move the credit risk off the balance sheet.

Concept Checkers

1. Which of the following statements is *most accurate* concerning non-amortizing assets? They do not:
   A. allow principal prepayments.
   B. have scheduled principal payment amounts.
   C. have scheduled interest payments.

2. Which of the following is *least likely* to be used as an external credit enhancement for an asset-backed security (ABS)?
   A. Crossover agreements.
   B. Corporate guarantees.
   C. Bond insurance.

3. Which of the following is a general problem associated with external credit enhancements? External credit enhancements:
   A. can only be used after internal credit enhancements have been exhausted.
   B. are expensive because of the long-term nature of the agreements.
   C. are subject to the credit risk of the third party guarantor.

4. Daren Lea, JD, is a Level II CFA candidate. He recently joined the securitization group of RokStarr Innovative Investments. The firm's two most recent deals were the securitization of a stock of rough and polished diamonds and the securitization of $25 million in loans originated and serviced by First One Financing to finance rock concerts in the United States. As part of the deal structure, RokStarr created a special purpose vehicle called Red Heads Rule. Which of the following choices *most accurately* identifies the parties to the loan securitization?

	First One	Red Heads Rule
A.	Seller	Servicer
B.	Seller	Issues ABS
C.	Trust	Servicer

5. Rating agencies require interest rate swaps in collateralized debt obligation (CDO) deals because:
   A. cash flows are mismatched.
   B. the subordinated tranche investors have credit risk.
   C. the equity tranche investors have credit risk.

6. Which of the following is not considered to be an external credit enhancement?
   A. Insurer call.
   B. Bond insurance.
   C. Corporate guarantee.

7. If a credit card receivables asset backed security (ABS) has a lock-out feature:
   A. no payments are made to the ABS investor for a certain time period.
   B. no principal payments are made to the ABS investor for a certain time period.
   C. no investors may sell the ABS for a certain time period.

8. Rashid Miller is seeking to purchase an asset-backed security that is backed by automobile loans. However, Miller is extremely concerned about prepayment risk. Which of the following factors should *least concern* Miller?
   A. Loan refinancing.
   B. Trade-ins.
   C. Insurance payoffs due to thefts or accidents.

9. Which of the following is the *least likely* reason why an asset-backed security (ABS) generally requires overcollateralization while a mortgage-backed security (MBS) does not?
   A. Some ABS do not have any tangible property as collateral.
   B. Principal recovery in the event of a default is likely to be lower in an ABS.
   C. The interest rates on the underlying assets in an ABS are likely to be lower than the rates on the underlying assets in an MBS.

10. Which of the following is the *most likely* reason why asset-backed securities (ABS) are often assumed to have a larger degree of default risk than mortgage-backed securities (MBS)?
    A. Most ABS are secured by variable-rate loans while most MBSs are secured by fixed-rate loans.
    B. Most ABS are backed by non-amortizing securities, which have more risk of default than amortizing securities.
    C. MBS are secured by loans on traditional real property, which has greater relative stability in value.

11. Which of the following statements concerning arbitrage-driven cash collateralized debt obligations (CDO) is *least accurate*?
    A. CDOs pool only fixed-rate bonds but issue both fixed- and floating-rate tranches from the pool.
    B. Rating agencies typically require the CDO to have an interest rate swap.
    C. The senior tranche in the CDO is generally about 70%–80% of the deal.

CHALLENGE PROBLEMS

12. Consider the following asset backed security (ABS) structure:

Senior tranche	$150,000,000
Subordinated tranche A	$60,000,000
Subordinated tranche B	$20,000,000
Total	$230,000,000

If the assets in the pool are worth $250,000,000, what is the amount of overcollateralization and at what amount of losses will senior tranche investors begin to lose money?

	Overcollateralization	Senior tranche investors' losses
A.	$20,000,000	$100,000,000
B.	$40,000,000	$80,000,000
C.	$20,000,000	$80,000,000

13. Marg Kingston and Albert Loo, both Level II CFA candidates, are discussing asset-backed securities. Kingston states that prepayment risk is more of a concern for an investor in a traditional mortgage-backed security than an auto loan asset-backed security (auto loan ABS) because auto loans typically have smaller loan balances and greater depreciation than mortgages. Loo adds that there are two other reasons—the underlying assets are less liquid in an auto loan ABS and often the loans are initially made at below-market rates as part of sales promotions. With regard to the overall statements made by Loo and Kingston, these are *most likely*:
    A. both correct.
    B. correct in one instance, but incorrect in the other.
    C. both incorrect.

14. Angelique Uttaro, CFA, is reviewing a proposal for a collateralized debt obligation (CDO) from Pilot Investors. The CDO will be collateralized by a pool of emerging market bonds. The report offers two alternatives: a simple cash CDO and a synthetic CDO. The report contains the following statements:

    1. In the synthetic CDO, the junior bondholders receive income from the high-quality debt securities in the portfolio and pay the insurance premium on a credit default swap.

    2. Disadvantages of a cash CDO include a longer ramp-up period and the need to fund the senior section.

    These statements are:
    A. both correct.
    B. correct in one instance, but incorrect in the other.
    C. both incorrect.

15. Consider the following scenarios regarding parties analyzing the potential use of collateralized debt obligations (CDOs).
    - Half-Pass Investments structures a deal to add value by repackaging bonds into tranches. Half-Pass plans to capture for equity investors the spread between relatively high yielding assets and lower yielding liabilities.
    - Piaffe First Bank recently acquired Pirouette Financial. Adding Pirouette's portfolio of loans will result in Piaffe's not being in compliance with internal asset composition targets because its concentration of sub-prime loans will be too high.
    - Canter Consulting has been asked to advise a U.S. commercial bank on ways to reduce the risk-based capital requirement for the commercial loan portfolio. Currently, the bank must reserve 100% capital against the loan balances.
    - Renvers Holdings plans to put together a CDO that it believes can generate a profit from the spread between the return on the collateral and the funding costs.

    Which of the choices below *most accurately* reflects the motivations for the parties in the previous scenarios?

	Arbitrage-driven CDO	Balance sheet-driven CDO
A.	Piaffe & Canter	Half-Pass & Renvers
B.	Piaffe & Renvers	Half-Pass & Canter
C.	Half-Pass & Renvers	Piaffe & Canter

Answers – Concept Checkers

1. **B** Non-amortizing assets do not have *scheduled* principal payment amounts. Principal prepayments and curtailments are allowed, and regular interest payments based on the unpaid principal are required.

2. **A** Crossover agreements are not a type of external credit enhancement. Corporate guarantees, letters of credit, and bond insurance are all examples of external credit enhancement.

3. **C** A general problem with external credit enhancements is that they are subject to the credit risk of the third party guarantor.

4. **B** First One is the seller—it originates the loans and sells them to Red Heads Rule, which is the issuer/trust for the ABS.

5. **A** Bond rating agencies require interest rate swaps because the cash inflows from floating- or fixed-rate assets are mismatched with the cash outflows to floating-rate tranches.

6. **A** An insurer call is a type of call provision. The other choices are external credit enhancements to an ABS.

7. **B** During the lock-out period on a credit card receivables backed ABS, no principal payments are made to the ABS investor for a certain period of time.

8. **A** Refinancing of automobile loans is a low probability event due to the short maturity of the loans and the fact that the loans are frequently set below market rates due to promotional events by the manufacturers. The other items listed could all cause prepayments on auto loan-backed securities.

9. **C** The interest rates on the underlying assets for some ABSs may be lower than for MBSs (e.g., auto loans), and some rates on underlying assets will be higher (e.g., credit card receivables). In any case, this is not a reason for overcollateralization of ABS.

10. **C** Mortgage backed securities are secured by loans on traditional real property. In the event of a default on a given mortgage loan, it is unlikely that a substantial loss will be incurred because real property is relatively stable in value.

11. **A** CDOs pool both fixed- and floating-rate assets.

Answers – Challenge Problems

12. **A** The overcollateralization in the pool is the difference between the amount of the assets and the claims against the pool: $250,000,000 – $230,000,000 = $20,000,000.

    Senior tranche investors begin to lose when the overcollateralization is gone and when the subordinated A and B tranches have defaulted, so losses must be $20,000,000 + $20,000,000 + $60,000,000 = $100,000,000 before the senior tranche suffers any losses.

13. **B** Loo is incorrect and Kingston is correct. The market for cars is probably more liquid than the market for houses. In any case, it is not a major factor contributing to auto loan prepayments. Prepayments for auto-loan ABS are less frequent because the underlying loans are not as sensitive to refinancing. This is because loan balances are usually small, reducing the extent of savings resulting from refinancing, especially if used car refinancing rates are significantly higher than new car rates.

    The auto's value may depreciate faster than the loan balance in the early years, resulting in the value of the asset being less than the outstanding loan amount, particularly if the loans are done at below-market rates because of sales promotions.

14. **B** Statement 1 is incorrect; junior bondholders receive income from the insurance premium on the credit default swap. Statement 2 is correct.

15. **C** Both Half-Pass and Renvers are in situations in which there is a motivation to create an arbitrage-driven CDO, where the motivation is to generate an arbitrage return on the spread between return on the collateral and funding costs. Piaffe and Canter are both in situations that lend themselves to an balance-sheet driven CDO, where the motivation is to remove assets (and the associated funding) from the balance sheet.

The following is a review of the Fixed Income: Structured Securities principles designed to address the learning outcome statements set forth by CFA Institute. This topic is also covered in:

VALUING MORTGAGE-BACKED AND ASSET-BACKED SECURITIES

Study Session 15

EXAM FOCUS

This topic review is the Level II fixed-income grand finale. It brings together concepts from the prior fixed-income material, where we discussed mortgage-backed securities (MBS) and asset-backed securities (ABS) and illustrated how cash flows could be distributed to different tranches to alter exposure to prepayment and credit risk. Here we address the important issue of how to value these securities and quantify their exposure to interest rate risk. Make certain you (1) understand the difference between nominal spreads, *Z*-spreads, and option-adjusted spread (OAS), (2) are able to apply OAS analysis to value MBS and ABS, (3) can determine which model is appropriate for valuing any specific type of fixed-income security, and (4) can analyze the interest rate risk of MBS and ABS.

LOS 47.a: Explain the calculation, use, and limitations of the cash flow yield, nominal spread, and zero-volatility spread for a mortgage-backed security and an asset-backed security.

CFA® Program Curriculum, Volume 5, page 522

Cash Flow Yield and Nominal Spread

The **cash flow yield** is the discount rate that makes the price of a mortgage-backed security (MBS) or asset-backed security (ABS) equal to the present value of its cash flows. To compute the cash flow yield:

- Estimate the future monthly cash flows.
- Calculate the monthly rate of return that makes the present value of these future cash flows equal to the security's current market price.

The monthly cash flow yield is usually converted to a bond-equivalent basis for comparison to yield-to-maturity:

$$\text{bond-equivalent yield} = 2[(1+\text{monthly cash flow yield})^6 - 1]$$

The challenge in applying this concept is that the cash flows from the MBS or ABS are uncertain because we don't know what future prepayment rates will be. In order to compute a cash flow yield for an MBS and ABS, we must make a prepayment assumption. Furthermore, if the security is not an agency issue, we also need assumptions about default and recovery rates.

The cash flow yield has three major deficiencies. When we use cash flow yield as our estimate of the bond's expected return, we assume:

1. The cash flows will be reinvested at the cash flow yield prevailing when the MBS or ABS is priced. In past topic reviews, we've called this **reinvestment risk.**
2. The MBS or ABS will be held until the last loan in the pool is paid off (i.e., expected maturity, not stated maturity). If the security is sold prior to maturity, uncertainty is introduced regarding terminal cash flows. This is called **price risk.**
3. The cash flows will be realized as expected. This assumption is more likely to be violated for MBS and ABS than for many other fixed-income securities because of prepayment risk.

Nominal spread is the difference between the cash flow yield on an MBS and the YTM on a Treasury security with a maturity equal to the average life of the MBS. A portion of the nominal spread represents compensation to the investor for exposure to prepayment risk.

The limitation of using nominal spread to analyze MBS is that we don't know how much of the nominal spread reflects the significant prepayment risk associated with MBS. This is particularly true for support (companion) collateralized mortgage obligation (CMO) tranches.

Let's look at an application of nominal spread and explore its limitations. Suppose the yield curve for U.S. Treasury bonds (T-bonds) is as shown in Figure 1.

Figure 1: U.S. Treasury Yields

Maturity	*5-year*	*7-year*	*9-year*	*12-year*	*20-year*
YTM	6.0%	6.2%	6.5%	6.9%	7.2%

Now consider a Ginnie Mae passthrough certificate with a stated maturity of 20 years and an average life of 12 years. Assume that the bond equivalent cash flow yield for this MBS is 7.75% based on a prepayment assumption of 150 Public Securities Association (PSA). Suppose a 12-year AA corporate bond with a YTM of 7.50% is also available.

The nominal spread for an MBS is traditionally measured relative to a Treasury security with a maturity equal to the average life of the MBS:

7.75% – 6.9% = 85 basis points

The nominal spread for the corporate is also computed relative to the 12-year Treasury:

7.50% – 6.9% = 60 basis points

We can't necessarily conclude from this relative value analysis that the MBS is a better investment, despite the fact that it has a higher spread and slightly lower credit risk than the AA bond. The reason is that some or perhaps most of that 85 basis point spread reflects the significant prepayment risk of the MBS. What we need is a spread measure that explicitly accounts for the prepayment option embedded in MBS.

Zero-Volatility Spread

Zero-volatility spread is another commonly used measure of relative value for MBS and ABS. The zero-volatility spread (also known as the *Z*-spread or static spread) is the spread that must be added to each Treasury spot rate that will cause the discounted value of the cash flows for an MBS or ABS to equal its price, assuming that the security is held until maturity. Note that there is a Treasury spot rate associated with each of these cash flows but only one value for the *Z*-spread that must be simultaneously added to each of the rates. A computer-assisted, iterative process can be used to determine the zero-volatility spread.

The zero-volatility spread and the nominal spread converge as the average life of the MBS decreases. Also, the difference between the zero-volatility spread and nominal spread increases as the slope of the yield curve increases.

The key limitation of the Z-spread is that it only considers one path of interest rates: the current Treasury spot rate curve. In contrast, the option-adjusted spread, which we discuss next, is added to the spot rates along *each and every path* in an interest rate tree. The key is to use the option-adjusted spread (OAS) for bonds with embedded options that are sensitive to changes in interest rate volatility (such as MBS).

LOS 47.b: Describe the Monte Carlo simulation model for valuing a mortgage-backed security.

CFA® Program Curriculum, Volume 5, page 524

There are five steps in the valuation of an MBS using the Monte Carlo simulation model:

Step 1: Simulate interest rate paths (e.g., 1,000 different paths) and cash flows using assumptions concerning benchmark rates, rate volatility, refinancing spreads, and prepayment rates. Non-agency MBS also require assumptions regarding default and recovery rates.

Step 2: Calculate the present value of the cash flows along each of the 1,000 interest rate paths.

Step 3: Calculate the theoretical value of the MBS as the average of the present values along each path.

Step 4: Calculate the OAS as the spread that makes the theoretical value equal to the market price.

Step 5: Calculate the option cost as the zero-volatility spread minus the OAS.

LOS 47.c: Describe path dependency in passthrough securities and the implications for valuation models.

CFA® Program Curriculum, Volume 5, page 525

Due to the path dependence of MBS cash flows, the Monte Carlo simulation technique is used to value these securities instead of the binomial model. Recall that when valuing a callable bond using backward induction methodology with the binomial model, the relevant cash flow to be discounted at any given node is either the call price or the theoretical value, whichever is less. An important assumption of the binomial valuation process is that the value of the cash flows at a given point in time is independent of the path that interest rates followed up to that point. Thus, the decision to use the call price or the theoretical value at a node in the binomial tree is determined by the assumed interest rate at the time the decision must be made, not past interest rates.

In contrast to the typical callable bond, the cash flows for MBS are dependent upon the path that interest rates follow and, therefore, cannot be properly valued with the binomial model or any other model that employs the backward induction methodology. The cash flows for passthrough securities are a function of prepayment rates, and prepayment rates in any given month are affected by interest rates in the past. There are two sources of path dependency:

1. If mortgage rates trend downward over a period of time, prepayment rates will increase at the beginning of the trend as homeowners refinance their mortgages, but prepayments will slow as the trend continues because many of the homeowners that can refinance will have already done so. This prepayment pattern is called **prepayment burnout**, and it applies to MBS and other types of passthrough security cash flows as well as CMO tranches.

2. The cash flows that a particular CMO tranche receives in any one month depend on the outstanding principal balances of the other tranches in the structure, which in turn depend on the prepayment history and the interest rate path.

LOS 47.d: Explain how the option-adjusted spread is calculated using the Monte Carlo simulation model and how this spread measure is interpreted.

CFA® Program Curriculum, Volume 5, page 530

The **option-adjusted spread** (OAS) estimated from a Monte Carlo simulation model is computed using the same general principle as the OAS from a binomial model. We want to determine the spread that makes the MBS value derived from the model (the present value of the projected cash flows) equal to the current market price. This process is a little more complicated with Monte Carlo models because the OAS is the spread that we have to add to *every* spot rate along *every* interest rate path.

We can interpret the OAS as the MBS spread after the "optionality" of the cash flows is taken into account. It can be used to express the dollar difference between price and theoretical value as a spread.

We can also use the relationship between the *Z*-spread and the OAS to estimate the cost of the embedded prepayment option inherent in MBS and ABS. The implied cost of the embedded option can be expressed as:

option cost = zero-volatility spread – option-adjusted spread

Note that here the option cost is derived from OAS analysis as opposed to an option pricing model.

To see how OAS is used in practice, consider a manager who computes the theoretical value of an MBS with the Monte Carlo model using Treasury rates as the benchmark. To compute this theoretical value, the manager must add a "risk-appropriate" spread to the spot rates along the model's interest rate paths. Recall that the monthly rates along the paths generated with the Monte Carlo simulation model using the Treasury yield curve as a benchmark are Treasury spot rates that have been adjusted to be arbitrage-free. Thus, the OAS measures the average spread over Treasury spot rates, *not* the comparable Treasury yield.

In general, you want the OAS to be large, all else equal. A wider OAS indicates a larger risk-adjusted spread, which leads to a lower relative price.

In our examples, the benchmark rates used to create the Monte Carlo Model are Treasury rates, so we can interpret the OAS for an MBS as the additional compensation for credit risk, liquidity risk, and modeling risk after the cost of the embedded prepayment option has been removed. We've already discussed credit risk and liquidity risk in previous topic reviews, so let's discuss modeling risk here.

Modeling risk is the uncertainty in the MBS value that results from the use of assumptions in the complicated Monte Carlo model framework. The MBS value derived from a Monte Carlo model is very sensitive to the interest rate volatility assumption and the prepayment assumption, for example.

The interpretation of the OAS depends on the security's credit risk, liquidity risk, and modeling risk relative to the benchmark.The appropriate interpretation of an OAS using Treasury securities as a benchmark for agency and non-agency passthrough and CMO issues is shown in Figure 2.

Figure 2: Interpretation of OAS Using Treasury Securities as a Benchmark

	Does the OAS using a Treasury Benchmark reflect:		
Security	*Credit Risk?*	*Liquidity Risk?*	*Modeling Risk?*
Ginnie Mae passthroughs	No	Yes	Yes
Ginnie Mae CMOs	No	Yes. Support tranches have more than PAC I.	Yes. CMOs have more than passthroughs. CMO support tranches have more than PAC I.
Freddie Mac/ Fannie Mae passthroughs	Yes, but small.	Yes	Yes
Freddie Mac/ Fannie Mae CMOs	Yes, but small.	Yes. CMO support tranches have more than PAC I.	Yes. CMOs have more than passthroughs.CMO support tranches have more than PAC I.
Non-agency MBS and real estate backed ABS	Yes	Yes, more than agency issues.	Yes

From a statistical perspective, as the number of paths generated by a Monte Carlo model increases, the "better" is the resulting estimate. Vendors, however, often employ computational procedures that reduce the full number of sample paths while maintaining the accuracy of the Monte Carlo analysis. The reduced set of paths is referred to as a set of **representative paths**. The theoretical value of the MBS is then the weighted average of the present values of each representative path, weighted by "path weights."

Example: Estimating OAS from a Monte Carlo model

The following figure shows the present values for six representative paths and corresponding path weights resulting from the Monte Carlo simulation analysis of a CMO tranche. Three present values for each path are shown because they were calculated using three different discount rates. Each discount rate is the short-term rate on the path plus the spread indicated at the top of the columns.

OAS Simulations

		Present Value of Representative Path		
Representative Path	*Path Weight*	*If Spread Is 65 bps*	*If Spread Is 70 bps*	*If Spread Is 75 bps*
1	18%	$80.00	$78.00	$76.00
2	15	82.00	80.00	77.00
3	20	78.00	75.00	74.00
4	9	81.00	78.00	77.00
5	23	88.00	86.00	85.00
6	15	85.00	84.00	81.00
Theoretical value = Σ(weight × PV)		$82.58	$80.44	$78.66

The last row in this figure represents the theoretical value for the CMO tranche based on the different discount rates. As indicated, this value is the weighted average of the present values of the cash flow for each representative path. Suppose that the actual market price of this tranche is $80.44. Determine the OAS of the CMO tranche.

Answer:

The OAS is the spread that, when added to the interest rates along an interest rate path, makes the theoretical value equal to the market price. When the spread is 70 basis points, the figure indicates the theoretical value from the model is $80.44, which is equal to the market price. Therefore, the OAS is 70 basis points.

LOS 47.e: Evaluate a mortgage-backed security using option-adjusted spread analysis.

CFA® Program Curriculum, Volume 5, page 530

We can identify rich and cheap securities (on a relative valuation basis) by comparing the OAS and option costs of the various tranches in a CMO deal. The OAS is the spread adjusted for the embedded options in the security, and the option cost is the difference between the *Z*-spread and the OAS. Typically, securities with longer effective durations have larger OAS and option costs because of their higher interest rate exposure. Therefore, *for a given Z-spread and effective duration*:

- *Cheap* securities will have high OAS relative to the required OAS and low option costs.
- *Rich* securities will have low OAS relative to the required OAS and high option costs.

Cheap securities are undervalued on a relative basis, and we want to buy them; rich securities are overvalued, which means we should sell them.

Example: OAS analysis of an MBS

Let's apply some of this by evaluating the following two tranches for a hypothetical sequential-pay CMO structure. Identify which CMO tranche is less expensive ("cheap") on a relative basis and justify your answer.

Pricing Data on CMO Tranches

Tranche	*OAS (bps)*	*Z-spread (bps)*	*Effective Duration*
I	92	142	4.25
II	118	134	4.25

Answer:

The first thing we have to do is compute the option cost of each tranche:

Tranche I option cost = 142 – 92 = 50 basis points

Tranche II option cost = 134 – 118 = 16 basis points

Tranche II has a higher OAS and lower option cost than Tranche I, and the effective durations of the two tranches are equal. Therefore:

- Tranche II is undervalued on a relative basis ("cheap"), and we should buy it.
- Tranche I is overvalued on a relative basis ("rich"), and we should sell it.

On an *absolute* valuation basis, note that:

1. Tranches trading at a premium (discount) will see gains (losses) when the assumed prepayment rate decreases.

2. Increases (decreases) in assumed interest rate volatility increases (decreases) the option cost and reduces (increases) the value of the MBS (which is short the prepayment option).

Additionally, for both changes in prepayment rates and changes in interest rate volatility, the gains (or losses) in value are more pronounced for tranches with higher effective duration.

LOS 47.f: Explain why effective durations reported by various dealers and vendors may differ.

CFA® Program Curriculum, Volume 5, page 539

Duration measures the sensitivity of a security's price to changes in interest rates. It can be determined by changing the interest rate in a security pricing model up and down by a small amount and observing what happens to the price.

Recall that **effective duration** can then be calculated as:

$$\text{effective duration} = \text{ED} = \frac{\text{BV}_{-\Delta y} - \text{BV}_{+\Delta y}}{2 \times \text{BV}_0 \times \Delta y}$$

where:

Δy = change in required yield, in decimal form
$\text{BV}_{-\Delta y}$ = estimated price if yield decreases by Δy
$\text{BV}_{+\Delta y}$ = estimated price if yield increases by Δy
BV_0 = initial observed bond price

The Monte Carlo simulation model may be used to compute $\text{BV}_{-\Delta y}$ and $\text{BV}_{+\Delta y}$ in the previous equation when measuring effective duration for MBS.

The assumptions used to calculate effective duration are important and can have a material impact on estimates of effective duration reported by different vendors and dealers.

- *Differences in* Δy. If Δy, which is the incremental change in interest rate, is too large, the effects of convexity contaminate effective duration estimates.
- *Prepayment model differences.* Prepayment models vary among dealers.
- *OAS differences.* OAS is a product of the Monte Carlo simulation model. Differences in the inputs to the model will affect the measurement of OAS. This has particular relevance to the volatility assumption and the prepayment model used with a particular Monte Carlo model.

- *Differences in the spread* between 1-month rates and refinancing rates. The assumed spread between 1-month rates and refinancing rates affects the computed values of MBS. Thus, different assumptions about this relationship will provide different values for $BV_{+\Delta y}$ and $BV_{-\Delta y}$ in the effective duration computation.

LOS 47.g: Analyze the interest rate risk of a security, given the security's effective duration.

CFA® Program Curriculum, Volume 5, page 539

Analyzing Interest Rate Risk With Effective Duration and Convexity

Remember that interest rate risk is the risk that the price of a fixed-income security will change as yields change. Effective duration is a measure of interest rate risk: the larger the duration of a security, all else equal, the greater the interest rate risk. However, duration only gives us an estimate of the actual change in the price of a bond for small changes in yields. The convexity adjustment gives us a more precise estimate for larger changes in yield. For a given duration, the greater the convexity, the lower the interest rate risk.

Given a bond's duration and convexity, we can estimate the percentage price change in the bond for a given change in yield as:

$$\begin{aligned}\%\text{ change in bond price} &\approx \text{duration effect} + \text{convexity effect}\\ &\approx (-ED \times \Delta y \times 100) + \left(EC \times \Delta y^2 \times 100\right)\end{aligned}$$

Example: Assessing interest rate risk, part 1

Durable, Inc., bonds have a duration of 5.6 years and a convexity of 38.2. Conversion Force, Inc., bonds have a duration of 7.3 years and a convexity of 38.2. Determine which bond is exposed to more interest rate risk.

Answer:

Conversion Force bonds have a larger duration than Durable bonds, but the two have equal convexities. That means Conversion Force bonds have greater interest rate risk exposure. To see this, calculate what happens to the price of both bonds if rates increase by 100 basis points:

$$\begin{aligned}\%\text{ change in Conversion Force bond price} &= (-7.3 \times 0.01 \times 100) + \left(38.2 \times 0.01^2 \times 100\right)\\ &= -6.9\%\end{aligned}$$

$$\begin{aligned}\%\text{ change in Durable bond price} &= (-5.6 \times 0.01 \times 100) + \left(38.2 \times 0.01^2 \times 100\right)\\ &= -5.2\%\end{aligned}$$

Example: Assessing interest rate risk, part 2

Suppose that Durable, Inc., bonds have a duration of 5.6 years and a convexity of 38.2, and Universal, Inc., bonds have a duration of 5.6 years and a convexity of 134.0. Determine which bond is exposed to more interest rate risk.

Answer:

Now the two have the same duration, but Universal bonds have greater convexity. That means Universal bonds are less exposed to changes in yields than Durable bonds. To see this, calculate what happens to the price of both bonds if rates increase by 100 basis points:

$$\text{\% change in Universal bond price} = (-5.6 \times 0.01 \times 100) + (134.0 \times 0.01^2 \times 100) = -4.3\%$$

$$\text{\% change in Durable bond price} = (-5.6 \times 0.01 \times 100) + (38.2 \times 0.01^2 \times 100) = -5.2\%$$

LOS 47.h: Explain cash flow, coupon curve, and empirical measures of duration, and describe limitations of each in relation to mortgage-backed securities.

CFA® Program Curriculum, Volume 5, page 542

Cash flow duration is a version of effective duration that allows for cash flows to change as interest rates change. Unlike valuation with the binomial or the Monte Carlo models, cash flow duration uses a static valuation procedure to determine $BV_{+\Delta y}$ and $BV_{-\Delta y}$. This procedure uses the following steps:

- Make a prepayment rate assumption (e.g., 100 PSA), and use it to estimate cash flows.
- Compute the cash flow yield based on the market price and the cash flow estimates. (Recall that cash flow yield is the discount rate that makes the present value of the cash flows equal to the price.)
- Increase the cash flow yield by Δy and, with the use of a prepayment model, recompute prepayment rates. These rates are normally lower than those in the original prepayment rates due to the higher interest rates. For example, if the original prepayment assumption was 100 PSA, the new prepayment rate might be 90 PSA.
- Recompute the cash flows using the prepayment rates generated in the previous step, and discount these cash flows at the higher cash flow yield to get $BV_{+\Delta y}$.
- Decrease the cash flow yield by Δy, and with the use of a prepayment model, regenerate prepayment rates. These rates are normally greater than those in the original prepayment rates (e.g., 140 PSA) due to the lower yield.
- Recompute the cash flow using the prepayment rates from Step 5, and discount these cash flows at the lower cash flow yield to get $BV_{-\Delta y}$.

The values for $BV_{+\Delta y}$ or $BV_{-\Delta y}$ obtained from this procedure—the initial value BV_0 and the imposed cash flow yield change Δy—can be substituted into the effective duration equation to obtain the cash flow duration.

A *major criticism of cash flow duration* is that it is based on the unrealistic assumption that the new MBS's prepayment rate is constant over its entire life for a given shock to interest rates. The Monte Carlo simulation does allow for changing prepayment rates, and therefore, *effective duration computed using the Monte Carlo simulation is much better than cash flow duration* for MBS.

Coupon curve duration is based on the relationship between coupon rates and prices for similar MBS. Let's look at an example of the process for determining $BV_{-\Delta y}$ and $BV_{+\Delta y}$ in the computation of coupon rate duration. Note, however, that the LOS doesn't ask you to "calculate."

Consider the coupon curve for a hypothetical passthrough shown in Figure 3.

Figure 3: Passthrough Coupon Curve

Coupon Rate:	7%	8%	9%	10%	11%	12%
Price:	93.06	96.07	99.55	103.25	105.90	110.35

Assume that we want to compute the effective duration for a 10% coupon passthrough (BV_0 = 103.25). If rates decrease 100 basis points, it is assumed that prices will increase to the price of the 11% coupon security ($BV_{-\Delta y}$ = 105.90). Similarly, for an increase of 100 basis points, $BV_{+\Delta y}$ will be 99.55. Plugging these values into the (familiar) duration equation yields a coupon curve duration equal to:

$$\frac{105.90 - 99.55}{2 \times 103.25 \times 0.01} = 3.075$$

The *advantages* of the coupon curve duration method are that it:

- Is easy to apply.
- Uses market prices that presumably reflect market expectations.

The *limitations* of the procedure are that it is:

- Only applicable to generic MBS.
- Not readily applicable for CMO structures and other mortgage-based derivatives.

Empirical duration (or implied duration) is determined using a regression analysis of the historical relationship between security prices (the dependent variable) and yields (the independent variable).

Empirical duration has three *advantages*:

- It requires few assumptions.
- The required parameters are easy to estimate with regression analysis.
- The time series data for Treasury prices and yields is readily available.

Disadvantages of empirical duration include:

- Time series price data on mortgage securities may be difficult to obtain.
- Embedded options can distort the results.
- The volatility of the spreads over Treasuries can distort the price reaction to interest rate changes.

LOS 47.i: Determine whether the nominal spread, zero-volatility spread, or option-adjusted spread should be used to evaluate a specific fixed income security.

CFA® Program Curriculum, Volume 5, page 544

The **nominal spread** is expressed as the spread between the cash flow yield and the yield on a Treasury security with the same maturity as the average life of the MBS or ABS under analysis. It is the spread at one point on the Treasury yield curve. We should never use the nominal spread for MBS and ABS because it masks the fact that a portion of the spread is compensation for accepting prepayment risk.

The **zero-volatility spread** is the spread over the entire Treasury spot rate curve if an MBS is held until maturity. It is suitable for assessing the value of option-free bonds. *Z*-spread analysis should not be used with bonds that have prepayment options because it does not reflect the possibility that cash flows may change as interest rates change.

The **option-adjusted spread** (OAS) should be used to assess the value of fixed-income securities that have embedded options that make it possible for cash flows to change as interest rates change.

- If the amounts of the cash flows are *not interest rate path dependent* (i.e., they may depend upon the *current level* of interest rates, but not the *path* that led to the current level), such as those associated with putable and callable bonds, OAS should be used with the binomial model.
- If the amounts of the cash flows are **interest rate path dependent**, like those associated with ABS and MBS, the OAS should be used with the Monte Carlo simulation model.

The appropriate valuation model for an ABS is dependent on whether a prepayment option is available on the underlying collateral and whether that option is typically exercised:

- Credit-card-receivable-backed ABS have no prepayment option. Automobile loans have a prepayment option, but it is not typically exercised as a result of changes in interest rates. In either case, the *Z*-spread is the appropriate measure.
- ABS backed by high-quality home equity loans have a prepayment option that is frequently exercised when rates drop and borrowers refinance. Furthermore, the amounts of the cash flows are path-dependent, so an OAS derived from a Monte Carlo model is appropriate.

Figure 4 summarizes this discussion.

Figure 4: Appropriate Spread Measures for Fixed Income Securities

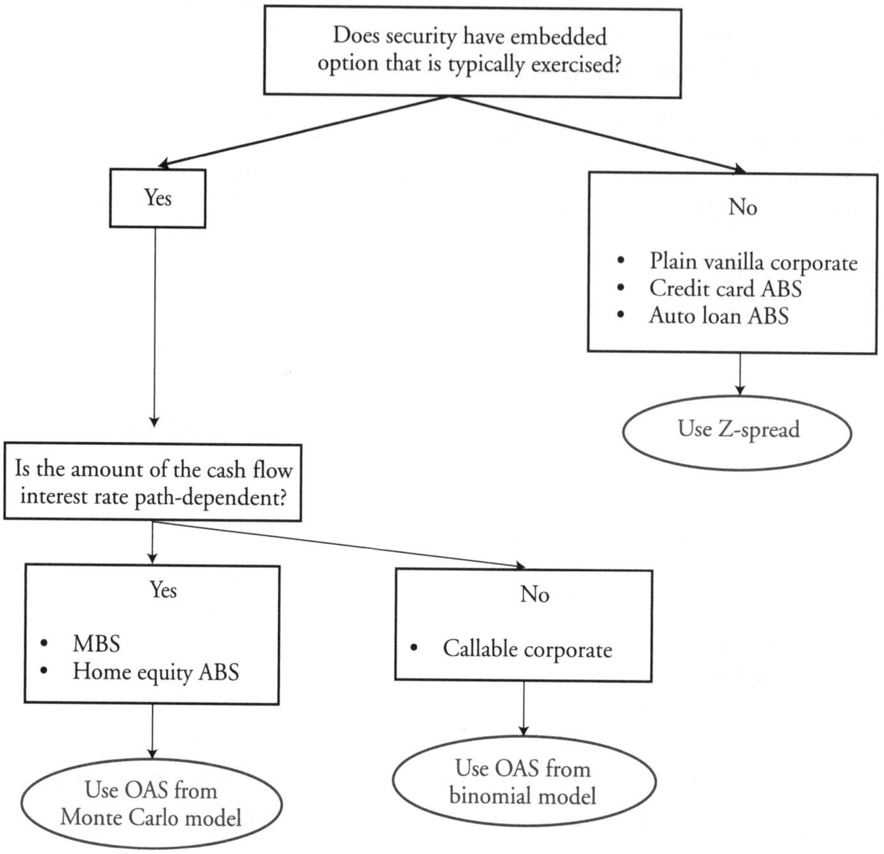

Does security have embedded option that is typically exercised?

Yes

Is the amount of the cash flow interest rate path-dependent?

Yes

- MBS
- Home equity ABS

Use OAS from Monte Carlo model

No

- Callable corporate

Use OAS from binomial model

No

- Plain vanilla corporate
- Credit card ABS
- Auto loan ABS

Use Z-spread

KEY CONCEPTS

LOS 47.a

The cash flow yield is the discount rate that makes the price of an ABS or MBS equal to the present value of its cash flows. Cash flow yield for MBS and ABS has three major deficiencies: (1) it is implicitly assumed that the cash flows will be reinvested at the cash flow yield prevailing when the MBS or ABS is priced, (2) it is based on the assumption that an MBS or ABS will be held until expected maturity, and (3) it assumes that the cash flows will be realized as expected.

The nominal spread is the difference between the cash flow yield on an MBS and the YTM on a Treasury security with a maturity equal to the average life of the MBS. There are at least two problems with the interpretation of the nominal spread:

- Some unknown fraction of the nominal spread represents compensation for prepayment risk.
- The unknown fraction of the nominal spread that is compensation for prepayment risk may be more significant for the support (companion) tranches.

The zero-volatility spread (*Z*-spread or static spread) is the spread that must be added to each Treasury spot rate to cause the discounted value of an MBS's cash flows to equal its price.

- A computer-aided, iterative process can be followed to determine the *Z*-spread.
- Zero-volatility spread and nominal spread converge as the average life of the MBS decreases.
- The difference between the *Z*-spread and nominal spread increases as the slope of the yield curve increases.

LOS 47.b

The OAS computed using the Monte Carlo model is the spread that makes the MBS value derived from the model (the present value of the projected cash flows) equal to the current market price.

LOS 47.c

The size of the cash flows and value of the MBS are interest rate path dependent, which means they must be valued with a Monte Carlo Model rather than a binomial model.

LOS 47.d

OAS estimates from a Monte Carlo simulation use the same general principle as the OAS from a binomial model—a spread is added to every spot rate along every interest rate path until the spread causes the model price to equal the current market price. We can interpret the OAS as the MBS spread after the "optionality" of the cash flows is taken into account. The interpretation of the OAS depends on the security's credit risk, liquidity risk, and modeling risk relative to the benchmark.

LOS 47.e

Relative valuation—for a given *Z*-spread and effective duration:

- Cheap securities will have high OAS relative to the required OAS and low option costs.
- Rich securities will have low OAS relative to the required OAS and high option costs.

Absolute valuation:

- Tranches trading at a premium (discount) will see gains (losses) when the assumed prepayment rate decreases.
- Increases (decreases) in assumed interest rate volatility increases (decreases) option cost and reduces (increases) the value of the MBS.

These changes in values are more pronounced for tranches with higher duration.

LOS 47.f

The assumptions used to calculate effective duration are important and can have a material impact on estimates of effective duration reported by different vendors and dealers.

- Differences in Δy: If Δy, which is the incremental change in interest rate, is too large, the effects of convexity contaminate effective duration estimates.
- Prepayment model differences: Prepayment models vary among dealers.
- OAS differences: OAS is a product of the Monte Carlo simulation model. Differences in the inputs to the model will affect the measurement of OAS. This has particular relevance to the volatility assumption and the prepayment model used with a particular Monte Carlo model.
- Differences in the spread between one-month rates and refinancing rates. The assumed spread between one-month rates and refinancing rates affects the computed values of MBS. Thus, different assumptions about this relationship will provide different values for $BV_{+\Delta y}$ and $BV_{-\Delta y}$ in the effective duration computation.

LOS 47.g

Interest-rate risk is the risk that the price of a fixed-income security will change as yields change. *Effective duration* is a measure of interest-rate risk. The larger the duration of a security, all else equal, the greater the interest-rate risk. However, duration only gives us an estimate of the actual change in the price of a bond for small changes in yields. The *convexity adjustment* gives us a more precise estimate for larger changes in yield. For a given duration, the greater the convexity, the lower the interest-rate risk.

Given a bond's duration and convexity, we can estimate the percentage price change in the bond for a given change in yields as:

$$\%\text{ change in bond price} \approx \text{duration effect} + \text{convexity effect, or}$$

$$\%\text{ change in bond price} \approx (-\text{ED} \times \Delta y \times 100) + (\text{EC} \times \Delta y^2 \times 100)$$

LOS 47.h

In practice, there are several measures of duration that may be used with MBS:

- Effective duration is the appropriate measure for securities with embedded options, such as callable corporate bonds and MBS. Effective duration is computed using Monte Carlo simulation by "bumping" interest rates up and down and using the new values in the duration equation.
- Coupon curve duration is based on the relationship between coupon rates and prices for similar MBS. The values used in the duration formula are found by moving up and down the coupon curve. Coupon curve duration applicability is, however, limited to generic MBS only.
- Empirical duration (implied duration) is determined using a regression analysis of the historical relationship between security prices and yields. Limitations of empirical duration include the following: time series data are difficult to obtain; spread volatility could change; and presence of embedded options could distort results.
- Cash flow duration is a form of effective duration. It recognizes that cash flows can change as interest rates change and is based on the changes in value that occur after the initial cash flow yield is shifted up and down. This causes prepayment rates, expected cash flows, and values to change. The changed values are plugged into the duration equation. Cash flow duration is, however, based on an unrealistic assumption of single prepayment rate over the life of a MBS.

LOS 47.i

Embedded Option That is Typically Exercised?	*Path-Dependent Option?*	*Example*	*Spread Measure*	*Option Valuation Model*
No	—	Plain-vanilla corporate	*Z*-spread	—
No	—	Credit card ABS	*Z*-spread	—
No	—	Auto loanABS	*Z*-spread	—
Yes	No	Callable corporate	OAS	Binomial
Yes	Yes	MBS	OAS	Monte Carlo
Yes	Yes	Home equity ABS	OAS	Monte Carlo

CONCEPT CHECKERS

1. Which of the following is *least likely* to be considered a shortcoming of the cash flow yield as a process for the cash flow analysis of a mortgage or asset-backed security?
   A. All cash flows are assumed to be reinvested at the cash flow yield.
   B. All cash flows are assumed to be certain to occur.
   C. The term structure is assumed to be normal.

2. Brian Heltzel recently completed a Monte Carlo simulation analysis of a collateralized mortgage obligation (CMO) tranche. Heltzel's analysis includes six equally weighted paths, with the present value of each calculated using four different discount rates, as shown in the following figure.

Representative Path	*PV if spread is 50 basis points*	*PV if spread is 60 basis points*	*PV if spread is 70 basis points*
1	70	68	66
2	73	70	68
3	68	66	64
4	71	69	68
5	77	75	73
6	75	73	71

   The actual market price of the CMO tranche being valued is 70.17. The tranche's option-adjusted spread (OAS) is *closest* to:
   A. 50 basis points.
   B. 60 basis points.
   C. 70 basis points.

3. An asset-backed security (ABS) backed by automobile loans is issued. This security should be evaluated using the:
   A. nominal spread.
   B. *Z*-spread.
   C. OAS from Monte Carlo simulation.

4. A Ginnie Mae security with no call or put features is issued against a pool of conventional mortgages. This security should be evaluated using the:
   A. *Z*-spread.
   B. OAS from the binomial model.
   C. OAS from Monte Carlo simulation.

5. Which of the following statements concerning the measurement of interest rate risk of a mortgage-backed security (MBS) is *least accurate*?
   A. Coupon curve duration looks at other MBS issues with different coupons to determine how one MBS price will change when interest rates change.
   B. Empirical duration uses regression analysis to determine how the MBS price has responded to interest rate changes in the past.
   C. Cash flow duration allows the prepayment speed of the pool to vary over time.

6. A model that incorporates backward induction methodology, like the binomial model, cannot be used to value a mortgage-backed security (MBS) because:
   A. the cash flows are assumed to occur with certainty.
   B. the cash flows for an MBS are dependent upon the path that interest rates follow.
   C. effective duration measures cannot be computed using backward induction.

7. Which of the following statements concerning the nominal spread, the *Z*-spread, and the option-adjusted spread (OAS) is *least accurate*?
   A. The *Z*-spread is the spread that must be added to Treasury spot rates that will cause the discounted value of the cash flows for an MBS or ABS to equal its price, assuming that the security is held until maturity.
   B. The OAS is equal to the *Z*-spread plus the option cost.
   C. The OAS from a Monte Carlo simulation model is the spread that must be added to all of the spot rates along each interest rate path that will force equality between the average present value of the path cash flows and the market price for the MBS being evaluated.

8. Suppose that ten equally weighted representative paths are used in the Monte Carlo simulation model. For the different spreads used, the present value of each representative path is shown in the following figure for a collateralized mortgage obligation (CMO) tranche.

Representative Path	*Present Value if Spread is:*		
	75 bps	*80 bps*	*85 bps*
1	72	62	65
2	77	75	72
3	81	79	76
4	84	81	77
5	69	65	63
6	83	81	77
7	91	87	83
8	87	85	81
9	69	66	62
10	93	59	56

If the market price of Tranche X is 74, the option-adjusted spread (OAS) is *closest* to:
A. 75 bps.
B. 80 bps.
C. 85 bps.

9. Which of the following statements *correctly* identifies a limitation of the nominal spread for analyzing a mortgage-backed security (MBS)? The nominal spread does not:
A. account for differences in credit risk between the MBS and the Treasury security.
B. adjust for the prepayment risk inherent in the MBS.
C. result in an effective comparison because the effective life rather than the maturity of the MBS is measured against the maturity of the Treasury.

10. Which of the following is *least likely* to be considered an advantage of using the empirical duration approach?
A. The volatility of the spread to Treasury securities does not distort how the price of mortgage-backed securities reacts to yield changes.
B. Its calculation relies on few assumptions.
C. Required parameters are easy to estimate using regression analysis.

11. Which of the following statements is *least accurate* concerning valuation methodologies?
    A. A callable corporate bond should be valued using the Monte Carlo OAS approach.
    B. An auto loan-backed ABS should be valued using the *Z*-spread approach.
    C. A high-quality home equity loan ABS should be valued using the Monte Carlo OAS approach.

12. Does the OAS of a PAC I tranche from a CMO backed by Ginnie Mae passthroughs, calculated using Treasury yields as a benchmark, reflect credit risk and/or modeling risk?
    A. Yes, it reflects both risks.
    B. It reflects one risk, but not the other.
    C. No, it does not reflect either risk.

Challenge Problems

13. Consider the collateralized mortgage obligation (CMO) tranches shown in the following figure.

Tranche	*OAS (bps)*	*Z-spread (bps)*	*Effective Duration*
1	68	85	2.60
2	71	91	2.90
3	73	136	8.25

Is Tranche 3 relatively more expensive than Tranche 1 and/or Tranche 2?
A. Yes, it is relatively more expensive than both tranches.
B. It is relatively more expensive than one tranche, but not the other.
C. No, it is relatively less expensive than both tranches.

14. Quantitative Duration Associates estimates the effective duration of a mortgage-backed passthrough security to be 14.7. Sundial Partners estimates the effective duration of the same passthrough to be 18.9. Which is the *least likely* reason for the difference in the effective duration estimates provided by the two firms? Each firm used a different:
A. proprietary prepayment model.
B. refinancing spread.
C. effective convexity estimate.

15. Which of the following variables is *least likely* to change when using a Monte Carlo simulation model to compute the effective duration of a mortgage-backed security (MBS)?
A. Option-adjusted spread.
B. Prepayment rates.
C. Expected cash flows.

16. An investor is comparing securities that differ only in effective duration and effective convexity. The security with the lowest interest rate risk will have:
A. the lowest duration and the highest convexity.
B. the lowest duration and the lowest convexity.
C. the highest duration and the lowest convexity.

Answers – Concept Checkers

1. C The term structure is not assumed to be normal in order to appropriately interpret the cash flow yield.

2. B The question tells us that the market price of the CMO tranche is 70.17. The OAS is the spread added to the interest rates along the interest rate path that makes the market price and the theoretical value equal. The theoretical value of the CMO will be the weighted average of the values of each interest path. Because we are told in the problem that the paths are equally weighted, we simply find the arithmetic average for each path and choose the theoretical value that equals the market price. In this case, the average of the 60 bps spread column is:

$$\frac{68+70+66+69+75+73}{6}=70.17$$

Therefore, the OAS must be 60 basis points.

3. B Automobile loans have a prepayment option, but it is not typically exercised as a result of a change in interest rates. Therefore the *Z*-spread is appropriate for evaluating the security.

4. C The *Z*-spread is not appropriate because there is a prepayment option present. The binomial model is not appropriate because the future cash flows on the pool are dependent upon interest rates. The OAS based on Monte Carlo simulation is most appropriate.

5. C Cash flow duration, unlike effective duration based on Monte Carlo simulation, assumes a single prepayment speed over the life of the MBS.

6. B The cash flows for an MBS are dependent upon the path that interest rates follow and, therefore, cannot be properly valued with the binomial model or any other model that employs the backward induction methodology. The cash flows for passthrough securities are a function of prepayment rates, and prepayment rates in any given month are affected by interest rates in the past (e.g., refinancing burnout).

7. B The OAS is the *Z*-spread *minus* the option cost. All the other statements are correct.

8. B Because it is assumed that each path has the same weight, the theoretical value is simply the average of the present values of the interest rate paths. The average present value of each path using the four spreads is tabulated in the following figure.

	Present Value if Spread is:		
	75 bps	*80 bps*	*85 bps*
Average PV	80.6	74.0	71.2

Therefore the OAS of Tranche X is 80 basis points.

9. B The nominal spread does not adjust for the prepayment risk of the MBS.

10. A A *disadvantage* of the empirical duration model is that the volatility of the spreads with reference to Treasuries can distort the price reaction to interest rate changes.

11. **A** A callable corporate bond should be valued using the binomial OAS model, not the Monte Carlo OAS model. Given that the cash flows are not interest rate path dependent, the callable corporate bond can be valued more easily with the simpler binomial OAS model.

12. **B** If we use Treasury securities as the benchmark, the OAS on a CMO backed by Ginnie Mae passthroughs does not reflect credit risk, because Ginnie Maes carry the full faith and credit of the U.S. government. The OAS does, however, reflect modeling risk.

ANSWERS – CHALLENGE PROBLEMS

13. **A** First calculate the option cost of each tranche:

    Tranche 1 option cost = 85 – 68 = 17 basis points
    Tranche 2 option cost = 91 – 71 = 20 basis points
    Tranche 3 option cost = 136 – 73 = 63 basis points

    Tranche 3, despite its longer effective duration, has a comparable OAS and a much higher option cost than Tranches 1 and 2. A risk-averse investor would demand a higher OAS on Tranche 3 than on Tranches 1 and 2 because of its longer duration. Therefore, on a relative basis, Tranche 3 is relatively more expensive than Tranches 1 and 2. If you saw two tranches with the same effective duration, the tranche with the largest OAS is cheaper. In this problem, Tranche #3 has a tiny advantage in OAS in exchange for a large difference in effective duration; this is not adequate compensation.

14. **C** Effective durations reported by vendors and dealers are most likely to differ as a result of differences in the (1) size of the interest rate shock (Δy), (2) prepayment model, (3) option-adjusted spread, and (4) refinancing spread. Effective convexity would be estimated using the same procedure as for effective duration, but the convexity estimate is not used in the estimation of the effective duration.

15. **A** Calculating effective duration using a Monte Carlo simulation model starts by changing interest rates by a small amount (Δy) and observing the changes in the price of the MBS. The price of the MBS changes because the change in interest rates causes prepayment rates to change, which causes expected cash flows to change. The option-adjusted spread (OAS) is assumed to remain constant in this procedure.

16. **A** Effective duration is a measure of interest rate risk: the larger the duration of a security, all else equal, the greater the interest rate risk. For a given duration, the greater the convexity, the lower the interest rate risk.

SELF-TEST: FIXED INCOME

Use the following information for Questions 1 through 6.

Jonathan Song is a CFA candidate who recently took the Level II exam and is currently waiting to receive his test results. Song is also pursuing his MBA at a prestigious Ivy League university. He accepted a position as an intern at a large brokerage firm in New York for this year's summer break. Over the course of his internship, he will rotate among the different areas of the firm, spending two weeks in each. His current rotation is in the brokerage firm's Research department, where he will report to Bill Dixon, a managing director whose group is responsible for economic forecasting and analysis. Dixon is evaluating all of the interns that rotate through his department this Summer to identify possible candidates for permanent positions at the brokerage firm after graduation.

Song has successfully completed a course in the basic principles of finance, and Dixon seeks to assess Song's knowledge of various concepts that are of specific importance to his area. Dixon decides to focus first on the term structure of interest rates, because this area is directly applicable to economic forecasting. To this end, Dixon supplies Song with some fundamental market information, asks him to interpret the shape of the yield curve, and to forecast how a portfolio might react to various changes in interest rates. Dixon also wants to explore Song's knowledge concerning the various theories of the term structure of interest rates, including their similarities, differences, and appropriate usage.

Dixon has constructed a sample portfolio of Treasury bonds with different maturities to simulate an actual portfolio management situation. This portfolio is similar to a barbell portfolio that Dixon is considering for a client of the firm.

Sample Treasury Portfolio

Security	*Weight*	*Current Yield*	*Key Rate Duration*
2-year	45%	4.50	0.91
10-year	15%	4.63	2.15
20-year	10%	4.82	3.89
25-year	30%	4.97	4.12

Dixon has asked Song to determine exactly how the sample portfolio value would react to several specific interest rate scenarios.

1. A recent change in interest rates has caused the Treasury yield curve to become significantly more curved. This change in shape of the yield curve is often called a:
   A. butterfly shift.
   B. negative butterfly shift.
   C. positive yield curve twist.

2. Dixon has asked Song to construct a theoretical spot rate curve. Dixon will have the greatest degree of confidence in the accuracy of the spot curve if Song uses:
   A. treasury strips.
   B. on-the-run Treasury securities.
   C. all available Treasury coupon securities and bills.

3. Dixon asks Song for his interpretation of the yield curve represented by the sample portfolio. Which of the following statements regarding term structure theories is *most accurate*?
   A. According to the pure expectations theory, the bond yields imply that investors expect short-term rates to remain constant.
   B. According to the liquidity theory, the bond yields imply that investors demand a premium for exposure to interest rate risk.
   C. According to the preferred habitat theory, the risk premium of the 20-year bond is 32 basis points greater than that of the 2-year security.

4. The effective duration for the portfolio for a parallel shift in the yield curve is *closest* to:
   A. 2.36.
   B. 4.69.
   C. 11.07.

5. Now Dixon wants Song to assume that the yield curve shifts in a nonparallel fashion. The anticipated change for the 2-year and 10-year rates is an increase of 50 basis points, while the 20-year and 25-year rates are expected to increase by 100 basis points. Song correctly calculates the effect of this yield shift as:
   A. 0.70% decrease in value.
   B. 2.00% decrease in value.
   C. 2.73% decrease in value.

6. The swap rate curve (based upon LIBOR rates) is preferred by some market participants as a yield benchmark. Which of the following statements is *least* valid regarding why these participants may prefer the swap rate curve over the traditional treasury curve?
   A. The swap market is highly regulated, which makes swap rates more consistent among markets.
   B. Swap pricing depends only on supply and demand, and is not affected by technical market factors.
   C. Unlike government bond yield curves, swap curves do not reflect sovereign risk unique to a particular country.

SELF-TEST ANSWERS: FIXED INCOME

1. **B** Yield curve butterfly shifts describe changes in the degree of curvature in the yield curve. A negative butterfly shift means that there is more curvature to the yield curve.

2. **B** On-the-run issues are the most-recently issued Treasury securities. These have the largest trading volume and are the most accurately priced issues. The main drawback to relying only on on-the-run issues is that there are likely to be large gaps between maturities available. To fill in the gaps, the analyst could use some off-the-run securities. This has the potential to reduce the accuracy of the spot rate estimates.

3. **B** According to the liquidity theory of the term structure, investors require a liquidity premium to compensate them for exposure to interest rate risk. The longer the maturity of the issue, the greater the interest rate risk, and the greater the liquidity premium. The other answers are incorrect or cannot be substantiated.

4. **A** The key rate duration of a portfolio is simply the weighted average of the key rate durations of the individual securities.

$$
\begin{aligned}
D_2 &= (0.45 \times 0.91) + (0.15 \times 0) + (0.10 \times 0) + (0.30 \times 0) = 0.41 \\
D_{10} &= (0.45 \times 0) + (0.15 \times 2.15) + (0.10 \times 0) + (0.30 \times 0) = 0.32 \\
D_{20} &= (0.45 \times 0) + (0.15 \times 0) + (0.10 \times 3.89) + (0.30 \times 0) = 0.39 \\
D_{25} &= (0.45 \times 0) + (0.15 \times 0) + (0.10 \times 0) + (0.30 \times 4.12) = \underline{1.24} \\
&\qquad 2.36
\end{aligned}
$$

5. **B** Using the individual key rate durations calculated above, a change in portfolio value can be derived by computing the change in value associated with each bond. Remember that an increase in rates will cause a decrease in value.

   Change in Portfolio Value:

   Change from 2-year: $-0.50\% \times 0.41 = -0.21\%$
   Change from 10-year: $-0.50\% \times 0.32 = -0.16\%$
   Change from 20-year: $-1.00\% \times 0.39 = -0.39\%$
   Change from 25-year: $-1.00\% \times 1.24 = \underline{-1.24\%}$
   -2.00%

6. **A** In fact, the swap market is lightly regulated (if at all) by any government, which makes swap rates in different countries more comparable.

FORMULAS

STUDY SESSION 13: ALTERNATIVE INVESTMENTS

net operating income:

rental income if fully occupied
+ other income
= potential gross income
– vacancy and collection loss
= effective gross income
– operating expense
= net operating income

capitalization rate:

cap rate = discount rate – growth rate

$$\text{cap rate} = \frac{\text{NOI}_1}{\text{value}} \quad \text{or} \quad \text{cap rate} = \frac{\text{NOI}_1}{\text{comparable sales price}}$$

value of a property using direct capitalization:

$$\text{value} = V_0 = \frac{\text{NOI}_1}{\text{cap rate}} \quad \text{or} \quad \text{value} = V_0 = \frac{\text{stabilized NOI}}{\text{cap rate}}$$

value of a property based on net rent and "all risks yield": $\text{value} = V_0 = \frac{\text{rent}_1}{\text{ARY}}$

value of a property using gross income multiplier:

$$\text{gross income multiplier} = \frac{\text{sales price}}{\text{gross income}}$$

value = gross income × gross income multiplier

term and reversion property valuation approach:

Total property value = PV of term rent + PV of incremental rent

$$= \frac{\text{term rent}}{\text{term rent cap rate}} + \frac{\text{estimated rental value}}{\text{ERV cap rate}}$$

NCREIF Property Index (NPI) calculation:

$$\text{return} = \frac{\text{NOI} - \text{capital expenditures} + (\text{end market value} - \text{beg market value})}{\text{beginning market value}}$$

debt service coverage ratio (DSCR): $\text{DSCR} = \dfrac{\text{first-year NOI}}{\text{debt service}}$

loan-to-value (LTV) ratio: $\text{LTV} = \dfrac{\text{loan amount}}{\text{appraisal value}}$

capitalization rate based on comparable recent transactions:

$$\text{capitalization rate} = \frac{\text{net operating income}}{\text{property value}}$$

capitalization of a property's rental stream: $\text{property value} = \dfrac{\text{net operating income}}{\text{capitalization rate}}$

Net Asset Value approach to REIT share valuation:

  estimated cash NOI
÷ assumed cap rate
= estimated value of operating real estate
+ cash and accounts receivable
– debt and other liabilities
= net asset value
÷ shares outstanding
= NAV/share

price-to-FFO approach to REIT share valuation:

  funds from operations (FFO)
÷ shares outstanding
= FFO/share
× sector average P/FFO multiple
= NAV/share

price-to-AFFO approach to REIT share valuation:

  funds from operations (FFO)
– non-cash rents:
– recurring maintenance-type capital expenditures
= AFFO
÷ shares outstanding
= AFFO/share
× property subsector average P/AFFO multiple
= NAV/share

discounted cash flow approach to REIT share valuation:

value of a REIT share
= PV(dividends for years 1 through n) + PV(terminal value at the end of year n)

exit value:

investment cost + earnings growth + increase in price multiple + reduction in debt = exit value

NAV before distributions:

= NAV after distributions in prior year + capital called down − management fees + operating results

NAV after distributions:

= NAV before distributions − carried interest − distributions

venture capital method:

the post-money portion of a firm purchased by an investment is:

$$f_1 = \frac{\text{investment } 1}{PV_1(\text{exit value})}$$

the number of new shares issued is:

$$\text{shares}_{VC} = \text{shares}_{EQUITY}\left(\frac{f_1}{1-f_1}\right)$$

where shares_{EQUITY} is the pre-investment number of shares, and share price is:

$$\text{price } 1 = \frac{\text{investment } 1}{\text{shares}_{VC}}$$

Study Sessions 14 and 15: Fixed Income

yield on an option-free corporate bond:

yield = real risk-free interest rate + expected inflation rate + maturity premium + liquidity premium + credit spread

yield spread = liquidity premium + credit spread

return impact of spread changes: return impact $\approx$ –duration × Δspread

or more accurately: $\text{return impact} \approx -\text{duration} \times \Delta\text{spread} + \frac{1}{2}\text{convexity} \times (\Delta\text{spread})^2$

standard deviation of daily yield changes:

$$\sigma_{\text{annual}} = \sigma_{\text{daily}} \times (\text{number of trading days in the year})^{1/2}$$

value of embedded call option: $V_{\text{call}} = V_{\text{noncallable}} - V_{\text{callable}}$

value of embedded put option: $V_{\text{put}} = V_{\text{putable}} - V_{\text{nonputable}}$

effective duration: $ED = \dfrac{BV_{-\Delta y} - BV_{+\Delta y}}{2 \times BV_0 \times \Delta y}$

effective convexity: $EC = \dfrac{BV_{-\Delta y} + BV_{+\Delta y} - (2 \times BV_0)}{2 \times BV_0 \times \Delta y^2}$

convertible bonds:

conversion value = market price of stock × conversion ratio

$$\text{market conversion price} = \frac{\text{market price of convertible bond}}{\text{conversion ratio}}$$

market conversion premium per share = market conversion price – market price

$$\text{market conversion premium ratio} = \frac{\text{market conversion premium per share}}{\text{market price of common stock}}$$

$$\text{premium payback period} = \frac{\text{market conversion premium per share}}{\text{favorable income difference per share}}$$

$$\text{favorable income difference per share} = \frac{\text{coupon interest} - (\text{conversion ratio} \times \text{dividends per share})}{\text{conversion ratio}}$$

$$\text{premium over straight value} = \left(\frac{\text{market price of convertible bond}}{\text{straight value}}\right) - 1$$

mortgage prepayment speed:

$$\text{single monthly mortality rate} = 1 - (1 - \text{conditional prepayment rate})^{1/12}$$

mortgage prepayment:

$$\text{prepayment}_m = \text{SMM}_m \times \left(\begin{matrix} \text{mortgage balance at} \\ \text{beginning of month m} \end{matrix} - \begin{matrix} \text{scheduled principal} \\ \text{payment for month m} \end{matrix} \right)$$

commercial MBS credit analysis:

$$\text{debt-to-service coverage ratio} = \frac{\text{net operating income}}{\text{debt service}}$$

$$\text{loan-to-value ratio} = \frac{\text{current mortgage amount}}{\text{current appraised value}}$$

absolute prepayment speed (ABS) and single monthly mortality rate (SMM):

$$\text{SMM} = \frac{\text{ABS}}{1-[\text{ABS} \times (\text{m}-1)]}$$

monthly cash flow yield converted to a bond-equivalent basis:

$$\text{bond-equivalent yield} = 2[(1+\text{monthly cash flow yield})^6 - 1]$$

implied cost of an embedded option:

$$\text{option cost} = \text{zero-volatility spread} - \text{option-adjusted spread}$$

percentage price change in the bond for a given change in yield:

$$\begin{aligned} \%\ \text{change in bond price} &\approx \text{duration effect} + \text{convexity effect} \\ &\approx (-\text{ED} \times \Delta y \times 100) + \left(\text{EC} \times \Delta y^2 \times 100\right) \end{aligned}$$

Index

D

E

F

G

H

Notes